# Fiscal Sociology and the Theory of Public Finance

NEW THINKING IN POLITICAL ECONOMY

**Series Editor: Peter J. Boettke**
George Mason University, USA

New Thinking in Political Economy aims to encourage scholarship in the intersection of the disciplines of politics, philosophy and economics. It has the ambitious purpose of reinvigorating political economy as a progressive force for understanding social and economic change.

The series is an important forum for the publication of new work analysing the social world from a multidisciplinary perspective. With increased specialization (and professionalization) within universities, interdisciplinary work has become increasingly uncommon. Indeed, during the 20th century, the process of disciplinary specialization reduced the intersection between economics, philosophy and politics and impoverished our understanding of society. Modem economics in particular has become increasingly mathematical and largely ignores the role of institutions and the contribution of moral philosophy and politics.

New Thinking in Political Economy will stimulate new work that combines technical knowledge provided by the 'dismal science' and the wisdom gleaned from the serious study of the 'worldly philosophy'. The series will reinvigorate our understanding of the social world by encouraging a multidisciplinary approach to the challenges confronting society in the new century.

Recent titles in the series include:

Governance and Economic Development
A Comparative Institutional Approach
*Joachim Ahrens*

Constitutions, Markets and Law
Recent Experiences in Transition Economies
*Edited by Stefan Voigt and Hans-Jiirgen Wagener*

Austrian Economics and the Political Economy of Freedom
*Richard M. Ebeling*

Anarchy, State and Public Choice
*Edited by Edward Stringham*

Humane Economics
Essays in Honor of Don Lavoie
*Edited by Jack High*

Public Choice and the Challenges of Democracy
*Edited by José Casas Pardo and Pedro Schwartz*

Fiscal Sociology and the Theory of Public Finance
An Exploratory Essay
*Richard E. Wagner*

# Fiscal Sociology and the Theory of Public Finance

An Exploratory Essay

Richard E. Wagner

*Holbert L. Harris Professor of Economics, George Mason University, US*

NEW THINKING IN POLITICAL ECONOMY

**Edward Elgar**

Cheltenham, UK • Northampton, MA, USA

Published by
Edward Elgar Publishing Limited
Glensanda House
Montpellier Parade
Cheltenham
Glos GL50 1UA
UK

Edward Elgar Publishing, Inc.
William Pratt House
9 Dewey Court
Northampton
Massachusetts 01060
USA

A catalogue record for this book
is available from the British Library

**Library of Congress Cataloguing in Publication Data**

Wagner, Richard E.
   Fiscal sociology and the theory of public finance: an exploratory essay /
Richard E. Wagner
      p. cm. — (New thinking in political economy series)
   Includes bibliographical references and index.
   1. Finance, Public.  2. Fiscal policy.  I. Title.
   HJ131.W34  2007
   336.001—dc22

                                                            2006102956

ISBN 978 1 84720 246 8

Printed and bound in Great Britain by MPG Books Ltd, Bodmin, Cornwall

# Contents

# Figures

# Preface

This book examines some of the material of public finance (or public economics) through 'a different window', to borrow a phrase from Friedrich Nietzsche. The object of analytical interest in the theory of public finance is a government's activities, mostly its revenues and expenditures (though any budgetary operation can be mirrored by a regulation). But through what window is this object viewed? The most commonly used window is one where government is portrayed as an entity that intervenes in society to alter the equilibrium pattern of market-generated outcomes. When seen through this window, public finance appears as the activity of developing knowledge about the consequences of different interventionist actions by governments.

When viewed through my alternative window, public finance appears as a form of social theorizing. If the aim of market theorizing is to explain how people are able to generate generally orderly patterns of activity when they relate to one another through private property, the coordinate aim of fiscal theorizing is similarly to explain how orderly patterns of activity emerge when people relate to one another in the particular form of collective property that constitutes a state. A comprehensive social theory might thus be thought to entail a combination of market theory and fiscal theory, taking care to incorporate the forms of civic association as well.

Through this alternative window, government appears as one of several interrelated arenas within which people interact inside a society. The pure theory of a market economy treats property rights as absolute. The alternative that I pursue here treats property as non-absolute, perhaps as illustrated by John Paul Sartre's closing declaration in *No Exit* that 'hell is other people'. Rights of property not only depend on what other people allow but are also subject to variation over time through societal processes that form part of the subject matter of the material I present here. Both political and economic activities emerge within the same societal process, a process that entails both cooperation and conflict. Societies have multiple arenas of interaction, and a government is just one of those arenas. Fiscal activities are thus assigned to the realm of catallaxy or interaction and not to the realm of interventionist choice. To be sure, catallaxy is generally regarded as denoting exchange. Knut Wicksell's vision of unanimity would be such a representation of catallaxy. But I use catallaxy to represent interaction, and in this I include duress as well as consent, as Wicksell recognized in his pragmatic retreat from unanimity.

The relationship between economy and polity is sequential in conventional fiscal theorizing: market equilibrium is first established, with government then intervening to shift society to some alternative equilibrium. This is, of course, as it must be with systems design, for an existing system is to be followed by some alternative. In contrast, when public finance is treated as a facet of social theorizing, the relationship between economy and polity must be coeval within a societal catallaxy. Moreover, primacy of analytical focus is placed on emergent processes of development and not on states of equilibrium. Moreover, much of that development is set in motion by conflict among people and their plans.

The book's material is presented in eight chapters. The first two chapters treat preliminary considerations. Chapter 1 explores the contrasting architectonics for the alternative approaches to public finance that I have just adumbrated: the predominant approach treats public finance as a branch of economic systems design; the alternative that I sketch here treats it as a form of social theorizing. To be sure, systems design and social theorizing are not antagonistic to one another. One person can practice both approaches to public finance, but not at the same instant. Chapter 2 examines the treatment of property rights within the context of a social-theoretic public finance, and shows how some incongruities between politically-generated and market-generated institutions can promote societal tectonics and not some placid equilibrium. The main point of this chapter is to explain the non-separable character of polity and economy, and to sketch some of the implications for a theory of public finance.

The next four chapters divide a social-theoretic treatment of public finance into four conceptual modules. Each module, moreover, reflects an enterprise-centered approach to public finance. By this, I mean that the aggregate pattern of activities undertaken by a government is generated in bottom-up or emergent fashion through entrepreneurial activity that is pursued politically. Chapter 3 conceptualizes a society as possessing two forums through which entrepreneurial activity can be pursued: a market square and a public square. These two forums reside within the same society, so they are connected; moreover, those points of connection serve as hubs of contested exchanges. The abstract notion of state is assimilated not to some such form of organization as a firm or club but to a particular type of transactional nexus; a parliamentary assembly is thus construed as a peculiar type of market forum. Chapter 4 characterizes political entrepreneurship as supplying the organizational momentum for the public square. With the political enterprise treated as the central unit of analysis for a theory of public finance, Chapter 4 locates political entrepreneurship as the generative source of the pattern of fiscal activity within a society. Chapter 5 examines the arrangements of governance within political enterprises with respect to their ability to promote the success of those enterprises. Chapter 6 explores how political enterprises go about securing revenues to support their activities, recognizing the complementarity between the taxing and the spending sides of the budget.

The final two chapters explore analytical extensions of the preceding analysis. In the earlier chapters, a society was implicitly characterized as possessing a single public square out of which the phenomena of public finance emerge. Most people, however, live inside multiple public squares. Chapter 7 examines federalist forms of public square, and does so within a polycentric vision that contrasts with the allocationist-centered vision that is common in the literature on fiscal federalism. Pareto efficiency, as generally interpreted, is a coherent analytical construction only within the framework of a closed system of equilibrated relationships. My alternative analytical window, however, entails an open system of emergent relationships, which renders Pareto efficiency incoherent. Chapter 8 presents an alternative exploration of the object of concern that has been addressed by welfare economics, and does so by working with some ideas that inhabit the domain of fiscal sociology.

This book is not written as a textbook. It assumes that the reader has a working knowledge of the standard conceptual framework within which the theory of public finance is commonly presented. It is written as an essay that offers a personal statement regarding the theory of public finance when that theory is understood to be one aspect of a broader scheme of social theorizing. It is elemental in character, in that it addresses some foundational conceptual issues in a straightforward manner, even as it presumes a general familiarity with the standard conceptual framework. The book seeks to explore some of the contours of what a theory of public finance might look like when it was oriented toward social theorizing and not systems design.

The modern development of public choice theorizing has, of course, sought to probe some of the interaction between market and public squares, and I embrace that development. The development of public choice theorizing, moreover, is to a significant extent a continuation of the social-theoretic orientation toward public finance that was developed by Italian scholars during roughly the period 1880 to 1940, as I have explained elsewhere (Wagner 2003). At the same time, however, much public choice theorizing treats governments as acting units of intervention and seeks to uncover the logic of such state intervention. In contrast, I treat democratic forms of government not as organizations but as orders, inside which many particular organizations operate.

I should like to express my appreciation to the Earhart Foundation and the J.M. Kaplan Fund for support that hastened the completion of this project, as well as to the numerous graduate students who during the spring semesters of 2004 and 2006 participated with me in exploring the thoughts presented here. I am also grateful to Jürgen Backhaus, of the University of Erfurt, and Domenico Da Empoli, of the University of Rome 'La Sapenzia', for extensive discussions over several years on a good number of the matters treated here, and especially for sharing with me their insights into the German and Italian literatures that have treated public finance as a form of social theorizing. I am likewise grateful to my George Mason colleague Peter Boettke for sharing with me some of his extensive knowledge of the Austrian tradition that likewise treats economic theory as a facet of a broader program of social theory pursued from an emergent orientation. Finally, I am deeply grateful to James Buchanan for providing inspiration and encouragement, starting in 1963 with my graduate student days at the University of Virginia, where he introduced me to the challenges of approaching public finance from a social-theoretic orientation.

# 1. Contrasting architectonics for a theory of public finance

Philosophers of science have occupied the foreground in reminding us that the sense we make of our observations about reality is conditioned by the mental frameworks or maps we use to organize those observations. This is an important point that bears heavily upon the selection of an architectonic framework for a theory of public finance. We are all necessarily captives of the mental maps we employ in making sense of our observations. There is nothing wrong with this, for there is no way to avoid this situation. Those maps can focus our observations on important matters and help us to avoid what is insignificant. They can also keep us from understanding accurately or clearly our chosen object of examination. For millennia people thought that the sun rose in the east and set in the west. This expression arose as part of a mental map that placed the earth at the center of the universe. Astronomers mapped the heavens to reconcile their observations of the heavenly bodies in terms of this Ptolemaic mental map. Then came Copernicus with his alternative mental map where the earth revolved around the sun, and we came subsequently to understand differently our observations of the heavenly bodies. While we still speak of the sun rising in the east and setting in the west, we now know that we are speaking figuratively and not literally.

In the Preface to his epochal *General Theory of Employment, Interest, and Money*, John Maynard Keynes (1936) referred to the difficulties of escaping 'from habitual modes of thought and expression'. He continued by noting that the 'difficulty lies, not in the new ideas, but in escaping from the old ones, which ramify, for those brought up as most of us have been, into every corner of our minds'. The specific context for Keynes's lament was the conventional, equilibrium-based theorizing that dominated economics at the time he wrote. According to this standard mental map, economic observations were observations of equilibrium relationships among prices and outputs, as conveyed by notions of stationary states. For Keynes, societies and economies were anything but stationary. They were continually in motion. He sought to contribute to the development of an alternative mental map centered on motion and not on stationarity. His work, however, was subsequently reinterpreted as a contribution to equilibrium theorizing, as Axel Leijonhufvud (1967) explains, and the distinctive features of his attempted contribution were lost in the process. In this respect, it is worth noting that even at the time of Copernicus, the Ptolemaic maps of astronomical observations, with earth at the center, were successful in describing those observations.

The specific context of Keynes's statement aside, he was pointing to a general problem of how the thoughts we have about phenomena are both assisted and shackled by our mental maps. A mental map designed to characterize the logic of stationary states, where economic life continues indefinitely without change, is unlikely to be suitable to characterize processes of continual innovation and development, where the one certainty is that a strategy of standing still in commercial activity is the short route to oblivion. While this book embraces processes of continuing development over the equilibrium of stationary states, as illustrated nicely by Jason Potts (2000), its subject matter is the theory of public finance and not general economic theory. The problem Keynes identified has bearing upon public finance, as many of the common patterns of thinking about public finance were fashioned at a time when governments were monarchies, in which case fiscal activities could reasonably be described as reflecting a monarch's choices. Modes of thought that were fashioned for monarchical times have been carried forward to democratic regimes without giving sufficient attention to the challenge for fiscal theorizing created by this institutional change. Hence, states are commonly treated as entities that stand outside the social economy and intervene in it. In contrast, in this book democratic states are treated as arenas of participation within the social economy: states are treated as orders and not as organizations, corresponding to Friedrich Hayek (1973).

## I.   ORDERS AND ORGANIZATIONS: TWO WINDOWS FOR FISCAL THEORIZING

The object of study for a science of public finance is a government's budget, its taxes and expenditures. To say that budgeting constitutes the object that fiscal scholars study says nothing about the types of questions they seek to address as they go about their studies. There are different sets of questions that fiscal scholars can pose, and have posed to their material, with each set representing an effort to look at the phenomena of public finance through some particular analytical window.

Suppose two territories, equal in terms of such things as population and wealth, and each containing a democratically-elected parliament, are observed to differ in both the size and composition of their governmental activities, and on both sides of the budget. Perhaps one government finances its activities through a proportional tax on income, with a low rate and a broad base. The other finances its activities through a progressive tax on income, with marginal rates of tax rising to perhaps more than 50 per cent, with numerous exemptions, exclusions and deductions incorporated into the tax base. On the expenditure side, one government spends heavily on draining swamps and building subways, while the provision of retirement annuities and poor relief is organized through market-based insurance companies and charities. In contrast, the other government spends relatively little on draining swamps and building subways, but is heavily involved in transferring wealth through a wide variety of programs for retirement insurance and poor relief.

What questions might a fiscal scholar bring to bear in examining this situation? Depending on the types of questions posed, different conceptual windows will be suitable for organizing thought about fiscal phenomena. The most commonly used window is one through which the state is viewed as a goal-directed organization. The alternative window is one where it is viewed as an order that accommodates myriad participants who pursue differing goals. A business firm is an organization: people must be invited to join an organization, it can reasonably be described as having goals (such as maximizing a firm's net worth) that its members act to achieve to the degree the organization is well ordered, and its activities can be characterized as choices made in pursuit of those goals. Societies and markets, however, are orders and not organizations, even though their processes proceed in a generally orderly fashion. People don't require invitations to participate in market or society, they just do it. Markets and societies don't have goals; these are just arenas that encompass the participating individuals and organizations that do have goals. The aggregate patterns and outcomes that arise within societies and markets are not products of choice, but are the emergent by-products of interaction among the participants.

The preponderance of scholarship on public finance treats the state as an organization. To be sure, there are substantial differences among fiscal scholars in how they portray the goals they regard the state as pursuing, or think it should pursue. The majority of those scholars treat the state as an organization that either does or should correct market failures through providing public goods and correcting for misallocations created by externalities. Other fiscal scholars treat the state as an organization that to a significant degree plunders outsiders for the benefit of those who control the apparatus of the state.[1] In either case, the state is treated as a goal-focused organization.

When viewed through this organizational window, the state chooses its pattern of activities in reflection of the goals it pursues. Two tasks appear for a science of public finance when it is viewed through this window. One is to advise the state on how it should conduct its activities. The other is to explain the responses of market participants to those activities. Fiscal activities are treated as exogenous insertions by the state into the market economy, and the task of the fiscal scholar is to portray the market-generated responses to and consequences of those insertions. This window is by far the most commonly used window for fiscal analysis these days. For instance, a government extends a subway in one direction where the relevant alternative was to extend it in a different direction.[2] The subway extension will reduce travel time in that direction, which will increase the demand for and value of land located along the route, particularly in the vicinity of exits. Indeed, the rise in the value of land can even be used to gauge the value that market participants place upon that extension. An economist could thus estimate a rate of return from the expenditure on the subway extension by comparing the added land value with the expenditure.[3] Alternatively, a government might increase sharply its taxes on alcohol and tobacco, while perhaps increasing personal exemptions under its income tax to keep total revenues approximately constant. Once again, market participants would respond in various ways to this exogenous fiscal imposition. Among other things, it would be reasonable to expect increases in cross-border shopping, counterfeiting of tax stamps, and smuggling in response to the tax increase, with the strength of those responses varying directly with the magnitude of the increase.

Analytical efforts of this type are the predominant activity of fiscal scholars. By starting from the existence of a state's budgetary activities and exploring their implications for market interaction, a fiscal theorist treats the state as an entity that is exogenous to the social-economic process. Public finance is thus a branch of applied microeconomic theory where budgetary activities are treated as exogenous shocks whose consequences are capable of being analyzed. While fiscal activities do pretty much appear to individual citizens as exogenous events, this window does not exhaust the analytical possibilities within a democratic polity. For a hereditary monarchy it might be plausible to treat fiscal activities as exogenous shocks injected into the society by the ruling monarch. For a democratic polity, however, there is no place from which such exogenous injection can occur. A second analytical window invites the fiscal theorist to explore the origination of fiscal activities and to explain a government's pattern of taxing and spending. The subway line didn't extend itself, but was extended through some process of choice or interaction among some portion of the citizenry. Likewise, the higher taxes on alcohol and tobacco, as well as the increase in the personal exemption, didn't just happen, but happened because some person or persons made them happen. The challenge for this alternative schema for fiscal analysis, which is the prime concern of this book, is to explain just how those fiscal patterns come into existence and subsequently change.

The alternative analytical window invites the fiscal scholar to treat fiscal activities as products of institutionally-mediated interaction among people who inhabit the society under examination. Fiscal activities emerge out of catallactical relationships just as do market-based activities.[4] At this point, a theory of public finance calls for integration with the concerns of institutional economics, for it is through institutionally-mediated relationships that fiscal activities emerge and evolve. Once these institutionally-mediated relationships become germane to fiscal theorizing, fiscal and political institutions become central to the theory of public finance in two respects, as noted by James Buchanan (1967). First, fiscal institutions provide the framework that shapes and constrains the interactions among fiscal participants, just as property and contract provide the framework that shapes and constrains the interactions among market participants. Second, those institutions are contestable and subject to change through processes that are capable of analytical examination, as explained with particular clarity by Samuel Bowles and Herbert Gintis (1993).

## II. TWO SEMINAL AUTHORS AND THEIR ANALYTICAL WINDOWS

In his treatment of the history of fiscal theorizing, Orhan Kayaalp (2004) organizes that history according to five distinctive national windows: British, Italian, German, Austrian and Swedish (for my review of Kayaalp see Wagner 2005). Kayaalp's treatment organizes fiscal theorizing according to the national origins of the theorists. There is certainly merit in doing this because fiscal scholars often chose their analytical topics from matters of interest where they are living. Fiscal scholars from nations that tax on the basis of value added are more likely to take their analytical material from this form of tax than are American scholars, where the taxation of value added is only an object of speculation. The examples that fiscal scholars use in developing their analyses tend to reflect topics of particular interest in the lands where the authors reside, as can be seen readily by comparing such prominent texts as Beat Blankart (1991) for Germany, Georgio Brosio (1986) for Italy, John Cullis and Philip Jones (1998) for the United Kingdom, and Harvey Rosen (2005) for the United States.

Yet what surely comes across particularly clearly from reading Kayaalp's presentation is the complementarity among the four continental bodies of fiscal scholarship, along with the sharp differences between those bodies and the British orientation. The four sets of continental scholars are using the same window to organize their fiscal scholarship, while the British scholars are using a different window. In this respect, Jürgen Backhaus and Richard Wagner (2005a, 2005b) present the theory of public finance in terms of a dichotomy between continental and Anglo-Saxon orientations.

A sharp presentation of this dichotomy appeared one year apart with the publication of classical pieces of work by Knut Wicksell (1896) in Sweden and Francis Edgeworth (1897) in Great Britain. Edgeworth asked how a government should impose taxes if it wanted to raise those taxes with a minimum amount of sacrifice to taxpayers. If taxpayer effort was independent of the rate of tax and if marginal utility declined with income, the least aggregate sacrifice would be attained by a tax that pared incomes down from the top until the required amount of revenue was raised. To be sure, Edgeworth noted that this was only a first approximation, because the effort to impose a 100 per cent marginal rate of tax would eliminate the incentive to earn those incomes. This insight was later formalized in what has become known as the theory of optimal taxation, initiated by Frank Ramsey (1927) and surveyed extensively in a variety of contemporary texts (see, for instance, Atkinson and Stiglitz (1980), Mirrlees (1994) and Salanié (2003)). The problem of optimal taxation is construed as one of how to slice the pieces of a pie equally, when the size of the pie shrinks as what were initially larger slices are reduced and transferred to what were initially smaller slices. While this formulation construes the budget as an instrument of wealth redistribution so as to maximize some notion of a social welfare function, this literature generally concludes in favor of only modest rates of taxation, because of presumptions about the rate at which increases in marginal tax rates will reduce the amount of effort supplied.

Regardless of particular beliefs about elasticities, the Edgeworthian-inspired branch of fiscal theorizing construes the state as an autonomous and choosing agent, a sentient being that intervenes in society to reform what would otherwise have been its characteristic features as these would otherwise have been generated through the process of open-market competition. The appropriate method of analysis is that of comparative statics, where the analytical focus is centered on the equilibrium properties of different allocative interventions by government. Public finance within the Edgeworthian tradition views the state as an autonomous and reforming sentient being, and uses a methodology of comparative statics to analyse and order the various end states over which that being is exercising choice. To be sure, there is also a fiscal literature that treats states as non-benevolent forms of organization, as forms of organized predation within a society.[5] While this literature offers a nice counterweight to the roseate character of

Edgeworth-inspired treatment of fiscal activity, it still conceptualizes the state as a goal-directed entity and not as an institutionally-mediated order of human interaction.

When Wicksell lamented in 1896 that 'with some very few exceptions the [theory of public finance] seems to have retained the assumptions of its infancy in the seventeenth and eighteenth centuries, when absolute power ruled almost all Europe (1958 [1896], p. 82)', he would surely have brought Edgeworth into that lament had he not published one year before Edgeworth. The orientation set forth by Wicksell stands in sharp contrast to the Edgeworthian orientation in most respects. For Wicksell, government was not some autonomous agent of societal reformation, though he did have a strong interest in societal reformation. Indeed, reformation and not explanation surely dominated the foreground of Wicksell's fiscal theorizing. That theoretical effort, however, treated government as a process of interaction and not as a sentient being. Individual participants might be modeled as maximizing creatures, but government itself was not some maximizing creature but simply an arena within which such maximizing creatures interact. Within the Edgeworthian orientation, people write their parts of the first draft of the manuscript of social life, with government then revising and polishing the manuscript. Within the Wicksellian orientation, people write the complete manuscript, with government serving simply as one of the many locations where the manuscript is worked on. Fiscal phenomena emerge out of interaction among participants, and those interactions are shaped by both customs and habits and by constitutive institutional rules. True to his catallactical orientation, Wicksell combined proportional representation with a principle of unanimity as a way of placing government and market activity on the same plane.

Wicksell was aware of the disjunction between treating government as a process of interaction and treating it as a sentient being. A holder of absolute power exercises choice and is only remotely engaged in catallactical processes. If government is treated as an arena of catallaxy, the explanation of observed outcomes becomes a more complex matter that involves patterns of interaction among participants, with those patterns being shaped in turn by a wide variety of institutions and customs that themselves have to some extent been generated through previous interaction. While treating government as a unitary being that intervenes in polyarchically organized market processes leads to simple and tractable models, it also misrepresents the tasks of organizing public governance. The situation for governance is one where people participate in the governance of their own activities, and not one where 'the state' governs people. Recognition of this distinction leads to a polycentric formulation of governance, where various governmental organizations provide arenas where people participate in the governance of their relationships and activities (as articulated nicely by Vincent Ostrom 1999).

## III.   INSTRUCTION FROM A VITRIOLIC TIRADE

Some interesting instruction about the different windows that might be employed in observing fiscal phenomena can be gleaned from the dueling book reviews that were penned in response to a book by the Italian fiscal scholar Antonio de Viti de Marco. The object of this duel was the 1934 publication of his *Principii di Economia Finanziaria* (De Viti de Marco 1934), the original scheme of which De Viti set forth in 1888 (De Viti de Marco 1888). This book, along with the German translation of a 1928 precursor to *Principii*, was reviewed by Fredric Benham in the August 1934 issue of *Economica* (Benham 1934). Benham began by asserting that De Viti's book 'is probably the best treatise on the theory of public finance ever written'. He continued by noting that De Viti's influence had been confined to Italy, along with perhaps some modest influence in Sweden. Benham likened De Viti's *Principii* to Alfred Marshall's *Principles of Economics* in its broad range combined with deep insights, and claimed that the sorry state of public finance in England could be perked up through a strong infusion of De Viti's orientation. Among the noteworthy figures that Benham took to task as reflecting this sorry state of English public finance were F.Y. Edgeworth and A.C. Pigou. Benham compared De Viti's approach with that common to English public finance by declaring that 'to turn from [English public finance] to the pages of the present volume [De Viti] is like turning from a Royal Academy exhibition into a gallery of Cézannes'. Benham continued by noting that Knut Wicksell's *New Principle of Just Taxation*, published in 1896 (Wicksell 1958 [1896]), constituted a complementary addendum to De Viti. Benham closed his review by musing that the 'lack of an English translation is a great misfortune and loss to all students of public finance in English-speaking countries'.

An English translation of De Viti appeared in 1936 (De Viti de Marco 1936), and it was reviewed in the October 1937 issue of the *Journal of Political Economy*. Henry Simons began this review by observing that:

> the Italian literature of public finance has long been held in high esteem; but its claims to distinction have rested mainly upon works which have been inaccessible to those of us who lacked facility with the language. The translations [both German and English translations were being reviewed by Simons] of De Viti's famous treatise are thus doubly welcome, for they will make possible a more informed consensus, both as to the merits of Italian economics and as to competence of the interpretation and appraisal which it has received in other countries.

After describing this initial sense of eager anticipation, Simons offered his summary judgment of what he found upon reading these translations: 'Careful reading . . . has left the reviewer with no little resentment toward the critics who induced him to search in this treatise for the profound analysis and penetrating insights which it does not contain. The *Principii* is revealed to him, not as a great book, but as a . . . monument to . . . confusion.' Simons continued by asserting that 'there is not a single section or chapter which the reviewer could conscientiously recommend to the competent student searching for genuine insights and understanding'. Simons concluded by taking on Benham's review: 'If his book is "the best treatise on the theory of public finance ever written", one hopes that it may be the last. . . . To say that it is distinguished among treatises in its field is to . . . comment bitterly on the quality of economic thought in one of its important branches.'

This clash cannot be attributed to any kind of deep ideological cleavage about the desirable extent of governmental activity. Both reviewers, along with De Viti, took a generally classically liberal orientation toward markets and politics. That clash rather reflected sharply the different conceptualizations of what a theory of public finance should seek to accomplish. For Simons, the theory of public finance was to serve as a direct instrument of statecraft. The purpose of fiscal theorizing was to advise governments on what to do to make society better. People might write the first drafts of their economic lives through their market activities, but it was the task of government to improve and perfect those lives through appropriate budgetary action. The theory of public finance was to provide assistance in discerning the contours and requirements of those perfecting interventions in the market economy. The state itself stood outside the market process and intervened in it according to a logic that was unrelated to that pursued by participants within the market process.

In sharp contrast, De Viti looked at government budgets through a different window, one where those budgets emerged according to the same economizing logic that pertained to the generation of market patterns and outcomes, with due allowance made for institutional differences between the two settings. De Viti sought to portray the rhyme and reason, the logic of the taxes and expenditures that comprise a government's budget. His theory of public finance was not designed to serve directly as an instrument of government-guided reformation. It was rather designed to serve as a complementary component of an adventure in social theorizing, where the task is to characterize how such universal economic categories as utility, demand, cost, exchange and entrepreneurship play out in the governance of that subset of human relationships and activities that are organized politically. For a passionate reformer like Henry Simons, the disinterested detachment of De Viti and Benham must have been disturbing and apparently infuriating as well.

In his Preface, De Viti explained that he approached public finance as a theoretical science, while many of the critics of his work construed public finance as a technique of practical statecraft. Simons certainly viewed his own work as oriented toward practical statecraft, as an adventure in what is now called economic systems design. The object of fiscal theorizing was to develop improvements in systems of political-economic order. Public finance involved the application of economic theory to particular issues of statecraft. In contrast, De Viti viewed public finance as a theoretical discipline whose object was to explain observed patterns of statecraft. Public finance was a branch of social theorizing and not a subset of economic systems design. For De Viti, the amount of effort that people devoted to economic systems design should be explainable according to the same underlying principles as those used to characterize the production of dog food, tomato juice or marriage counseling.

While the dichotomy between systems design and social theorizing is sharp, both have legitimate places within the overall scheme of human thought. Contrary to the appearance created by those dueling book reviews, there is no need to accept one approach as legitimate while rejecting the legitimacy of the other. Public finance is a conventional term that describes two distinct activities, one being participation in statecraft and the other being theorizing about society and societal processes. This book follows De Viti in pursuing public finance as a branch of social theorizing whose particular object is that portion of human activity that is organized through governmental offices and processes.

A focus on social theorizing, moreover, is surely more foundational than a focus on systems design. Systems design follows the presumption that institutions are the rules that shape social outcomes, so those outcomes can be changed by changing those institutional rules. Social theory, however, counsels some caution in making this leap from rules to outcomes. In 1919, the United States adopted rules that prohibited the production and consumption of alcoholic beverages. This change in rules, however, did little to reduce the use of alcohol while at the same time it generated a lot of violence, bribery and resort to underground commerce.[6] Among other things, social theorizing explores the reach and limits of systems design. Both Prohibition in the 1920s and efforts to prohibit recreational drugs today play out quite differently from efforts to regulate the flow of automobile traffic in cities. Social theory can provide instruction about the variable capacity of systems design to change societal outcomes in a predictable fashion. It can also provide insight into the creation and perpetuation of measures that, like Prohibition, are rampantly destructive.

## IV.  STATE AND MARKET: THE DISJUNCTIVE VISION

The object of Wicksell's complaint was a model of political economy wherein individuals governed their private activities through market relationships and where the state intervened autonomously into the market economy. The historical record presents plenty of instances where this model of a disjunctive political economy seems reasonably accurate. Louis XIV's oft-attributed assertion that 'the state is me' is a limiting illustration of a model of disjunctive political economy, as is the contemporary literature on the welfare economics of optimal taxation. Raghbenda Jha's (1998) treatise on public finance is quite typical in this respect when it opens by asserting that 'public economics [is] the study of government intervention in the marketplace' (p. xii).

For hereditary monarchies among other forms of absolutist government, it is perhaps reasonable to model subjects as relating to one another within a market economy and to model rulers as intervening in the market economy on terms of their choosing. Kings could, of course, differ greatly in the choices they made, but fiscal phenomena would arise out of *their* choices in any case. One branch of choice-theoretic public finance, of which Edgeworth and Ramsey are the prime initiators, has sought to lay down norms for some relatively benevolent ruler, as illustrated by maxims to minimize the excess burden from taxation. Another branch of choice-theoretic public finance, which Amilcare Puviani (1903) illustrates nicely, has sought to portray maxims that could be construed as heuristics by which a ruler or ruling clique could maximize the present value of their personal account. In either case, the state is conceptualized as an autonomous entity that intervenes into market-based relationships as it chooses, with the only differences residing in the utility function that is ascribed to the ruler.

Figure 1.1 presents a simple graphical portrayal of a disjunctive political economy. The circles denote individual citizens and the squares denote members of a ruling cadre, or perhaps a royal family. In this figure, the members of the ruling cadre are fully connected, to indicate that they act as a single unit (or, equivalently, as an equilibrated collection of people). A king and his family would be a sociological instantiation of such an analytical construction. In contrast, the individual citizens who relate to one another within the market economy form an incompletely connected network, following Jason Potts's (2000) formulation for modeling processes of continuing development. The double arrow denotes state intervention in the economy; one direction points to the ruler's demand for revenue while the other shows the subjects' compliance with that demand. This analytical model captures pretty well the characteristic features of a hereditary

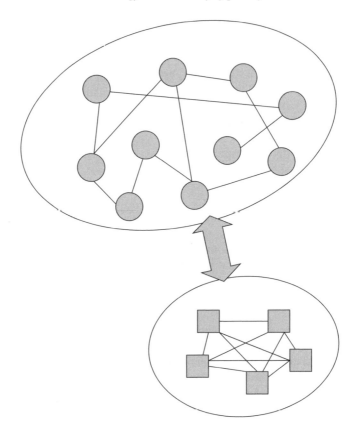

*Figure 1.1    Disjunctive political economy*

monarchy. It likewise fits well with the systems design orientation of contemporary fiscal theorizing, where an exogenous state intervenes in market-
generated arrangements.

Within this orientation, the analytical agenda of a theory of public
finance contains two primary components. One component seeks to articulate standards or criteria for enlightened intervention. To be sure, this literature has not been penned under any presumption that rulers are necessarily
enlightened, or even under a presumption that most of them are. Setting
aside such formulations as those of Puviani (1903), it has apparently seemed
second nature that such exercises should aim at some beneficent rather than
malevolent standard. Substantial controversy has accompanied the articulation of such standards, but the controversies themselves all concern what
would comprise benevolent intervention in market-generated patterns
and outcomes. The agent of intervention must stand outside that market

process, and cannot arise within and participate in that process. Or alternatively and in line with Buchanan (1959), the fiscal expert could simply advance a proposal for change under the hypothesis that it was generally beneficial, and with the correctness of that hypothesis subsequently judged by the degree of consent it obtained within the citizenry.

The second analytical component for a theory of public finance within a framework of disjunctive political economy is an analysis of the properties of different fiscal measures. A theory of public finance in the disjunctive mode has two analytical levels. The first level concerns the articulation of norms; the second level concerns the consequences of actual fiscal interventions. At the level of normative analysis, a claim might be advanced that fiscal measures should reduce the inequality that arises through market interaction. The positive level of analysis examines actual fiscal measures to determine such matters as their distributional impact. To the extent that benevolent power rules society at the first level, the results of positive analysis at the second level will either affirm those first-level choices or will lead to modifications of those choices.

It seems reasonable to model the fiscal activities of some absolute ruler in choice-theoretic fashion.[7] Those activities represent choices by those rulers, and the observation of those choices will provide insight into the preferences and values of those rulers. The model represented by Figure 1.1 fits a particular form of society where rulers are distinct from and stand apart from the society over which they rule. Societies with democratic polities, however, are not represented accurately by Figure 1.1, for the disjunction between market and state that characterizes hereditary monarchies gives way to a conjunctive political economy, as Richard Wagner (2006a) explains.

## V.  STATE AND MARKET: THE CONJUNCTIVE VISION

As a hereditary monarchy gives way to some democratic or republican regime, a transformation occurs in the connective structure of the society. Royal families lose their lands and privileges, get jobs, and become relatively ordinary. The disjunction between rulers and ruled erodes. The situation after this erosion is portrayed in Figure 1.2, where the squares and circles shown in Figure 1.1 have commingled to produce the society represented by Figure 1.2. In this alternative representation, government is no longer a creature that lords it over society, for it is an order and not a single-minded organization. It is, of course, always possible to aggregate over the activities of the various squares depicted in Figure 1.2, and refer to this aggregate as indicating something called *government output*. But this would

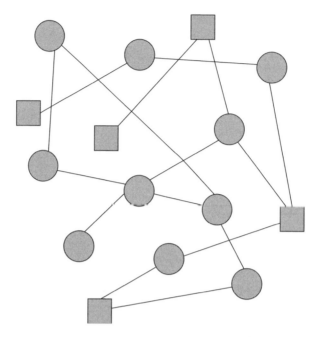

*Figure 1.2    Conjunctive political economy*

be little different from aggregating over the circles and calling the result *market output*. Figure 1.1 implies a society with a strong separation between rulers and ruled. Figure 1.2 implies a society where some members of a family staff political positions while others staff commercial and industrial positions. A brother might be in politics while a sister is in commerce. Throughout the land, classrooms, clubhouses and pews will contain members who operate inside each type of activity.

Within the framework of a conjunctive political economy, the state is not a sentient being that intervenes in the market but rather is an institutionalized process or forum within which people interact with one another. Social-theoretic public finance is the study of means by which people govern themselves. This is not to say that everything that governments do is agreeable to everyone. It is only to say that state activity arises from within a society, and that the same economizing drives and urges that generate market activity generate state activity as well.

The difference between the disjunctive and conjunctive visions can be illuminated with a simple illustration. Somewhere a city establishes an enterprise whereby it offers broadband service to city residents. Of what interest would this establishment be to a theory of public finance? A disjunctive orientation could examine a city's provision of broadband services from any of several possible teleological perspectives. For instance, someone might advocate municipal broadband as a means of offsetting alleged failures of market-based provision. Someone else might dispute those claims, as illustrated by Joseph Bast (2002). Rather than offsetting market failures, municipal broadband might be characterized as a means of subsidizing politically-favored clients and supporters. In any event, the insertion of municipal broadband would be treated as an interventionist act whose consequences could be subjected to teleological analysis: where some analysts might ascribe market perfection to that act, others might describe it as market deformation.

In contrast, a social-theoretic public finance would seek first of all to investigate the establishment of such an enterprise. There is an act of entrepreneurship that establishes the enterprise. Capital is deployed into the enterprise that could have been used in other ways. Just as there is a cost of capital, so must there be an anticipated return. To be sure, there are not explicit shareholders for the municipal enterprise. Still, the enterprise would never have been created without the promise of returns to sponsors. The challenge for a theory of public finance in the conjunctive orientation is to characterize fiscal entrepreneurship according to the same essential economizing logic as is used to characterize the founding of market-based enterprises, taking due account of the pertinent institutional differences between market squares and public squares. The challenge for a social-theoretic orientation toward public finance is to explain the rhyme and reason of governmental activity as emergent from within a society, as this emergence is shaped and channeled by institutionally-mediated relationships.

## VI.  THE PUBLIC, THE PRIVATE AND THE ORGANIZATION OF GOVERNANCE

The theory of public goods is one of the primary foundations upon which the theory of public finance has been erected, at least with respect to the disjunctive version of that theory. The dichotomy between private and public goods seems to map directly and immediately into a dichotomy between markets and governments as methods of economic organization, with markets organizing the supply of private goods and governments organizing the supply of public goods. The effort to work with this dichotomy has spawned much analysis and disputation about the public or private character of numerous goods and services, most of it relatively inconclusive.

The theoretical dichotomy is sharp, as presented in Samuelson (1954, 1955). The aggregate consumption of a private good is determined by addition across the amount consumed by different individuals. For public goods, however, what is produced is equally available to everyone. If the mere production of a good is to render it available to everyone, one might reasonably wonder how its production would be paid for. Some would argue that so long as the equivalent of fences can be placed around public goods, markets can organize their supply and the problem posed by public goods vanishes. Not quite, though, at least with respect to the requirements of Paretian welfare economics. A fence will keep out people who aren't willing to pay the price of admission. But no cost is involved in excluding someone, so exclusion violates one of the standard first-order conditions for Pareto-efficiency.

Short of its capacity, an auditorium that shows a film is providing a public good. If the capacity is 500 and if 300 people pay the $5 admission fee, the outcome is Pareto inefficient so long as there are people who would be willing to gain admission for something less than $5. To label this situation as inefficient, however, does not imply that there is any better way of organizing the supply of movies. For one thing, a private vendor has strong incentives to expand patronage so long as the resulting marginal revenue exceeds marginal cost, which itself is presumed to be zero in the theoretical formulations. What this means is that some system of multiple pricing will typically be established in these circumstances (as Brancato and Wagner (2004) explore), with the enormous variety of airline fares on a single flight serving as a good illustration. This does not imply that profit maximization gives the same allocative outcome as Paretian efficiency might give. There is simply no way to know, and in this realization lies the primary infirmity of the common dichotomy between public and private goods: its inability to address in any reasonable way questions concerning the organization of productive activity within a society.

There are numerous instances where similar enterprises are organized in both market-based and politically-based manners. Just as there are privately-organized hospitals, so are there governmentally-organized hospitals. There are tennis courts and golf courses organized by governments, and there are golf courses and tennis courts organized through market-based arrangements. It is the same for parks, for libraries and for educational services. There are governmentally-sponsored enterprises that help people learn foreign languages, and there are market-based enterprises that do the same thing. It is the same for the provision of security services. In short, the theory of public goods would seem to have only weak connection with the phenomena of public finance. The dichotomy between public and private goods seems to map naturally into a disjunction between domains, with government providing public goods and market-based organizations providing private goods. This disjunction, however, does not conform at all well to reality.

Perhaps it is the very dichotomy between private and public goods that is disabling, particularly in the resulting shift of attention away from concerns about institutional arrangements to concerns with resource allocation.[8] The extent of the public is surely broad and not narrow. Most economic activity takes place in organized public arenas. Places of commerce are public arenas. A public exists whenever a multiplicity of people comes together. In many instances, the composition of a public is continually changing, as illustrated by the customers of a retail store; nevertheless those customers do constitute a public. Anyone who has been disturbed in a theatre by someone talking nearby can attest that watching a movie in a theatre is a public experience, in contrast to watching it at home. For the most part, though, the organization and governance of a wide variety of publics is secured in open and polycentric fashion, and not through the hierarchical ordering suggested by formulations from the theory of public goods.

For a conjunctive political economy, the institutional arrangements of human governance command the foreground of analytical attention while concerns about resource allocation occupy the analytical background. Resources, after all, cannot allocate themselves. Only people can allocate resources, and they do so within an institutional framework that constrains, facilitates and channels those efforts. The object of study for a conjunctive political economy is how people participate through government to achieve their various ends, realizing, moreover, that people can differ in the particular ends they pursue. Fiscal phenomena emerge through interaction among people just as do market phenomena. This interaction might be beneficial for everyone or nearly everyone, or it might be beneficial for only a few, and costly for many others. The state is simply a nexus of contractual and exploitive relationships in which everyone participates to varying degrees, even if not always willingly. The extent to which those relationships are contractual or exploitive depends on the constitutive structure of governance that is in place.

It is fine to say that taxes are the price we pay for civilization. This doesn't mean, however, that the relationship between citizens and state is the same as the relationship between customers and the retail outlets they frequent. A customer can refuse to buy and, moreover, can generally return merchandise that turns out to be defective or otherwise unsatisfactory. There is no option to do this in politics. To say that civilization is being priced too highly and to withhold payment will only land the protester in prison. And there is certainly no point in asking for a refund by claiming that the state's offerings weren't as good as its advertisements claimed them to be.

To speak of a catallactical approach to public finance is only to say that those phenomena arise through interaction among people, the very same people who interact with one another within the market economy. Many of the phenomena of public finance surely arise through duress and not through genuine agreement. This aspect of duress was emphasized in a good deal of the Italian scholarship on public finance, which is surveyed in James Buchanan (1960), as well as in Richard Wagner (2003). A catallactical approach toward the organization of the public economy leads directly into a conceptualization of polycentric public finance. Within that conceptualization, there is open competition within the public square for the organization and operation of enterprises that provide services to clients and offer returns to sponsors, all mediated within an institutional framework of civic governance within the public square.

A general treatment of a polycentric public economy leads to a recognition that many different enterprises are involved with the provision of services within the public square. As Vincent Ostrom (1962) explains, it is not the case that water is supplied either by market-based organizations or by governments. Rather, it is that myriad different enterprises participate in the provision of water, and these enterprises operate under a variety of organizational frameworks. It is a straightforward matter to conceptualize a municipal services industry, as this was articulated by Vincent Ostrom, Charles Tiebout and Robert Warren (1961), and elaborated further in Vincent Ostrom (1973).

Resources cannot allocate themselves nor can functions assign themselves. Only people can do these things, and they do so while encased within institutional arrangements that channel and constrain what they know and how they act. Government is simply a subset of the myriad arenas for human interaction within the public square; those interactions generate a wide variety of enterprises, some established within market forums and others established within political forums, with varying degrees of complementarity and competitiveness existing among those enterprises. Within a social-theoretic orientation toward public finance, the establishment and subsequent support of political enterprises, along with their relationships to market-based enterprises, provides the focal point of the analytical effort.

## VII.   ENTERPRISE-BASED PUBLIC FINANCE

The key unit of analysis in an enterprise-based theory of public finance is the political enterprise, which is the political equivalent to the firm within the context of market theory. What we call the state or government is not itself an enterprise. It is rather an arena within which enterprises are created, exist, operate and even die. All enterprises are public creatures, in that they involve a multiplicity of people, a public. To call that multiplicity a public does not mean that it constitutes a government in the sense used within the theory of public goods. There are numerous specific ways through which the governance of the myriad publics that comprise a society can be constituted, the examination of which forms a good part of the domain of a science of human association.

The myriad associations that exist within a society constitute its enterprises. Those enterprises will in turn be organized within a variety of different arenas. The theoretical exposition of a pure market economy postulates one particular arena for the organization of enterprises. This is an arena characterized by private property and freedom of contract. To be sure, in actuality private property is not absolute and liberty of contract is restricted in numerous ways, as will be examined more fully in Chapter 2. Still, we may consider the market as an abstract noun that, among other things, denotes the framework of principles and rules of human interaction through which people can seek to organize enterprises and promote them.

But the market is not the only arena within which enterprises may be organized. The polity provides another arena. Vincent Ostrom (1962) describes how the organization of water supply involves both market-based and politically-based enterprises. Just as the relationship among different market-based enterprises may be complementary or competitive, so may be the relationship among different politically-based enterprises. Furthermore, the same principles of complementarity and substitutability can characterize relationships between market-based and politically-based enterprises. Political- and market-based enterprises interact with one another, and in myriad ways. Some of those interactions might produce widespread, general advantage. Others might provide advantage for some people at the expense of others, as manifestations of duress in the operation of political enterprises. Regardless of the particular character of those interactions, government is not some choosing agent but is a nexus or arena of contractual and exploitive relationships. In any event, the same operation of such universal economic categories as demand, costs, profits and entrepreneurship would be found useful in explaining the operation and governance of political enterprises as characterizes ordinary commercial activity and relationships, except that they would play out differently owing to differences in institutional frameworks.

It is easy enough to think of an urban transit industry that contains many different participants. To start, suppose the consensual framework of a market economy governs the relationships among all participants. Accordingly, some people might drive their own cars each day, while other people might create taxi or limousine companies. Still others might establish a bus service, others might try to provide a monorail service, and yet others might try to establish a subway service. All of these enterprises might be operated privately by profit-seeking companies, but if so this would be an emergent feature of the process and not something dictated in advance. There might also be some cooperative enterprises that participate in this industry, and there could even be some municipally owned operations.

The prospect of municipal operation brings forth possible conflicts among enterprises organized within political and market forums, as recognized by Maffeo Pantaleoni (1911) and elaborated by Richard Wagner (1997b). It is one thing for government-sponsored enterprises to participate within polycentric societal processes on the same terms as other participants. This would require municipally sponsored transit enterprises to compete for customers on the same basis as all other enterprises. Governments, though, can subsidize enterprises that might otherwise fail in open competition with private transit enterprises. They can also impose disabilities on competitive enterprises through regulation, as discussed in Daniel Klein (1997). The competitive ability of a privately organized bus company might be degraded by requiring it to maintain routes and schedules that are not profitable. The competitive ability of a municipal transit company might be strengthened by restricting the numbers of parking spaces that can be created within buildings located downtown. There are an indefinitely large number of ways by which a government can use taxation and regulation to secure advantages for the enterprises it sponsors relative to other enterprises within a society.

To say that governments secure advantages for enterprises that they sponsor is not necessarily to offer a negative evaluation. Several lines of cogent argument have been advanced as to why the market-based organization of urban transit might fit standard claims of market failure. For instance, Roger Sherman (1967) argues that the private ownership of automobiles creates a bias against the use of public transit facilities. Once a decision to own a car has been made, a driver's comparison between using a car and using public transit is based only on the marginal cost of using the car, whereas the price of public transit might include depreciation on the capital equipment. In a related line of argument, Donald Shoup (2005) argues that the provision of free parking in urban areas similarly presents a bias against mass transit. But these arguments get into the domain of systems design, whereas this book pursues a social-theoretic orientation whose object is to give a coherent characterization of the patterns of activity undertaken within public squares.

Within the social-theoretic orientation, the political enterprise provides the analytical starting point. At any instant, a society contains a network of enterprises. Some of those enterprises are organized through market forums while others are organized through political forums. One analytical task is to explain the characteristic features of the ecology of enterprises that exist within a society. The standard dichotomy between public and private goods will be of little help in this task. Prior to undertaking this analytical task, it is necessary to consider the place of property in the theory of public finance. The pure theory of a market economy is based upon an idealization of universal private property and full liberty of contract. The phenomena of public finance, however, are based upon a denial of those idealizations. There are some significant incongruities between the theory of a market economy and the theory of public finance that must first be addressed before proceeding to an exposition of a social-theoretic public finance.

## VIII.   A BRIEF EXCURSUS ON SCOPE AND METHOD

In cooking, you don't want to do without spices and seasonings, and yet you are aware that these ingredients are but a sideshow in your overall culinary effort. Methodology would seem to occupy a position similar to spices and seasonings: some methodology is desirable but it must not be allowed to overwhelm the substance. While methodological points will be addressed at several points in this book, a summary statement might be helpful at this point to avoid misunderstanding as to what I am trying to accomplish here, for this book differs from most contemporary public finance both in its substance and in its methodology. There are four related themes of methodological significance that inform this book and which set it apart from much scholarship in public finance: (1) a treatment of a bi-directional relationship between mind and society, in contrast to mind being independent of society; (2) an emphasis on inside-out rather than outside-in modeling; (3) a focus on processes of development and not on states of equilibrium; and (4) an adoption of intelligibility and not prediction as the prime object of fiscal and social theorizing.[9]

Most economic theorizing follows George Stigler and Gary Becker (1977) in working with minds that are independent of and autonomous from societal interaction, whereas, borrowing from Georg Simmel (1978 [1900]), Vilfredo Pareto (1935) and Norbert Elias (1982, 1991), I work with a bi-directional relationship between mind and society. From one direction, the interaction among minds generates and transforms societal formations; from the other direction, those formations channel and shape both the ends people choose to pursue and the means they employ in doing so. Similar to Tony Lawson (1997, 2003), I regard both mind and society as real categories of existence, in that society cannot be reduced to an individual even though a society cannot exist without members. Object-oriented programming offers insight in this respect, as can be illustrated by Mitchel Resnick's (1994) computational model of a traffic jam. In that model, all cars always move forward, and yet the jam itself moves backward. The jam is an object in its own right, distinct from the individual cars even though it is constituted by those cars. It is the same for the relation between mind and society.

Theorizing about people is different from theorizing about termites or trees, because with respect to people we live inside the objects we theorize about. For termites or trees there is no option but to theorize from the outside looking in, and the only test of reasonable theorizing must be some measure of the coherence between theoretical predictions and observed outcomes. In contrast, the human sciences can also call upon theorizing from the inside looking out. Indeed, much social theorizing can only be done from this perspective. The claim that people seek to be effective in applying means to the pursuit of ends is not a conclusion of outside observation and inference, but rather is a feature of our self-awareness. To be sure, theorizing from the inside looking out is an instrument that must be used with care, for a danger that comes with it is that it can turn into a battle among contending prejudices and intuitions. Yet there are many statements about successful human action that can be rendered intelligible in terms of a pure logic of choice because such a logic maps directly into a logic of successful conduct – and we know from the inside that people do not seek to fail at what they try.

Equilibrium is a sensible even if perhaps peculiar notion to apply to an individual, for it merely signifies coherence in the person's planned pattern of conduct regarding the employment of means in the pursuit of ends. It is an entirely different matter to apply notions of equilibrium to societies. A society is not an acting creature from which we would expect coherence, but rather is an arena within which acting creatures interact. It is true that societal processes unfold in generally orderly fashion, though not always and never completely. People seek to be successful in action, and have over the years developed various customs and conventions that facilitate such success. While there is a good deal of permanence in social life, particularly over relatively short periods of time, there is also a fair amount of turbulence, much of which manifests itself through capital gains and losses. In my view the most foundational features of social life are not repetition, reproduction and stagnation, but are creation, novelty and turbulence. The challenge for fiscal theorizing, as well as social theorizing more generally, is to render intelligible social life and social patterns in such a setting of continual and turbulent development.

A desire to render social life intelligible in terms of people pursuing plans stands, of course, in some contrast to claims that theory should seek to predict societal outcomes. To be sure, next month will be a lot like this month, and from such regularities weak forms of prediction are possible. For instance, it is easy enough to predict that a government that increases its tax on alcohol or tobacco will find that its residents resort increasingly to underground sources of supply. But societal interaction yields much more than this, as illustrated by increased bribery, violence and disrespect for law. These other consequences are more products of interaction than of direct choice, though in principle they too could be brought under the rubric of prediction. Yet pragmatically speaking the scope of what can be addressed by prediction is narrower than what can be addressed by intelligibility. What we can predict is limited to the availability of externally generated data, while our ability to understand has a wider range. Moreover, prediction is plagued by a problem of knowledge that does not bother intelligibility. One might seek to predict next month's societal patterns based on what people know now. However, as people live they learn, which in turn changes what they do, thus undermining the basis for the earlier prediction. The serenity of steady-state equilibrium gives way to the turbulence of emergent development. Prediction is a reasonable standard for any closed system to which equilibrium pertains. But for an open system characterized by turbulence injected through novelty, the appropriate objective of theoretical activity is to seek to render social life intelligible in terms of people pursuing plans within a societal setting.

## NOTES

1. For a sharp contrast between these visions, presented by two of the major fiscal theorists of the past half-century, see Buchanan and Musgrave (1999).
2. To be sure, there are many possible options to the particular subway extension. Different expenditure programs could be increased. Taxes could be reduced, there being numerous ways of doing so.
3. The subway extension might also reduce congestion and travel time elsewhere, which would also have to be incorporated into a benefit–cost calculus.
4. The choice-theoretic and catallactical options are portrayed in Wagner (1997a).
5. For exemplary treatments, see Brennan and Buchanan (1980) and Usher (1992).
6. See, for instance, Miron and Zwiebel (1991), Benson and Rasmussen (1991) and Thornton (1991).
7. Even the notion of an absolute ruler is a conceptual abstraction, as Norbert Elias (1982, 1991) explains in his examination of social relationships within court-based societies.
8. For a seminal effort to formulate a theory of public goods with institutional arrangements in the foreground, see James Buchanan (1968).
9. Five references that I have found particularly valuable in this regard, arrayed chronologically, are: Alfred Stonier and Karl Bode (1937), Karl Bode (1943), Ludwig von Mises (1966, esp. pp. 1–199), Ludwig Lachmann (1971) and Ludwig Lachmann (1977).

# 2.   Property, state and public finance

A creature of high intelligence who could not communicate with us humans and who had recourse only to direct observation would surely conclude that we are like social insects or mammals. We live in groups and form organized patterns of activity, as the literature on social biology illustrates (Tullock 1994; Wilson 1971, 1975). We specialize across activities through a division of labor just as do the social insects and mammals. Termites build skyscrapers just as we do; indeed, they build taller skyscrapers relative to their height than we do. In social biology, specialization and the division of labor are explained as genetically programmed. Worker ants do what they do because their biology compels them, as do queens; worker ants don't aspire to become queens.[1]

The very nature of ants and termites allows them to participate within their colonies without questioning their participation or their roles. While genetics is important also to the organization of human activity, language and property are unique components of organized human activity. We are social creatures that need each other, but our ability to enter into cooperative association resides to a large degree in language and the property-based relationships and institutions we generate. Our social nature requires property-governed relationships to accommodate peaceful and productive human interaction within society. Property, after all, connotes propriety or properness in human conduct.

The Marxist ideal was that of human society organized as if it were a colony of ants or termites, at least once people had acquired a true consciousness of their natures and had been freed from the warping character of private property and market-based interaction within society. The communist experiment has surely rendered dubious any Marxist fantasies about our ant-like natures. For us humans, the cooperative living together that our natures compel is promoted through property-governed relationships. Such relationships involve a disjunction between mine and thine, and also require a supporting institutional framework to instantiate that disjunction. Conflict arises when the boundary of that disjunction is contested. Nonetheless, our very natures require both property as the framework by which we govern our relationships and procedures for resolving the boundary disputes that will invariably arise.

While the point of this chapter, and indeed, of the entire book, is to assimilate fiscal phenomena to property-based governance, it will facilitate the exposition to start by reviewing the relation between private property and a market economy. Doing this makes it possible directly and readily to appreciate some challenges regarding property, market and state that accompany any effort to pursue a social-theoretic orientation toward public finance. The theory of a market economy seeks to explain how generally orderly patterns of human activity emerge within a society when people relate to one another through private property.

The phenomena of public finance, however, do not arise out of private property but out of abridgements of private property. Taxation transforms private property into collective property. This transformation creates several analytical challenges. Both forms of property arise within the same society among the same people. One challenge is to characterize or explain the boundary between private and collective property. That boundary, moreover, is multidimensional and has a structure; using a bundle-of-sticks analogy, it is not that some sticks are collective and some private but is rather that many of the sticks have attributes of both. Another challenge arises because action cannot be characterized in the same way when it concerns collective property as when it concerns private property. With private property, trade between two people is easy to characterize and understand. It is different with collective property because collectives aren't sentient beings who can choose and act. Collectives simply denote a web of connections and relationships out of which actions emerge. Collective property must be defined in terms of particular institutional frameworks that establish relationships among participants. Taxation does not transfer property into some acting entity called State, but rather transfers it to some complex network of relationships within the public square. What emerges are the fiscal phenomena that are the object of interest in a social-theoretic orientation toward public finance.

## I. PRIVATE PROPERTY AND THE THEORY OF A MARKET ECONOMY

The pure theory of a market economy is an intellectual construction that explores the logic of human interaction when those interactions are governed by private property and freedom of contract. Every object that people value is owned by someone and the owner has the right to use or trade those objects. Within this institutional framework, all market activity is voluntary. Complex commercial enterprises can be created and operated through this framework of simple rules (Epstein 1995). Anyone who wants to establish a commercial enterprise is free to try to do so. The ability to try is, of course, no guarantee of success. To be successful, the voluntary cooperation of other property owners will have to be secured. The promoter of the enterprise will have to convince investors or lenders to support the enterprise. That accomplished, it will be necessary to convince many other participants to provide labor, supplies, places of work and all of the other inputs that the enterprise will require. And it will be necessary to convince yet other people to buy the enterprise's products and services.

The economic theory of a market economy seeks to explain how orderly patterns of economic life arise when human relationships are governed by a simple recognition of the disjunction between mine and thine. For instance, several people can agree to form a commercial association, with that association governed by rules and procedures that those participants select. Economic activity is an illustration of self-organization that emerges when human relationships are governed by private property.[2] Where the model of the Edgeworth Box illustrates how both parties can gain from a trade, a market economy is generalized as an aggregation of such trades. If both parties to any particular trade gain, or at least if neither loses, the generalization holds that trades will continue so long as opportunities for gain remain unexploited. The logic of a market economy explains that markets possess a strong tendency to promote the exploitation of all opportunities for mutual gain within their reach. This tendency is, of course, the claim that a competitive equilibrium is Pareto efficient. While this Paretian construction is irrelevant to the analytical formulations pursued in this book, it is central to the organization of the systems design orientation toward public finance.

While the theory of a market economy is typically presented with reference to an equilibrated pattern of relationships, also noteworthy is the self-transformative character of market-generated relationships. This transformation occurs through invention, both technological and organizational, both of which are facilitated by the degenerative character of an institutional framework characterized by private property and freedom of contract and association.[3] In terms of the logic of a market economy, degeneracy means that there is no particular person whose consent is necessary for an entrepreneurial plan to go forward. While any such plan will require cooperation from many people, there is no particular, identifiable person whose participation must be secured. For any node in a network where someone refuses to participate in someone else's plan, other nodes can be substituted to carry the plan forward. While such alternative nodes might not be as desirable in the entrepreneur's judgment, the plan can go forward nonetheless because there is no particular person whose participation is indispensable for the pursuit of an entrepreneurial plan.

It is easy enough to see the transformative character of technological invention. Anyone who has walked through a densely populated barn and breathed deeply can get a sense of what life in large cities must have been like before the automobile replaced horses. While the automobile transformed life on a massive scale, destroying many occupations and activities while generating myriad new ones, a market economy continually generates such transformations as a feature of its ordinary mode of operation. The central mode of operation of a market economy is surely creative transformation and not some steady-state equilibrium.

Such transformation also occurs organizationally through such activities as developing new forms of commercial organization and new forms of contract. For instance, with the proliferation of automobiles in the aftermath of World War II and the accompanying expansion in highway construction, travel by automobile increased markedly. Accompanying this increase in mobility was the development of franchise-based commercial organizations, particularly for lodging and dining. By virtue of hindsight, it is easy to understand how entrepreneurs would have seen opportunities present in creating forms of commercial organization that would accommodate the desire that most people have to avoid being unpleasantly surprised while traveling in unfamiliar places. The creation of franchised chains is one organizational method for injecting loci of familiarity into unfamiliar places.

A market economy even has the flexibility to accommodate the generation of organizational forms that are implicitly critical of market-generated outcomes. Nonprofit forms of organization are readily created within the framework of private property and its associated framework, and yet such forms of organization often denote a demurral from what would otherwise have been market-generated patterns of conduct. Among the nonprofit organizations that people develop are fraternal institutions to provide mutual assistance, charitable organizations to help those who are experiencing particularly hard times, and scientific and cultural associations to advance the common interests of their members (Beito 2000). It is no little irony that many of the nonprofit organizations that are created within the framework provided by private property represent internally-generated contestations of some substantive features of market-generated outcomes.

The historical record is replete with people who establish museums, libraries and charitable organizations. In each such instance, private property is being used to contest substantively though not formally some characteristic feature of what would otherwise pertain to the market economy that was also generated through private property. For instance, a donor who founds a library is using wealth accumulated through market-based activity to contest the amount or type of reading that would otherwise be undertaken within the society. Similarly, a donor who founds a museum devoted to Etruscan art is contesting the awareness of Etruscan art that would otherwise be present within the society. Hence, the institutional framework that people can generate by acting according to the principles of private property will lead not only to the creation of profit-seeking commercial organizations but also to a wide variety of non-commercial organizations whose existence reflects some element of uneasiness with the societal landscape otherwise generated through commercial activity. Property-governed relationships can accommodate continual transformation in the substantive character of economic relationships while conforming to the formal framework of private property. Social reformation occurs continually within the framework of a market economy.

## II.   TELEOLOGY, WELFARE ECONOMICS AND PUBLIC FINANCE

A market economy is not the object of prime analytical interest for fiscal theorizing. Rather, that object is government or state. State activity, however, is not organized within the framework of private property and freedom of contract. Governments are not clubs or other forms of voluntary association, although it is possible normatively speaking to assimilate some idealization of state to a club (Backhaus 1992). Governments are not just particular firms that operate within the framework of private property. To be sure, many analytical efforts have sought to reconcile governmental force with private property.

For the most part, the systems design orientation toward public finance proceeds through a set of exercises on the notions of externalities and public goods. What results is an analysis that divides society into two regions. One region is characterized by property-based governance that results in economic interaction that works well. The other region is one that is characterized by a failure of property-based governance to accommodate what nonetheless are presumed by an analyst to be patterns of interaction that people would find desirable, if only those patterns could somehow be organized. This claimed failure of property-based governance is typically accompanied by a claim that governmental organization can potentially fill the gaps that property-based governance cannot. Claims about market failure through externalities and public goods form the contours of the systems design approach to public finance.[4] The various claims about market failure, moreover, have also evoked contrary arguments that dispute those claims.

One of the archetypical claims of externality-based market failure can be illustrated by bees and pollination, as advanced by James Meade (1952). He illustrated his argument with beekeepers and apple farmers, claiming that markets would fail to secure efficient production. On the one hand, apple growers would plant too few trees because they don't take into account the value that their trees provide to beekeepers. On the other hand, beekeepers would supply an insufficient number of hives because they don't take into consideration the increased apple production that results from the pollination services the bees provide.

This tale of externality and market failure is something that might seem sensible at first glance; however, a closer examination shows it to be dubious. Someone who actually examines the market relationships within which honey and apples are produced will find that there exists a wide variety of contractual agreements among beekeepers and apple growers, as detailed by Steven Cheung (1973) and David Johnson (1973). For instance, apple blossoms provide little honey but bees offer valuable pollination services, so apple growers pay beekeepers to provide their bees for such services. On the other hand, clover does not require pollination but yields much honey, so beekeepers pay to bring their bees into fields of clover. In either case, property-based governance leads people to craft contractual and organizational arrangements that facilitate the very exchanges that are presumed to be absent by conventional analyses of market failure.[5] Any claim of market failure implies that market participants are failing to seize some of the mutual gains from trade that exist among them. Such situations doubtlessly exist, but at the same time they are being hunted by entrepreneurs who are seeking to devise organizational and contractual arrangements that will seize those mutual gains.

Lighthouses have long served as an archetypical example of the public goods form of market failure, in conjunction with a claim of how fiscal action can fill the gaps left open by property-based governance. While lighthouses have been subject to dispute ever since Ronald Coase's (1974) examination, it is worth exploring the matter in some detail because doing so will point to several topics that will be explored subsequently. Figure 2.1 can be used to represent the various ideas in play and at issue. Ships that pass through some shallow and rocky area face some prospect of running aground and sinking, and this creates a demand for protection against that prospect. Without a lighthouse, ships would take lengthier and more costly journeys to reduce the prospect of running aground. The lighthouse offers a gain both through a reduced risk of running aground and through an ability to shorten travel time.

The demand curves $d_i$ and $d_j$ represented in Figure 2.1 illustrate the value that two ship owners place on the protection offered by lighthouse beams of varying strength. Whatever strength of beam is offered to one

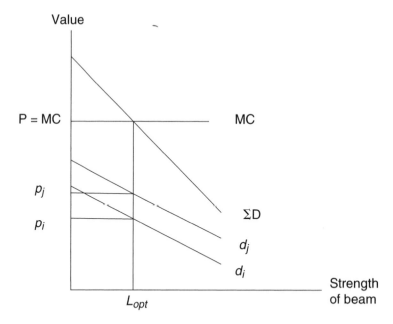

*Figure 2.1    Lighthouses as public goods*

ship is necessarily offered to the other ship as well. This is the condition
of equal consumption, where one unit of production supplies the same,
indivisible amount of consumption to everyone. For any particular
strength of beam, the total value of that beam to ship owners is derived
by adding the value that each owner places on that beam. This aggregate
demand for the lighthouse's service is indicated by $\Sigma D$. The Pareto
efficient strength of the lighthouse beam is indicated by $L_{opt}$, which is
where the sum of the valuations that each individual ship owner places on
that strength of beam is equal to the marginal cost of producing that
strength of beam.

At this point, the theory of public goods injects a claim of market failure,
with this claim based on a presumption about particular organizational
arrangements. In many cases, market-governed arrangements operate on a
basis that can be described as a form of build-it-and-they-will-come, as
illustrated by *Field of Dreams*, a movie about someone turning a cornfield
in Iowa into a baseball field. In this typical setting, someone builds the facility in anticipation that a demand will exist for its use. The actual strength
of demand is revealed subsequently when people decide how much use to
make of it. It is easy enough to use Figure 2.1 to portray the ball park. The
different demands might correspond to a demand for cheaper seats by $d_i$

while $d_j$ represents a demand for box seats. In any case, the same event is viewed by all, regardless of the strengths of their individual demands, as shown by $\Sigma D$.

A ball park can be fenced and admission charged. It is a collective good in that one unit of production supplies consumption to a collection of people, and is subject to the same analytical issues as was illustrated by the movie theatre in Chapter 1. The ability to exclude those who don't pay makes market-based provision possible, with complex pricing arrangements securing the exploitation of gains from trade that could not be exploited under uniform pricing. However, there will be no market provision of the build-it-and-they-will-come form if there is no possibility of exclusion. In this case, the theory of public goods is typically used as a vehicle for arguing in support of government provision. The argument is that if lighthouses were first built, with the owners then having to rely upon voluntary contributions from ship owners, the setting portrayed by Figure 2.1 would fail to materialize. People would not contribute what it was truly worth to them, as indicated by what they would have paid had it been necessary to do so to receive the lighthouse beam. Some might not contribute at all, while others might contribute some but less than they would have contributed had some means of exclusion been in place.[6] The option is either to get along with fewer and smaller lighthouses with weaker beams, or to have government provision. A theory of market failure maps into a teleological vision of government as filling gaps in market-based arrangements.

As Coase (1974) explains, lighthouses were erected as commercial ventures in 17th century England. The presence of commercial lighthouses has spawned some significant controversy as to its meaning, with some claiming that this shows the fallacies of public goods theorizing while others claiming that it shows the pivotal place of government activity in promoting successful market operation. Actually, it shows a bit of both and a bit of neither. Lighthouses were not produced by government and financed through taxes. They were produced by commercial enterprises and were financed by charges to ships for their use of lighthouse services. While lighthouses were commercial enterprises, they were not put in place through the common process whereby the owner supplies the facility and then awaits the response of customers through their expressions of desires to buy the service. Rather, tolls were levied upon ships as they came into port, and the collection of these tolls was enforced by government.

This situation happens to be the way the history of the period unfolded. There was clearly some state presence. The situation was not one of entrepreneurs first building lighthouses and then awaiting contributions from grateful ship owners. So, does this case point to market success and the inaptness of market failure claims made on behalf of public goods? Or does it offer an illustration of market failure, where government correction took the form not of direct production but of creating a kind of regulated utility status for lighthouses? The public utility claim has merit, but it is also incomplete, because the sequence of building something first and than awaiting consumer judgments is not the only sequence for economic organization.

This sequence is common when fences, gates and other means of exclusion are used, but what if exclusion is not possible, or perhaps is just not practical in the light of cost? Ships that crash upon the rocks are costly to their owners, as are ships that take longer journeys to deliver their cargos. An association of ship owners could conceivably provide the arena within which the production and financing of lighthouses was organized. The world of experience presents us with many such instances. On occasion, a ship that did not belong to such an association might use a protective beam sponsored by the association. Such incidental events, however, would generally be infra-marginal and present no Paretian-type issues, as Buchanan and Stubblebine (1962) explain.

A more difficult case arises with the introduction of change through time. A number of ship owners may well commit themselves through an association they form. As time passes, however, new ship owners may enter the picture. It is understandable that members of the existing association would like to incorporate the new ship owners, or at least to derive revenue from them. It is equally clear that the new ship owners might prefer to use the existing lighthouse services without payment. The English system that Coase studied resolved this situation by effectively incorporating new ship owners into the association on the same terms as incumbent members. But alternative approaches to organizing the realization of mutual gains are also conceivable.

These issues arise because sea lanes are not subject to ownership. If they were, there would be no problem of charging for lighthouse services. In this respect, all nations assert sovereignty over offshore territory. Just as oyster beds are often leased to private persons, so could sea lanes be leased to lighthouse associations. Disputes might still arise and these might be brought before state-sponsored forums for resolution. Debating whether this possibility means we are dealing with private or public goods seems irrelevant, for surely what it points to is the inadequacy of approaching these matters from an orientation that posits distinct spheres of private and collective property, as against seeking an alternative orientation that locates property inside the social setting through which the specific contours of property are shaped. The lighthouse presents a setting of conflict among institutional arrangements, and such conflict points toward entrepreneurial opportunities that can include the development of new organizational arrangements.

Before turning to such entrepreneurial activity, there are some conundrums of public goods theorizing that should be examined. The standard public goods claim is one of market failure, which in terms of Figure 2.1 means that the actual supply of lighthouse services will be something less than $L_{opt}$. Government supply is thought to be the remedy for such deficiency. This raises the question of accuracy or validity. On what basis can a claim of some discrepancy between actual and optimal amounts be judged? There really isn't any way to do this. It could simply be asserted that state supply enters when market provision fails, as illustrated by Donald Wittman (1995). This is an argument that can be neither confirmed nor disconfirmed, and rather represents a particular metaphysical orientation that interprets all economic activity in terms of a universalized efficiency standard, as explained by Richard Wagner (1994). To claim otherwise is simultaneously to embrace the claim that market outcomes could be attained through planning without markets. If Figure 2.1 is taken to be a portrait of what markets would generate if they could work, but it is also claimed that they can't, this raises the question of how anyone would know this.

To say this involves a claim that models can serve as a recipe or grammar for the application of expertise. In other words, such constructions as Figure 2.1 represent some information about the categories of cost and demand that are available independently of the choices that people actually make in real market settings. To say that the world does not look like Figure 2.1 because market processes are presumed not to operate is to claim to be able to say what markets would generate without ever resorting to market-generated information and action.

These days, no one supports planning to replace market organization. Ants can operate under these arrangements, and indeed, can operate only under these arrangements. Humans, however, require property to operate in society, and our natures allow it to be no other way. Economic models are not recipes for calculation; they do not represent a grammar in terms of which the expertise of planners can operate in place of actual market arrangements. To the contrary, models are merely predictions of the patterns of outcomes that tend to emerge through human interaction within a framework of property, as embellished by such attendant features as contracts and associations. Hence, something like Figure 2.1 can reasonably be used to organize observations about the actual supply of lighthouse services when private property constitutes the core of human governance, even if the data portrayed in Figure 2.1 cannot be calculated independently of actual human action.[7]

## III.  PROPERTY-GOVERNED RELATIONSHIPS: A FORK IN THE THEORETICAL ROAD

The theory of a market economy represents the effort of myriad scholars over many years to give a coherent account of patterns of societal organization when human relationships are governed by the various institutional arrangements we associate with private property. While clubs and other forms of voluntary association can readily be incorporated into this analytical framework, the state presents a particular problem. If economics is the science of markets and public finance the science of state (to create a linguistic parallel with the Germanic concept of *Staatswissenschaften*), how is the latter related to the former?[8] Despite the analytical constructions of welfare economics, the state is not just another marketplace where people buy public goods to complement their purchases of private goods on ordinary marketplaces.

For public finance treated as a facet of social theory, property presents a challenge of which of two possible analytical paths to take. The more common path is to treat the state and its activities as reflections of people's use of their property rights. The analytical world begins with autonomous individuals who possess a feeble form of private property, and they pool some of those rights to create collective property that a government administers to secure the remaining rights. How successful they are in doing this depends on the ability of the constitutive arrangements they create to restrain and channel the use of state force. For instance, Barzel (2002) argues that paying fixed salaries to state officials rather than making them residual claimants serves to blunt what would otherwise be expansionary thrusts into the remaining private property.[9] Within this Hobbes-like analytical framework, people use some of their prior rights of private property to create a state that in turn operates to increase the value of the remaining rights of private property over what the value of the full bundle of rights would have been without the state.

State provision of security and welfare is thus explained according to the same principles as the market-based supply of dog food and shoes. The state is just one organization among many that is formed within a society, and people use their property rights to support states just as they use them to support other vendors. The threat of force, however, means that the state is not just another market participant. The common way of confronting this observation is to treat the state as initially created through the use of private property, only subsequently to abridge those rights of property. This approach is taken throughout the Hobbes-inspired formulations of the state. The extent to which the state subsequently abridges those prior rights of property is thought to depend on the ability of constitutive arrangements to control the state.[10]

In the various Hobbes-like formulations, the analysis begins with individuals who are seeking to protect themselves against predations from other individuals. People have property prior to state, but it is a puny form of property that is secured only through the strength of its possessor. People use their property to enhance their security of possession and action by forming a state. The state is an internally-generated agent that subsequently stands apart from the society, just as referees to a game stand apart from the game even though at some earlier stage they were selected by the players. What is most significant about this analytical orientation is that the state reflects a use of prior rights of property. At its founding, the state is conceptualized as a form of club or protective association. However, with monopoly over some piece of geography, the problem of guarding against predation by the guardian arises. The state may secure a position of dominance and autonomy that was not intended by those who participated in its creation (de Jasay 1985). The constitutional literature provides numerous formulations of this ancient problem, most of which seek to overcome the problem through some process of fragmentation and distribution that would evaporate, or at least reduce greatly, the position of an outside entity with a monopoly over the instruments of violence.[11]

The sequential order that places market prior to state is one that leads naturally to a formulation where one would speak of a market-generated distribution of income that to some degree might be redistributed through subsequent state action. In this respect, numerous studies have been made of how state budgetary activity redistributes income or consumption as compared with the initial, market-generated distributions.[12] In *The Myth of Ownership*, Liam Murphy and Thomas Nagel (2002) present an alternative form of sequential logic, wherein state precedes market. Murphy and Nagel argue that no economic activity is possible without a state presence, and so they start with collective ownership. What is commonly described as private property is thus a withdrawal of the state from the exercise of some of its rights of ownership. Murphy and Nagel do not distinguish redistribution from distribution because the market-generated distribution is attributable to state action, just as are all actions in society for that matter.

While Murphy and Nagel seem off base in their treatment of state as prior to property, their treatment is surely valuable in bringing to the analytical foreground the neglected relationship between property and theorizing about public finance. The customary treatment is to regard state as a use of prior property, even if the state subsequently turns into a Leviathan-like creature that devours much of the surplus that people thought they might have been protecting by creating a state. Murphy and Nagel are right to challenge this conventional treatment, but they still work with a sequential relationship between market and state and, moreover, treat the state as a goal-focused organization.

Whether one starts with individual ownership, however insecure it might be, or with collective ownership, however this might be instantiated institutionally, the sequential nature of the relationship between state and market has some significant problematical features. While the organization of market activity is treated as an emergent result of human interaction within a nexus of property-governed relationships, state activity is treated as teleological. Market participants are treated as *acting inside* the social world with distributed knowledge, and the resulting order is an emergent quality of those distributed actions and interactions. In sharp contrast, the state is conceptualized as *acting outside* the social world, based on global knowledge of the details that brought about the emergent market order. The phenomena of public finance are thus conventionally treated as disjunctive in character from those of market-generated activity. There are thus two realms of human activity, one whose characteristic features are explained in emergent terms and the other whose characteristic features are explained in teleological terms.

This disjunction seems deeply problematical. If one fork in the road of theoretical public finance treats property and state in a relationship of primary to derivative, even if scholars differ as to which is primary and which is derivative, the alternative fork treats the two as coeval. This alternative, lesser-traveled fork is the one I take here, with the journey accompanied by a treatment of state as an arena for human interaction and not as a goal-focused organization. The Hobbes-like fables are all tales of solitary adults who come together to form a state. And yet an adult could never get to adulthood alone. Adults start as infants who are raised in social groups of various types, with those settings implanting various psychological imprints upon those individuals, largely through habits generated through practice supported by instruction. There is interaction between mind and society, a central theme of such works as Norbert Elias (1982, 1991), Emile Durkheim (1933 [1893]) and Vilfredo Pareto (1935).[13] People arrive at adulthood with a sense of both I and we, to use the title of the third essay from Elias's (1991) formulation, with a tension between the two, and with the contours of that tension surely differing among people. In any case, what comprises proper conduct within society is not captured adequately by private property. Hence, property and property-governed relations must be articulated differently for a social-theoretic orientation toward the material of public finance. In this respect, I seek to ground property rights in human nature, with that nature seeking both autonomy and solidarity. This leads to a form of social theorizing wherein market and

fiscal phenomena are coeval products of human association and interaction, as illustrated nicely by Georg Simmel's (1978 [1900]) treatment of
the changing reach of alienability in human relationships.

Private property is often analogized with a bundle of sticks, with an
owner able to alienate some of those sticks while keeping possession of the
remainder. An owner might thus transfer a few sticks to the organizers of
a state. Within such a framework, private property would still govern
market-based relationships while the state was governed by the particular
form of collective property by which it was constituted. By this method of
separation, societal outcomes would be described by addition across the
two separate spheres of human interaction. Such separability between
spheres might ease analytical burdens and challenges, but it surely conflicts
with our experiences and observations about societal processes. To the contrary, collective property interbreeds with private property, often transforming the meaning of private property in the process. For instance, the
textbook literature contains numerous references to how agriculture provides perhaps an ideal exemplar of a competitive industry: there are many
producers, each so insignificant as to be price takers, products are relatively
homogeneous, and information is simple and easy to procure. Such references, however, are inapt, for perhaps nowhere in the world is agriculture
organized through private property and freedom of contract. To produce
wheat, milk, or just about any agricultural crop nearly anywhere is subject
to governmental requirements and impositions. Degeneracy clearly does
not characterize the economic organization of agriculture, and the same
can be said for many other forms of economic activity.

If market and state were separable spheres of human activity, degeneracy would still characterize market-based relationships because it is the
modus operandi of private property. If two people agree to exchange property, it is their choice to do so under private property. Yet reality presents
us with a seemingly unending supply of cases where this isn't so. Antitrust,
for instance, is a denial of this principle of private property, as are all
instances and forms of price control and other limitations and impositions
on free contracting.[14] My aim here is not to attack such measures. It is
rather to note that markets and states are non-separable arenas of human
interaction, and this condition cannot be captured adequately by thinking
of markets as that sphere where private property governs and the polity as
governed by some form of collective property that leaves undisturbed some
residual domain of private property.

Market and state are abstract nouns that pertain to the same people. A
unified treatment of property as an emergent phenomenon within society
would allow for the simultaneous generation of market and fiscal phenomena. This book seeks to bring the theory of public finance within the

ambit of an emergent and generative orientation toward the organization of property-based societal governance. Yet political phenomena involve force, both potential and actual, which is generally absent from market phenomena.[15] Both phenomena, however, emerge in the same place among the same people, so must surely be accorded a congruent explanation. The remainder of this chapter probes more fully the place of property in giving such a congruent account, and the rest of the book applies this account to some of the material of public finance.

## IV.   PROPERTY, TAXATION AND THE FISCAL COMMONS

Any effort to treat the actual organization and conduct of fiscal activity in an explanatory vein runs into a conundrum about property-governed relationships. Within a market economy, human relationships are organized according to the principles of private property and freedom of contract. Within a public economy, however, human relationships are organized according to principles of collective property. This presents distinct problems and situations because collectives are not sentient beings but rather are abstract nouns we employ to describe some products of institutionally-mediated interaction. Taxation entails a transformation in the institutional arrangements of human governance. To illustrate, suppose taxation is of a simple, flat-tax form where all income is taxed at some common marginal rate. Suppose that rate is doubled from 20 to 40 per cent. This increased taxation represents a transformation in the arrangements of human governance within a society (Wagner 2002a). Initially, 80 per cent of economic activity within society was governed by private property; subsequently, private property governed only 60 per cent. The reach of collective property governance doubles from 20 to 40 per cent. To be sure, there are many particular forms of collective property governance, just as Elinor Ostrom (1990, 2005) shows for common property governance. In any case, changes in taxation change the forms of property-based relationships within a society.

What consequences might stem from such transformation will be explored throughout the remaining chapters, but some anticipatory mention will be made here because it relates to the preceding reference to economic calculation. The most widely used model of outcomes under collective property is the median voter model. Figure 2.2 illustrates this setting by amending Figure 2.1. A third person, $k$, is added, and it is assumed that each person pays one-third of the aggregate tax bill. The collective choice will be that preferred by the median voter, which is still shown by

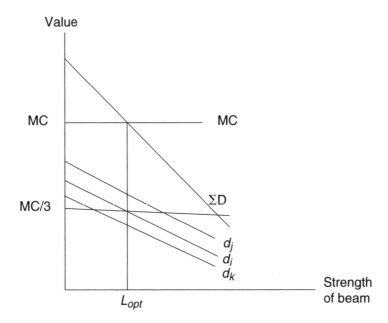

*Figure 2.2   Lighthouses with majority choice*

construction as $L_{opt}$ in Figure 2.2. This simplistic formulation surely invites thoughts of calculational simplicity, for all that is necessary is to estimate some mid-range demand in the vicinity of some mid-range quantity.

Note, however, that this exercise starts from the information summarized from observations of actual market interaction as previously portrayed by Figure 2.1. That figure, however, is just an *ex post* summarization of what has emerged out of interaction among people within some particular institutional arrangement. The theory of a market economy gives us good reason for thinking that such mental apparatus as supply and demand can usefully summarize a good deal of market-based activity. Someone who surveys data on sales of dog food and cat food could reasonably characterize the differences in prices and quantities in terms of demand and supply, for this would be a prediction of an institutionally-generated logic.

An institutional logic appropriate to private property can be plausibly carried over to common or collective property only if all other relevant considerations are invariant to the institutional change. This invariance, however, is surely something to be argued about and not something to be accepted for analytical convenience. It is not enough to stand on the outside and observe the outcome of relationships organized though private property, and then presume that collective property would proceed in the same or similar manner. It is necessary to theorize from the inside, as it were, so as to generate the characteristic features of such processes. While this task will be pursued starting in the next chapter, a brief preview will be offered here.

First of all, the only issue on the table in Figure 2.2 is the strength of a lighthouse's beam. With private property governance, entrepreneurs choose the strength of beam they will provide, along with such other features as the location and design of lighthouses, and then offer their product to the market. Private property provides a simple grammar through which lighthouses are constructed, along with the other activities organized through market-based relationships. This simple grammar, however, does not pertain to collective property. Suppose the collectivity is a tiny one, involving only 100 people, which would comprise but a very small representative assembly. We enter the assembly knowing only that people are generally concerned about ships coming aground and crashing against rocks, along with possessing some notion that strong light beams could militate against these situations.

How might 100 people come to some such outcome as that denoted by Figure 2.1 or 2.2? If the only relevant issue for collective action were the strength of beam, it is possible to imagine something like the demand-revealing process being used (Clark 1971; Groves and Loeb 1975; Tideman and Tullock 1976). To be sure, it might be wondered by what procedure the members of the assembly came to adopt that procedure, but this is a separate issue. But social organization under collective property is not so simple. To the contrary, it is complex because it involves a combinatorial grammar for putting enterprises together, in contrast to the simple grammar of market-based entrepreneurship. The strength of beam is a variable to be explored, but so is the number of lighthouses. So too, for that matter, is the height of lighthouses, and likewise their location. Further variables that would be at issue include their architectural design and the identities of the builders of lighthouses. If there are ten possible options to be considered for each of ten possible elements involved in lighthouse creation, there are ten billion ($10^{10}$) options for collective deliberation if everyone has an equal say in the matter. While the same number of options faces a private entrepreneur, he does not have to engage in collective deliberation. He also bears the value consequences of the choices he makes, in contrast to participants within a network of collective property.

Following Bertrand de Jouvenal's (1961) treatment of the problem faced by the disinterested chairman who wanted only to facilitate parliamentary exploration of an issue, it is easy enough to imagine what would be involved in trying to have a genuine discussion and debate among 100 people when the object is to arrive at some consensus based on truthful revelation. As de Jouvenal explained, no such collective discussion is possible as a basis for action. The basis for any such action will be oligarchic in that particular subsets of the 100 people will select what options will be considered.[16] The only reason to assimilate such settings to market-like settings is that we have a framework for treating market settings. Life on the fiscal commons, however, remains to be explored from the inside looking out; whether the resulting view will be reasonably summarized by something resembling Figures 2.1 and 2.2 remains to be explored.

## V. HUMAN NATURE, PROPERTY AND PUBLIC FINANCE

In his two seminal works that initiated a distinctive Austrian orientation toward economic and social theorizing, Carl Menger (1981 [1871], 1985 [1883]) argued that property, markets and states were common products of the economizing efforts of people within a social setting. Economizing is a meaningful activity only in the presence of scarcity, for only then is choice necessary. Property and markets emerge jointly, Menger argued, and in this most economists clearly concur. But Menger also listed the state as a product of spontaneous emergence, though he did not pursue this matter to any length.[17]

A world of wholly private property is an idealization that provides a framework for analysing the patterns of social interaction that emerge when people relate to one another within the framework of private property and freedom of contract. This framework of simple rules of interaction is sufficient to allow us to understand, in an inside-out manner, the generation and operation of the complex activities and organizations that are present in contemporary, market-based societies. Yet the world is not partitioned wholly into autonomous spheres of individual ownership. While there are large regions of individual ownership, there are also substantial regions where it is absent and where some form of collective ownership exists instead.

The general course of institutional development, moreover, has been one of a substitution of individual for collective ownership, though by no means a complete substitution and in some cases a movement in the reverse direction has taken place. Historically and anthropologically, the order of movement has generally been one from collective to individual attribution, as illustrated by a movement of ownership from tribe to family to individual and as noted in such works as Henry Maine (1864), Harold Berman (1983) and Georg Simmel (1978 [1900]). Even in the presence of tribal arrangements that support much collective consumption, procedures often existed to assign ownership. In one case the first hunter who caught up with a hunted animal would be the owner, in another the owner might be the person who first spotted the animal, while in a third ownership might be attributed to the person whose arrow or spear first hit the animal. In this manner, tribes might assign ownership over animals that were caught even if those animals were destined for tribal and not individual consumption. Once it is recognized that the attributed owner would host the subsequent feast, it is easy enough to argue that such arrangements would provide stronger incentive to hunt successfully than would be forthcoming under a full-blown commons.

The Greeks and Romans of ancient times owned slaves and thought this was a proper pattern of human existence. We no longer own slaves and think slavery is an abomination. In this change, there was a reduction in the range of objects that could be owned but there was an expansion in the number of people who were responsible for themselves. A millennia or so ago, family members were responsible for each other's debts. This is no longer so, though a debt will pass into a deceased's estate. A few centuries ago in the West, estates could not be subdivided and instead had to pass intact to the eldest son. Now owners can divide estates, pass them to their daughters or whomever else they might choose. A couple of centuries ago, wives did not hold property in their own names but only through their husbands. Now the value of property held by wives may well exceed that held by husbands.

These examples, and many more like them, illustrate a movement away from collective property toward private property. This direction of movement, however, is far from complete, and it is not even a universal direction of movement but only the prevalent direction. A half-century ago, someone who wanted to drain and fill a marshy piece of land could do so. This is no longer the case, as this use of land has shifted from private to collective control. Two sisters might want to help support their college education by preparing sandwiches and selling them in a public park across the street from their campus. A half-century ago they could generally do so, now they can't. Entry into such commercial activity is now governed less fully by private property and freedom of contract than it once was.

Numerous explanations have been advanced as to why private property does not serve wholly to order social relationships. Many of those explanations claim that societal ordering through private property performs poorly in certain circumstances, as illustrated by claims about market failure and distributive injustice. Alternative types of explanation reject claims about poor performance and claim instead that universal private property is not embraced because dominant groups within society are able to suppress the open competition that would accompany it. Hence, owners of developed property might be able to increase their rents by restricting entry and preventing the filling of marshy land that could otherwise hold competitive development, just as competitive vendors might increase their net worth by restricting entry.

Suppose we set aside for now such claims about market failure, rent seeking and rent extraction, and other claims that use private property as a point of departure for the derivation of their various analytical agendas. The pure theory of a market economy and private property is a tale that is woven around property-governed relationships among solipsistic creatures. All objects of ownership are partitioned among people, and those people relate to each other contractually. In this formulation, the objects of economizing action are limited to things. Yet our social character affirms that people and relationships are also objects of economizing action.

Our social nature surely places some limit on the domain of private property because what is proper etiquette is ultimately socially adjudicated, and property is a form of etiquette that speaks to propriety in personal conduct. This social nature, moreover, by no means implies harmony because conflict is also a social activity. A desire for approbation, for instance, is often used in support of claims that people seek to pursue projects of mutual gain because in so doing they become more highly esteemed by those whose ends they help to promote. Without doubt, this is true. But approbation also has a side that is less warm and fuzzy in the sentiments with which it is associated, as Arthur Lovejoy (1961) explains with especial clarity. Approbation implies ranking and judgment, wherein some actions and people are esteemed more highly than others. Such sentiments as envy reflect the same desire to rank but operate to different effect (see, for instance, Helmut Schoeck 1969). In any case, people have reactions to and preferences about the activities of one another, for good and for bad.[18]

Economists typically work with a concept of autonomous individuals with given preference functions. This makes for tractable modeling that facilitates the exposition of the logic of a market economy. Yet the domain of private property and a market economy cannot reach throughout society; a point of departure based on solipsistic creatures who relate to one another exclusively through private property will not arrive at society. Private property can operate only within a medium of common property. If two people own themselves, how can they shake hands? One might ask permission to do so from the other. But to do this is to violate the other person's air space by forcing sound waves into his ears. Some element of common property is essential to the social existence that is necessary for human flourishing. Yet because commons are common, they are susceptible to exploitation and degradation in ways that generally afflict private property to a lesser extent.

In any case, we are, among other things, sociable creatures, though of course, conflict is also a social activity (Coser 1964; Hirshleifer 2001). We live in groups, gaining from each other through such things as specialization and the division of labor. But our social groupings also impose limits and constraints, even if often these manifest themselves as duress and not forthright coercion. For purposes of fiscal theorizing, human nature can be represented as possessing a bivalent character. One pole contains our desire for autonomy, the other our desire for solidarity or community. Without doubt, each of these poles entails much more complexity and subtlety than can be explored here, but my only point in taking this approach is to locate the phenomena of public finance in human nature.[19] Hence, I do not follow the Hobbes-like approach of deriving state from individual uses of their prior property. But neither do I take the opposite approach of treating society as the point of departure.

The framework I seek to sketch entails a point of departure where desires for autonomy and solidarity are both present in the human mind, though surely in differing degrees across individuals. We are social creatures, but we also take pride in what we do and we all aspire to be First Violin in an orchestra of some type. Hence, both market and fiscal phenomena are latent in human nature, though there is huge variety in the institutional forms that can emerge within the context of this latency. This formulation entails a dialectical tension within any particular person, with further tension residing in differences among people in how they appraise the desires for autonomy and solidarity. This book does not offer a treatment of such mind-and-society themes, and I raise this topic simply to frame the coeval character of market and state within the institutional matrix of human governance.[20]

Consider two examples, one historical and the other conceptual, though the latter has clear historical basis. J.H. Thomas (1933) reports that in 16th century England it was common for refuse collection to be carried from homes to a public dump by privately organized carters. This would represent the market organization of refuse disposal. It appears that on occasion a carter dropped his load before reaching the approved town dump. When this happened those who were located near where the drop occurred were understandably upset. With the technology of the time, it was unlikely that the culprit would have been detected without a clear sighting, and such unauthorized dumping was unlikely to occur under a full moon.

Thomas reports that it was such circumstances as this that led to towns taking on responsibility for refuse removal. It is easy enough to imagine how this might have evolved. Snide jokes about refuse-dropping carters might have started to pass through town. People would generally be aghast at the prospect of waking up to the aroma of refuse passing through their rooms, and would sympathize with those who suffered such experiences. Refuse would be a topic of conversation at parties, and if refuse continued long to be on people's minds it would surely appear as an item of discussion at some town assembly. People who aren't carters care about what carters do. Indeed, a conscientious carter would be as much the brunt of jokes as a refuse-dumping carter. It is easy enough to see how a motion to have the town take over the carting of refuse might be generally approved by a town council. It might even be recognized that a town-sponsored carter might well work in a more lethargic manner than a carter who was a residual claimant to the difference between his fees and his costs, but at least town residents would know the source of unauthorized deposits of refuse. While it is easy enough to imagine that not everyone would support such a shift to town responsibility, I have nonetheless sketched an inside-out, emergent articulation of how this might come about. Such simple stories as these can thus provide a template for putting together an emergent and polycentric approach to public finance.

Alternatively, suppose a low-lying area along a river is subject periodically to flooding. The lay of the land is such that flood waters disperse pretty much uniformly throughout the area. It so happens that each resident's landholding includes a section that abuts the river. Some of the residents hatch the idea of raising and strengthening the river bank to reduce the threat from flooding. Much enthusiasm for the project develops among many of the residents, though not everyone is convinced that doing this is a good idea. If property were absolute, which means that each person acted solipsistically, those who didn't think the project was worthwhile would say so, and the project would not be pursued. Most people, however, don't have those types of sentiments and don't act in that manner. If there is sufficient sentiment for the levee project, it will be pursued and a claim of absolute property will falter in the process, one way or another, most likely through duress, as conveyed by the aphorism 'going along to get along'.

Private property is an idealized concept that recognizes that people have spheres of autonomous action. Yet the reaches of that autonomy are always limited. That limit, moreover, is present in the human mind and its valuation of both autonomy and solidarity. While the distinction between private goods and public goods seems to be of little use in distinguishing between market-based and state-based activities, it is nonetheless surely reasonable to distinguish between personal and social wants. To say this, however, is most surely not to assign wants to society. It is only to say that Crusoe and Friday will acquire wants by virtue of their living in close proximity that they would not have had they lived in isolation from each other. Among such wants are those that pertain to the conduct of the other, or at least certain features of that conduct. People will generally have wants regarding what other people do to their houses and yards. This might find political expression through codes and ordinances, or it might find informal expression through social relationships and possibly that vague sentiment called pressure. And no doubt some people will think other people should not have such sentiments, but they are pretty widespread nonetheless. Moreover, they are sentiments that arise only when people have preferences about the activities of other people. These settings present organizational problems, for they can generally be addressed through market and social arrangements outside of political processes or forums. But addressed they will be in any case, and it is in such social wants that the potential bedding ground for the emergence of phenomena on the public square lies.

## VI.  PUBLIC SQUARES AND MARKET SQUARES: A SOCIETAL ARCHITECTURE

There is no public square within the context of the pure theory of a market economy. The market is simply an abstract noun that describes the pattern of exchanges that takes place among utility-maximizing automatons. Our sociable natures mean, however, that people have desires concerning the actions and conduct of other people. In this book I work with an architecture that divides societies into market squares and public squares. This architecture is, of course, an abstraction that is suggested by my desire to give an exposition of fiscal phenomena that coheres with that given for market phenomena, and yet which allows both phenomena to emerge out of interaction among the same people.

This distinction serves the purely analytical purpose of setting forth a domain for the emergence of fiscal phenomena within the same society in which market phenomena also emerge, with all such phenomena emerging through interaction among economizing individuals. This market–state architecture might seem austere and possibly even frightening to those who stress the importance of the institutions of civic association that stand outside the ambit of both governments and profit-seeking firms. I don't regard market as a synonym for profit seeking, which would indeed leave profit-seeking firms and governments as the sole organizational forms within society. Profit-seeking firms are but a subset of all organizations that comprise the non-governmental portion of a society, and market denotes all such organizations. In other words, market denotes the arena where human effort is organized on the basis of handshakes alone, in contrast to state, where a fist will be used if a handshake doesn't suffice.

There is a significant distinction between constructing a model that stands on the outside and looks into a situation and one that stands inside a situation and builds out. Most economic modeling is of the former type, and this is the orientation taken by that creature of high intelligence with whom we cannot communicate to which this chapter referred in opening. Emergent-based theorizing, however, requires some effort to construct models that start from the inside and work outward to the macro or societal level. To say this is to require that social processes must ultimately be made intelligible in terms of people pursuing their plans through interaction with other people, and with that interaction sometimes being beneficial to everyone or nearly everyone while at other times it is beneficial to only a few and perhaps even harmful to many.

Some people might leave standing water on their property, where mosquitoes breed and plague those who live nearby. It is possible to reduce this setting to one of partitioned private property, and to claim that those mosquitoes belong to the owner on whose property they bred. This is surely one of those blackboard exercises that can give students practice in working with the logic of market-based relationships, but which finds no counterpart in the world of practice and experience. A mosquito that bites someone cannot be traced to some alleged owner, even though this is usually possible for dogs who bite people.

It is certainly possible to imagine someone filing suit against a property owner where mosquitoes are breeding, perhaps by claiming reckless endangerment. Whether such a case might get anywhere is another matter. As an alternative, it is also possible to imagine someone convincing a town council to hold a hearing on the problem of mosquitoes, and to consider any of several possible resolutions. One such resolution might be to pass an ordinance that requires property owners to keep their property free of standing water. An alternative resolution might provide for town-wide mosquito spraying. While there are a number of ways that the economic properties of these alternative approaches could be explored, what is most important to keep in mind here is that what we denote as property is not something that is absolute but is subject to the forbearance of others.

Courts and legislatures are both forums in the public square. Both forums are activated by a complaint. With courts, it is usually one citizen filing a complaint against another, as when someone who is plagued by roaming mosquitoes or wandering dogs files a complaint against some alleged owner or source of the irritant. With legislatures, it is usually a mass of citizens having a complaint filed on their behalf, along with a call for some form of redress. To be sure, a good deal of legislation is private in character. Moreover, class actions involve large collections of plaintiffs.

The central point in any case is that property is something that is continually contestable, though the space of contestation during any particular interval of time is but a small portion of the total size of potentially contestable space. An owner of land wants to build a shopping center on that land. Several objections might be raised. Hence, someone might own land, and yet not be able to put a shopping center on it; however, it might be possible to put a zoo for small animals on it. Once we leave behind a world of solipsistic automatons and enter a world where people have opinions about the conduct of other people, we can recognize the truth of Jean Paul Sartre's declaration in *No Exit* that 'hell is other people', and at the same time recognize that we are inevitably caught up in public processes where the spheres over which we exercise what appear to be our zones of autonomy contains regions of contestability that are attributable to our social natures in confrontation with the requirements of structured living-together, to borrow Wolfgang Dreschler's (2001) treatment of the tradition of *Staatswissenschaften*.

Public squares and market squares are thus coeval institutional patterns within a society. State and market both reside in human nature and evolve through interaction within society. The coeval character of public and market squares is rooted in our desires for both autonomy and solidarity, though probably in a manner that varies both among people at any instant as well as over time. The phenomena of public finance, as well as those of a market economy, are thus rooted in human nature. What emerges out of that nature when people interact, however, is contingent in that at any particular moment many paths lead into the future.

Let me illustrate briefly this contingent character with reference to Harold Demsetz's (1967) argument in support of the claim that common ownership gives way to private ownership when it becomes economically efficient for it to give way. In the 17th century setting in Labrador that Demsetz examined, such fur-bearing animals as beaver were once owned in common by tribes and subsequently were reduced to various forms of private ownership. Demsetz advanced an explanation for this institutional transformation that can be summarized in comparative static terms. Initially, beaver were plentiful and one person's harvest imposed no cost on other tribal members who were also seeking beaver. This situation changed with the emergence of trade in furs. With the increased demand, beaver harvested by some people would impose costs on others by forcing them to travel farther to find beaver. Hence, beaver were reduced to private ownership.

The bare historical facts as presented seem simple and straightforward. What is not considered, though, are the processes through which this transformation occurred and the other options that might have been pursued. In this vein, it would be possible in the fashion of Armen Alchian (1950) to envision a number of tribes facing circumstances similar to what Demsetz characterizes. All would have lived for some time without any concern about a scarcity of fur-bearing animals, which in turn means that there were no conflicts among people over which beaver belonged to whom. If Primo took a particular beaver, Secunda would simply take another beaver, and would not have to look harder, travel farther or hunt longer to do so.

To posit a transformation into scarcity in this setting is to postulate the arrival of conflict. Indeed, scarcity is a designation that is applied from the outside looking in; from the inside looking out, the scarcity is manifested in conflict. The creation of private ownership is one method of reducing conflict, but it is easy enough to imagine numerous other options that could be tried, all of which have been tried in our time. Beaver could remain subject to common ownership, only now the tribe would license hunting along the lines that hunting and fishing are typically regulated. Alternatively, a tribal sage might think that beaver is worn too ostentatiously and support a tax on beaver to restrict the amount of harvesting. Another sage might think that the conflict might go away if people came to appreciate more fully the sartorial splendors of wearing opossum coats, and so put together an educational program to achieve this end. These other options would, of course, involve more activity within the public square than the establishment of private property, although even with private property there is often a background state presence due to potential adjudication.

## VII. UNIVERSAL STATE, PARTICULAR GOVERNMENTS

The historical record presents us with immense variation in the institutional arrangements through which fiscal phenomena have emerged. These days we associate fiscal phenomena with states, with states in turn denoting territorial exclusivity over the use of force within their boundaries. This territorial exclusivity came about only over the past several centuries, as Hendrik Spruynt (1994) explains. Fiscal phenomena were present in feudal times even though territorial exclusivity was absent. At that time, fiscal phenomena manifested themselves mostly through a prince's use of his property rather than through taxation (Backhaus and Wagner 1987). Modern states, however, present forms of social organization quite different from those of feudal times and relationships. In any case, fiscal phenomena are latent in human nature and arise out of people living together in close proximity. Such living together, moreover, is a near-universal feature of human existence even though the historical record presents us with numerous particular forms in which this has occurred.

Fiscal phenomena are universal in societies, though their particular organization has been enormously varied. Our language often uses the same term to mean different things or concepts, and this seems rarely to cause problems of misunderstanding. Accordingly, I shall use 'state' to denote the locus of all fiscal phenomena, while accounting for the enormous historical variety through particular forms of government. Hence, 'state' is a universal category that maps into fiscal phenomena, while the variegated institutional details that vary across place and time are the province of particular forms of government, all of which are instantiations of the universal category of state.

Whereas the phenomena of public finance point to the place of state in human society, the concrete form taken by those phenomena emanate from the particular forms of government that are in place at any historical moment. State, then, is a universal category of existence that stems from our sociable and non-solipsistic natures. The universal form of state, however, can and has led to a huge variety of different forms of government. State, property and market all have common origins, but there is huge variety in concrete, historical instantiations.

Government refers to particular organizational forms that are generated through the sentiments and relationships that constitute the state. State is thus an enduring feature of human existence, as is property. Immense variety is possible in the actual forms of government, just as immense variety is possible in the particular forms that property can take. State is an order that speaks to the interest that people have in one another. There is an irreducible commons feature to life in society, and state denotes that commons. State, however, is an abstract concept that is distinct from particular governments. While the origin of state is located in human nature, the particular governments that spring forth in history are contingent events that are subject to immense organizational variability. This was recognized by James Madison when he asked in *Federalist* #51: 'what is government itself, but the greatest of all reflections on human nature?'

## NOTES

1. For an interesting effort by two economists to explain differences between ants and honeybees with respect to the nests they build, see Landa and Tullock (2003).
2. The centralilty of private property for a market economy is treated in many places, a few of which are Eucken (1952), Alchian (1965), De Alessi (1980), Barzel (1989) and Streit (1992).
3. Degeneracy is treated in Tononi, Sporns and Edelman (1999).
4. For a careful presentation of the relation between welfare economics and public finance, see Russell Sobel (2004). The modern classic statement of this teleological orientation is William Baumol (1965).
5. For a collection of essays on this theme, see Cowen (1988). For a more recent collection in the same vein though with different points of contention, see Cowen and Crampton (2002).

6. For a survey of the experimental literature which finds that free riding is less severe that standard economic models suggest, see Anderson and Holt (2004).
7. For a perceptive treatment of public goods theory along these lines, see Buchanan (1968).
8. For recent examinations of *Staatswissenschaften*, see Dreschler (2001) and Peukert (2001).
9. That state officials are officially compensated in this manner is clear. What is not so clear is the genuine absence of residual claimacy, once the indefinitely large number of alternative channels of compensation is considered.
10. For a few cogent treatments of this theme, see Buchanan (1975), Morris (1998), Gordon (1999) and Barzel (2002).
11. For a sample of thoughtful treatments of these matters, see Ackerman (1977), Epstein (1985), Ostrom (1997), Gordon (1999) and Voigt (1999).
12. For some examples, see Pechman and Okner (1974), Reynolds and Smolensky (1977) and Browning and Johnson (1979).
13. Also pertinent are, among other items, Michael Taylor (1982), Michael Sandel (1996) and Jeffrey Schoenblum (2006); moreover, Georg Simmel (1978 [1900]) expressed a similar orientation in work that pre-dated Elias.
14. For a collection of essays asserting that the domain over which freedom of contract operates is presently expanding, see Frank Buckley (1999).
15. Duress can appear as well in market relationships, but political phenomena surely involve a higher ratio of fists to handshakes than do market phenomena.
16. Plott and Levine (1978) offer a fascinating and absorbing examination of such a setting in the context of the purchase of aircraft by the members of a club.
17. In a review article on Friedrich Hayek's *Constitution of Liberty*, Jacob Viner (1961) chided Hayek for his failure to include government within the ambit of spontaneously emergent arrangements.
18. For a recent treatise on this topic, see Geoffrey Brennan and Philip Pettit (2004). For an effort to address taxation in the context of non-absolute property, see Eric Mack (2002, 2006).
19. For some elaboration on these brief remarks, see Stephen Buckle (1991), Fred Miller (1995) and Lloyd Weinrib (1987).
20. For a few treatments of a related type, though more sociological in character, see Coleman (1990), Fukuyama (1995), Homans (1958, 1974) and Vanberg (1975).

# 3. State and market: a two-forum societal architecture

Chapter 2 located the phenomena of interest to a theory of public finance as stemming from the bivalent character of human nature, wherein people seek both autonomy and community. Both fiscal and market phenomena derive from the same source: the efforts of economizing individuals to pursue plans so as to attain more highly desired states of being. That pursuit, however, is undertaken by social and not solipsistic creatures. Market and state are both emergent phenomena that spring from human effort to pursue plans within a setting of societal interaction. Desires for autonomy within a society map into the forms of interpersonal relationship that are constituted through what we designate as private property. Desires for community, however, limit the range of autonomy and private property by generating patterns of inter-personal relationship we designate as collective property. Private property pertains to actions that people undertake because they choose to, and about which the remainder of society forbears from contesting. The remaining residuum of human action is governed by collective property.

To be sure and as already noted in Chapter 2, a desire for community need not map exclusively into the pattern of conduct denoted by state, as a variety of civic associations also emerge out of that desire. It would be possible to consider a triangular social architecture, where the third pole would denote collective activity that is organized within the precincts of civic association. I have avoided doing this here because my object of interest is the theory of public finance and not societal organization more generally. Still, there is much of interest in the relationships among market, state and civil society, as conveyed, for instance, in David Beito (2000) and Gertrude Himmelfarb (1992, 1984).

Community enters when the limit of forbearance over individual action is reached. People care sufficiently about the actions of other people to desist from what would otherwise be forbearance. Notions of community and caring do not necessarily assimilate to any kind of warm and fuzzy sentiment. The quality of caring is simply an abstract term that conveys the absence of forbearance regarding individual conduct, with the substantive content of such absence subject to huge variation across time and place. Caring is a quality that can be nasty and invasive. A thief cares about the wealth of potential victims, as well as the marketability of that wealth. Theft is a social phenomenon, as is all conflict.

Consider some variations on the theme of the refuse-dropping carters mentioned in Chapter 2. It is easy to imagine a setting, probably comparatively rural in nature, where people keep refuse on their property until they decide to take it to some disposal site, at which time they have to pay for disposal. Refuse disposal would be market-based, and the patterns of activity would be similar to those we observe when people visit movie theatres. In this setting, it is easy enough to imagine manifold forms of potential conflict among people, even without bringing refuse-dropping carters into the picture. One person may be exceedingly tidy, even to the extent of washing the front steps each day as well as taking refuse promptly to a disposal site. Another might be more relaxed about such cleanliness, possibly because of spending long hours at work though also possibly because of simple lack of interest. Whatever the reason, conditions are present for the absence of forbearance over individual choices regarding refuse disposal. How that conflict plays out, moreover, will not be the result of some type of benefit–cost calculus by some detached observer, but will be generated within some form of societal network within which the participants are encased. In any case, the relationships of propriety or property that exert governance over this situation will not belong to the sphere of absolute privateness. Collective action will be crowd action of some form, and relationships of community and collective property may range from the sublime to the revolting, with the interval occupied by several intermediate points.[1] We can say this even though crowds are not acting entities, because the course of action within crowd-based relationships is generated through various patterns of interaction among the participants.[2]

We all live within a societal architecture wherein people experience life as some mixture of personally chosen undertakings and collectively sponsored undertakings which they might embrace or even reject but in which they are involved in any case due to their inclusion within that society. Within the spirit of this architecture, economic theory can be divided into market theory and fiscal theory. The economic theory of markets seeks to explain how those personal undertakings generate apprehensible patterns of societal activity. The economic theory of state that is pursued here seeks the same end: to explain how those collective undertakings generate apprehensible patterns of societal activity. The same explanatory orientation wherein people act to alleviate sensed uneasiness and subsequently generate societal formations in the process (Mises 1966, pp. 11–71), is at work universally throughout a society.

To posit this two-forum architecture is not, however, to treat the two spheres of action as separable. They are connected, though different forms of connection are both imaginable and have been found historically. The two realms of action and experience are woven together by virtue of cohabitation within the same territory, though the particular pattern of the weave is subject to variation across time and place. In one society people may be free to choose at which grocery store to shop, whereas in a different society they may be compelled to shop at some collective store, while in yet a third society their choice among stores might be limited to those that have been awarded licenses to operate by some state office. Even in the society where people are free to choose among stores that don't require state permission to operate, those stores might be prohibited by collective action from allowing people to buy such products as unpasteurized cheese that would otherwise be readily available. The personal and the collective occupy the same space, with the characteristic features of that occupancy emerging through societal interaction.

This chapter opens by examining some methodological issues concerning the place of fiscal theory within economic and social theory, as well as the place of institutional presumptions about specific forms of government within that theorizing effort. The point of this opening is to create a bridge between theoretical principles of universal validity and specific applications of that framework to the particular contexts presented by democratic polities. An architectural arrangement that separates a society between market squares and public squares has general validity, although the application of that analytical framework will differ across institutional arrangements. Within democratic arrangements, parliamentary assemblies can be usefully examined as particular types of catallactical arenas, just as are market squares. Both squares are present in the same society, with the conditions for their existence residing within human nature. Hence, the two squares must be connected. Whatever the institutional features of that connection, the relationship between the two squares will involve phenomena of mutualism and parasitism, as well as conflicts among enterprises occupying various boundary areas where the two squares come into contact. While market squares are constituted within an institutional framework we describe abstractly as private property, public squares are constituted within an institutional framework we describe abstractly as collective property. For both forms of abstract category, historical experience and possibility present us with a wide range of instituted practice.

## I.   ETERNAL VERITIES, HISTORICAL FORMS AND SOCIAL THEORIZING

Whether someone surveys the world cross-sectionally or travels through time to survey it historically, it would surely be relatively easy to recognize similarity in the forms of activity undertaken on the various market squares that are encountered. While the particular details of real estate transactions differ in many ways today from the transactions that would have been observed two centuries ago, the basic elements of title and trade are universally present. Alternatively, in some market settings buyers and sellers negotiate over prices while in others they don't; once again, universal principles of trade operate within differing contexts. The institutional arrangements that govern market transactions may differ in numerous particular details, but some universal features of governance through private property shine through clearly nonetheless. It is easy to recognize a universal notion of a market square beneath the surface details of particular, historical market squares.

At first glance, it might seem different when surveying the public squares that generate such collectively-sponsored activities as raising armies, building roads, regulating commerce or imprisoning people. The Pharaohs of ancient Egypt, the Princes of the many lands that constituted the Holy Roman Empire, the Doges of Venice, and the members of contemporary parliaments, were or are involved in the organization of those collectively sponsored activities. There is clearly great variation in the institutional details through which public squares operate, but in all such cases that operation implicates a collection of people within some regime of collective property. While autocracy appears to be categorically distinct from democracy, as illustrated by William Niskanen (2003), Mancur Olson (2000) and Gordon Tullock (1987), there is also a continuum present, as portrayed by Roger Congleton's (2001) treatment of the universal template provided by the king-and-council format. By itself, collective property must be inert because collectives can't act. Only people can act, and the set of actions we denote as collective will emerge through some constitutive institutional framework. By universal principles I mean little more than that people seek to use means at their disposal to pursue ends. For action within market squares, people choose their ends and the remainder of society forbears in those choices. Collective property resides in those spheres of action where forbearance does not prevail.

For any form of social theorizing, whether it pertains to organization through market-based processes or organization through politically-based arrangements, there are two principles in play. These are eternal principles that are invariant across regimes and contexts, and particular historical contexts and features that provide much of the material for detailed examination. Market theory and fiscal theory both rest upon the same eternal abstract principles of human nature and conduct, but the historical record, whether of commercial conduct or of fiscal conduct, is particularistic and variable. This book explores an abstract notion of collective property that is instantiated historically within public squares that are organized democratically, though with some American orientation showing through because this is the material the author knows best. My emphasis, however, is upon the comparatively general within the democratic genre and not upon American experience in particular.

That emphasis is also on processes of motion and development and not on states or conditions of equilibrium. This choice of emphasis maps into philosophical issues about whether analytical primacy belongs to processes or to states, a controversy that is surveyed by Nicholas Rescher (2000). Any analytical framework that uses universal concepts and categories to illuminate historical situations does, of course, contain both states and processes. Within this type of framework, the concepts and categories are universal states while the continual generation of historical particularity is the activity of processes. Processes are at work in history; equilibrium states stand outside history though are recognizable in history.

There are two perspectives from which societal phenomena can be portrayed. One perspective is from the outside looking in. This is the perspective of equilibrium analysis, where the grammar of equilibrium requires that all observations be accounted for as being consistent with one another and with the postulated conditions of equilibrium. The other perspective is from the inside looking out. Where equilibrium is the perspective of a spectator standing outside a society and looking in, process is the perspective of a participant whose activities are helping to generate the material that spectators observe. Statements about the one should in principle be capable of reconciliation in terms of statements about the other. Such alternative statements are implied by any treatment in terms of universals and particulars. Nonetheless, the question of primacy cannot be avoided. Take a film made of a horse running down a road, and cut that film into a sequence of snapshots. Some of those snapshots will show that all four of the horse's legs are off the ground. An equilibrium model would have to explain that observation by claiming that horses can fly. To reject this claim is to affirm the primacy of process to the apprehension of reality.

## II.   A SIDEBAR ON UTILITY AND THE STRUCTURE OF MIND

This book is grounded on a presumption that matters regarding emergent structure have important work to do in social inquiry. A distinction between market squares and public squares invokes a context in which to do important analytical work, even if both of those structures are treated as reflecting some universal principle of human action. To attribute a binary structure to human nature translates or maps into some structural notion of mind. To work with a structural notion of mind, moreover, must involve a denial of the universal validity of theorizing based on utility functions.

Standard economic theorizing is based on the twin presumptions that human action can be characterized as maximizing a utility function and that the results of human interaction constitute some equilibrium. A portrayal in terms of utility maximization allows no room for structure of any form, as it inexorably smashes all structure on to a plane. A utility function is a serviceable instrument for some purposes but it has limitations that present obstacles to the type of effort I undertake here. A key part of this effort involves an organizational structure within society that corresponds to an organizational structure within the mind.

A utility function denies organizational structure, for it treats mind as a *tabula rasa* or a computer disk. If $X$ is a vector of actions that yield utility, a utility function maps the elements of that vector on to some position on the real line: multidimensional variables are transformed into a single dimension pronounced as utility. For preferences to be represented by a utility function, they must be rational, as conveyed by postulates of completeness, transitivity and continuity. This last condition rules out of consideration any kind of conduct that would be described as leaps, jumps or gaps. Utility functions imply that mind and its mental patterns can be assimilated to a surface that is continuous and twice-differentiable.

Consider a simple utility function $U = f(B, P)$ where $B$ denotes beans and $P$ denotes peas. Such examples constitute the standard fare of economic theory, and moreover, the people to whom that utility function is claimed to apply could recognize their conduct as conforming to that representation. When it comes to choosing between beans and peas, the insight provided by the outside-in perspective of the economic theorist would surely be easily reconcilable with the inside-out perspective of the people who face those choices. The two perspectives would thus arrive at the same focal point, and in so doing would illustrate the proper use of abstraction in economic theorizing that Asik Radomysler (1946) articulated with lucid brilliance.

Not all abstraction is equally illuminating, Radomysler also noted. Suppose the symbols $B$ and $P$ are maintained as before, only now $B$ denotes birthrights and $P$ denotes pottage. To maintain twice-differentiability, a birthright can be leased for some interval of time, whereas Esau sold his birthright outright to Jacob.[3] The story of Jacob and Esau is, of course, a story of life options being destroyed as a result of treating the two as commensurable points on the same real line. The Ancients, moreover, plumbed the notion of the orderliness of the soul, with much of the work of classical drama unfolding as manifestations of various types of disorderliness of the soul; the soul's disorderliness is represented by a failure to recognize important distinctions, disjunctions and structures.

An alternative to theorizing in terms of utility functions and the rational choice formulations that come along in tow is to theorize in terms of lexicographic orderings. These impose a structure on the evaluating and appraising mind that cannot be mapped on to a one-dimensional real line. If a birthright may not be sold for pottage, there is no utility function that combines the two. Commandments and injunctions, for instance, are denials of utility functions, at least to the extent that people adhere to these, and the evidence is surely that most people do most of the time.

Without doubt, the utility apparatus could always be used *ex post* to 'explain' action. That one would sell a birthright while another refused would be explained as a matter of different rates of substitution in conjunction with price offers. Before traveling this road, however, it is worthwhile to remember that the Ptolemaic astronomers at the time of Copernicus were successful in making their maps fit their observations of earth sitting at the center of everything. Similarly, it is surely better to model the movement of a horse as a process than to treat it as some equilibrium that is disturbed by a parade of exogenous shocks to the horse. Furthermore, that outside-in orientation would not be recognized by most participants who view their activities from an inside-out orientation. For such participants, options for choice will have some structure, wherein substitution and trade-off occur mostly among a subset of entities.

A lexicographic ordering maps readily into notions of structure, where trade-offs may occur among entities that exist on the same plane while not occurring smoothly among entities across planes.[4] Lexicographic ordering also fits nicely with Ludwig Lachmann's (1971) pioneering examination of institutions, published in a book where he submerged his originality within the legacy of Max Weber, to cite the book's title. Lachmann works with a structural hierarchy of institutions, where some are more foundational or fundamental than others. Relatively more foundational institutions can be translated as more constitutive. There are principles that govern and guide the formation of less foundational principles. This feature of institutional arrangements with which Lachmann works is likewise a feature of the human mind, and can be illuminated by working with lexicographic orderings while it is obscured by the dark cloud of a misplaced utility function.

## III. PUBLIC SQUARES AND MARKET SQUARES: ALTERNATIVE FORUMS FOR INTERACTION

It is easy enough to envision a small town where a city hall stands adjacent to a market square. Market activity these days is not confined to some specific location, but neither is the conduct of collective activity. Regardless of the geographical reach of market activity, it can be conceptualized as organizing itself within the precincts of a market square. Likewise, collective activity can be denoted as originating within a public square no matter how dispersed such activities might actually be. Patterns of activity within a society thus emerge through one of these two arenas of human interaction, with the public square serving as the arena where fiscal phenomena are generated.

The two squares, moreover, bear a particular relationship to one another because neither can exist without the other. A market square cannot exist without some modicum of common property that is maintained through socially oriented processes of some type. This need not involve a state in the contemporary sense of territorial exclusivity, for such exclusivity has become predominant in history only over the past few centuries. There is, moreover, a libertarian literature that supports stateless societies, two fine expositions of which are Murray Rothbard (1977) and David Friedman (1978).[5] While I have no desire to rebut such sentiments, I would also note that to be banished from a tribe and removed from its protection could easily be a more frightful situation than anything people typically encounter in their dealings with contemporary states. In any case, a public square of some type will exist in all societies as a reflection of our social natures.

The core of the economic theory of markets seeks to explain how orderly patterns of economic activity can emerge when relationships among people are governed by private property and various associated institutions. In doing this, economic theory explains how the market square will be populated with activity, and how the patterns of activity undertaken there will change through innovation and experimentation. An important element in the story of the self-organizing character of market squares is the emergent character of market prices as a by-product of the exchange activities that are made possible by the alienability of property. The theory of a market economy is almost self-contained or self-reflexive, but not quite. Unlike ants and their genetically-programmed conduct, humans are not genetically programmed to conduct themselves in accord with some specific commands and dictates of private property, even though there is clearly a good deal of genetic programming involved in human conduct. To complete the story of the self-organization of market activity, it is necessary for there to be some source that maintains adherence to private property.

Market theory explains how human interaction within the market square can generate orderly patterns of activity, provided only that some form of activity outside the market square supports the framework of just conduct that is denoted by private property. Hence, a public square of some form must be populated for a market square to operate. But how much activity will take place on the public square and how will that square be constituted? Consider a limiting case where all activity is organized on the public square. This thoroughgoing communism characterizes the ideal condition portrayed by Karl Marx. For Marx, there would be no alienation of property, including labor. There would exist no commercial transactions, so there would exist no market prices, even of the barter form, because alienability would have been abolished. Production would be only for use and never for exchange. People would not act for the instrumental purposes of earning the means to obtain desired objects through exchange. Such alienation would be abolished and human activity would be apportioned according to use value and not exchange value, a distinction, incidentally, that is the same as Ludwig von Mises' (1966, pp. 587–88) distinction between introversive and extroversive labor.

So, how would society proceed if all activity were organized through its public square where property was collective and not severable or alienable? Suppose someone who participates actively within the public square were to propose making Atlanta a seaport by dredging the Chattahoochee and Appalachicola rivers and building the necessary locks and other devices. The first thing to be said about such a proposal is that it could not be appraised by making any kind of reference to the cost of the project or of any comparison with the cost of delivering goods to Atlanta by truck and rail. Prices are an emergent feature of alienable property, and would not exist when all activity was organized through the public square.

Such a project would, of course, divert resources away from other employments. It is normal that people would hold different opinions about this matter, but there is no way that information about pricing could be brought to bear in forming appraisals of this or any other project. The simple fact of the matter is that such economic calculation is impossible in a society where all activity is organized within the public square. To be sure, real socialist regimes operated with substantial market squares. This was noted with especial clarity by Craig Roberts (1971) and also Peter Boettke (2001), who explained that the Soviet Union was not a communally organized economy wherein alienation had been abolished. To the contrary, alienation was present in the Soviet Union, but its institutional framework was one that generated only awkward coordination, as was further noted by David Levy (1990).

We thus confront two impossibilities regarding property and society. On the one hand, a society ordered exclusively through a market square cannot generate and maintain the rules of just conduct that are required for such a society to reproduce itself. On the other hand, a society ordered exclusively through a public square cannot generate sustainable patterns of activity because the absence of alienation eliminates both knowledge of valuation and incentive to act so as to attain higher valuation. The two squares depend on each other and thus exist in a symbiotic relationship that involves a good deal of parasitism. A public square cannot operate on its own in any but the smallest of societies because economic calculation is impossible without alienable property, and that is the province of the market square. Without alienable property there can be no trade and hence no prices. Public squares require the presence of market squares. The two squares and the activities they host are related through various forms of mutualistic and parasitic relationships, a theme developed in Maffeo Pantaleoni (1911) and elaborated in Richard Wagner (1997b). The public square draws its sustenance from the market square. It also draws upon technologies and pricing from the operation of the market square. The public square both needs and supports the market square, though as in any parasitical relationship the public square can also debilitate the vitality of the market square.

A market square is the host that generates the technologies and prices without which activities could not be organized within the public square. Taxation, after all, is impossible without a market square. In this technical sense, the public square operates parasitically upon the market square. Parasitical relationships may be either beneficial or harmful to the host. Moreover, within the context of a conjunctive political economy with its emphasis on an emergence and structure, the public square parasite does not act upon the market square host in some aggregate, entity-to-entity manner. The market square is not the entity on which a public square parasite attaches. Rather the relevant entity is some particular enterprise or set of enterprises within the market square. Only rarely will a public square parasite attach itself uniformly to all enterprises within the market square.

Figure 3.1 gives a simple representation of an ecology of 15 enterprises, four of which are state enterprises denoted by triangles. The connecting lines denote patterns of complementarity. Thus the private firm at $A_1$ provides inputs to the private firm at $C_2$, with that chain of private connections continuing through $C_3$, $B_4$ and $A_5$. This network exists wholly within the market economy. As Figure 3.1 is drawn, no network exists wholly within the public economy. Any state enterprise must have some connection to market enterprises, as will be elaborated in Chapter 4.

That connection of state enterprises to market enterprises is necessary for the state enterprise, but is also a potential source of conflict. State enterprises require market enterprises to provide various forms of navigational guidance. Yet they can also use political power to degrade market enterprises, thereby overcoming what otherwise might be their natural inferiority. For instance, the enterprise at $A_5$ might exist at the consumer good level and produce some form of education (or perhaps hospitalization or

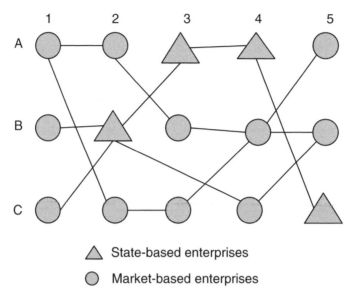

$\triangle$ State-based enterprises

$\bigcirc$ Market-based enterprises

*Figure 3.1    Network of enterprises, political- and market-based*

transportation, or anything else that comes to mind). The enterprise located at $C_5$ provides a similar service, but is organized politically. Even that enterprise has a point of market contact, denoted at $C_1$ (through the chain $C_5–A_4–A_3–B_2–C_1$).

Suppose the state enterprise is not able to compete successfully against the market enterprise on equal terms. If the state enterprise tried to do so, it would fail. If Figure 3.1 were presented as a motion picture, the territory covered by $C_5$ would shrink while that covered by $A_5$ would expand. As Chapter 4 explores, the state enterprise has investors and other supporters who do not want to see their enterprise fail. In their effort to avoid failure, they have tools at their disposal that private enterprises do not have, at least until those market-based enterprises form some alliance with state enterprises within their zones of activity.

State enterprises have two basic tools for promoting the interests of their supporters. One is that they can use regulatory powers to degrade the competitive capacity of such competing enterprises as $A_5$. Almost limitless are the particular ways in which this might be done. For instance, construction standards might be imposed on private schools to raise their expenses and prices. Private schools might be required to enroll five per cent of their students as scholarship students, thereby increasing the price that must be charged to other students. The state-sponsored enterprise at $C_5$ not only might be free of these requirements, but also might be able to derive revenues from tax extractions imposed on taxpayers who make no use of the school. This allows people with a relatively high demand for the enterprise's output to shift a share of the cost on to those who have little or no demand. If a state enterprise is not naturally competitive with market-based enterprises, we should expect to see both techniques being used when state enterprises are present.

It is not always the case that political and market enterprises are competitive with each other. It is also possible that there are zones of complementarity. For instance, the market enterprises at $C_3$ and $C_4$ might be competitive with one another. Yet $C_3$ might be faring better competitively, perhaps in consequence of all of its connections being through the market, in contrast to the political connections in which $C_4$ is implicated. While those political connections might degrade $C_4$'s competitive ability relative to $C_3$, it also provides $C_4$ with an opportunity to secure regulation favorable to it relative to $C_3$. Thus the public square becomes an arena within which some market-based enterprises secure advantages relative to other market-based enterprises, in addition to being an arena where state enterprises seek to degrade market-based enterprises that are located too close to them, competitively speaking.

## IV. PARLIAMENTARY ASSEMBLIES AS CATALLACTICAL ARENAS

From the social-theoretic orientation pursued here, the state or public square is an order wherein many particular organizations or governmental entities are established. Both market squares and public squares are open-access commons where people are free to try to establish enterprises. To be sure, the institutional arrangements that govern participation and determine success within the public square are different from those that pertain to the market square. Nonetheless, the public square in a democratic regime is an order and not an organization, and thus forms a complement to activities organized on the market square. To say that the relation between public square and market square is one of complements is not to say that the activities sponsored within the two squares are complementary to one another. In some cases they are, but in other cases they are competitive with one another. The two squares are complements only in that they pertain to the two sides of the limit of forbearance of autonomous individual activity. Both squares exist within society, and together they encompass society.

To conceptualize a society as comprising two types of forum for human interaction wherein people form and pursue plans raises instantly matters concerning the types of activities that will be pursued within those forums.

To some extent, the establishment of such boundaries is the province of constitutional discourse, as represented by charters that enumerate powers of government and establish structures of government. Whatever is established at one moment, however, will be subject to contestation and revision through time. Our so-called mixed economies contain tectonic regions where enterprises established within the market square collide with enterprises established within the public square. These tectonic rumblings and clashes are part of the normal course of operation regarding the relationship between market and public squares.

Maffeo Pantaleoni (1911) conceptualized a society as containing two bazaars, each operating with its own pricing system. Within the market bazaar prices emerged through alienable property and open competition. In contrast, the political bazaar operated with a set of political prices. These prices could not be established within the political bazaar, but rather were attached parasitically to the system of market prices. The precise character of those political prices depended on the particular tax system in place, for a tax is a parasitical attachment to a system of market prices. A proportional tax on income, for instance, sets prices in proportion to a person's income, whereas market prices are uniform for the same service regardless of income.

Parliamentary assemblies thus become a peculiar type of market forum. The particular enterprises that are sponsored within the parliamentary bazaar are determined through interaction among the people who hold seats in the assembly, in conjunction with interaction among assembly members and those people in society who are seeking parliamentary support for their enterprises. The political enterprise is the locus of energizing activity within the public square. Entrepreneurship is as much involved in the formation of political-based enterprises as it is in the formation of market-based enterprises. The institutional arrangements that govern the formation of political enterprises, as well as those that govern the subsequent conduct and performance of those enterprises, are certainly different from those that apply to market-based enterprises. In some cases, those differences across forms might be narrower than might appear at first glance while in other cases they might be quite wide. Nonetheless, all forms of enterprise emerge from within the same collection of people, so there must be connections across the various types of enterprises that exist within a society. The presence of such connections suggests the universal applicability of such economic categories as utility, demand, cost and profit throughout a society regardless of particular institutional or organizational forms.

Enterprises that can be observed within either of those arenas are emergent phenomena. This emergent character is well recognized for market phenomena, where the analytical core is based upon the impossibility of a command economy that operates without the guidance that market prices offer. The conventional approach to the theory of public finance then inserts the state into the picture by treating it as if it were a single firm. Accordingly, the problems of public finance are treated as if they were problems of someone exercising choice, with that choice guided by notions of public goods. As already noted, the dichotomy between public and private goods has only weak ability to distinguish between market squares and public squares as the sources of enterprise sponsorship. This observation might be troubling for teleological prescription, but it presents no particular problem for emergent theorizing. The mixture of public and private goods organized within the public square, or the market square for that matter, is an emergent feature of human interaction across the two forums, and remains to be explained, as noted by Robert McCormick and Robert Tollison (1981).

## V.  TWO HYATTS AND THEIR ECONOMIC ORGANIZATION

Suppose we ask what insight the theory of public goods provides for a comparative analysis of two types of organization, one type formed within public squares and the other type formed within market squares. Cities and towns and the activities they sponsor are formed within public squares. Hotels, along with apartment complexes and shopping centers, are formed within market squares. The distinction between cities and hotels reflects the operation of different principles of organization and governance, but those differences have nothing to do with the distinction between public and private goods. Cities and hotels are both frameworks for human governance, and both sets of arrangements confront the same situations.

It is commonly said that a city establishes what might be called an infrastructure of public goods that provides a framework through which people can conduct their personal activities. Thus people live in their private homes and travel to other private places to work and to shop. In the course of doing so, they travel over streets that are provided and maintained by the city. Those streets may be kept in good condition or allowed to become filled with potholes. They may be kept clean or allowed to become covered in litter. The city will also offer security services through a police department, and may also offer some protection against fires as well. To be sure, fire protection may be operated privately as a kind of regulated utility, but such fire protection will be present in any case. Cities also offer places for people to play. These various city services are financed largely through taxes, often on property, but there are a variety of other charges and fees that are generally found as well.

What is particularly notable about a hotel is that it contains the same types of activities as cities, as Spencer MacCallum (1970) explains and Fred Foldvary (1994) amplifies. Hotels have residents, just as cities do. The hotel provides various types of infrastructure that provide a framework within which people conduct their activities. Hotels operate mass transit systems, except that they run vertically and not horizontally. Just as roads and subways become congested at peak travel times, so too do hotel elevators. While some economists argue for pricing roads to reduce peak congestion, these suggestions have not been extended to elevators. Yet the settings are identical, which leads one to wonder why pricing is thought to be a solution to congestion in the one case and not in the other. A possible answer, as will be explored later, would seem to lie in the economics of different forms of property and their attendant organizational settings, but most certainly not in considerations of resource allocation. In these terms, the two settings are identical: both cities and hotels contain mixtures of private and collective consumption.

Hotels don't price elevators, and peak congestion is simply accepted as something that people must live with. Why is it different with cities? Hotels provide security and recreation services, again just as do cities. Not all of the residents of a hotel have a demand for all of the public goods the hotel provides. Nonetheless, it is plausible to think that the ownership of the hotel seeks to provide a combination of public goods that supplies the highest ownership value for the hotel. The hotel offers a rental price that entails a tied sale between a room and a set of public goods that are offered free of direct charge.

Allocatively speaking, a city has these same characteristics. The value of particular houses within a city depends not just on the value of the house as somehow evaluated in a state of nature, but also reflects the value of the associated services the city provides. Cities are typically referred to as municipal corporations. It is easy enough to de-emphasize the municipal relative to the corporation in this expression. In doing this, what would exist would be seen as the owners of places within the city likewise and simultaneously being the corporate owners of the city itself. The value that people place on staying at a hotel depends on both the value of the room itself and on the accompanying set of services that are packaged with the room. Similarly, the value that people place on living in a particular city includes both the value of their houses and the accompanying infrastructure assets that the city owns and operates.

From this simple recognition, it is easy to imagine a mental experiment whereby Hyatt the city is converted into Hyatt the hotel, or vice versa. The conversion would start from a change in the character of property. For Hyatt the hotel, property is held by owners who pool their property in an act of association, with that association governed by rules of corporate association. Residents are customers who purchase services from the hotel. There is a clear distinction between owners and customers. This distinction vanishes with the formation of Hyatt the city. Residents become owners. According to the rules of this political association, ownership rights cannot be transferred through transactions on an open market. A resident is necessarily an owner, and can cease being an owner only by moving out of Hyatt the city.

Besides a shift from alienable to nonalienable ownership, the conversion from Hyatt the hotel to Hyatt the city is accompanied by a change in the rules of association governance. With Hyatt the hotel, the aggregate bundle of ownership is split into units called shares, with each owner having a proportionate share. By acquiring more shares, an owner gains weight within corporate decision processes. With Hyatt the city, each owner–resident has the same weight within corporate decision processes, on the surface anyway.

Hyatt the hotel and Hyatt the city face pretty much the same sets of situations and problems, but they operate under different frameworks for association. For Hyatt the hotel, people participate in ownership to the extent that they choose to do so through their purchase of ownership shares. For Hyatt the city, a proportionate share in ownership is necessarily acquired upon taking up residence in the city, and the rules of association are likewise different. For Hyatt the hotel, a majority vote refers to a majority of the ownership shares. For Hyatt the city, a majority refers to a majority of the voting residents independently of what might be called their 'investments' in the city. A reflection on the two Hyatts surely suggests that the phenomena of public finance arise out of property and rules of organization or association as these govern human conduct and relationships, and not out of notions of public goods and related constructions which empirically map very poorly into any distinction between market-based and politically-based activity.

## VI. PROPERTY AND THE BOUNDARY BETWEEN CONCORD AND DISCORD

To work with a model of two squares or two bazaars within the same society leads one to ponder the character of the boundary between the two. The median voter notion suggests a seamless boundary. By contrast, the preceding mental experiment regarding the two Hyatts suggests a discontinuity, and one that entails several dimensions. Those discontinuities, moreover, can be traced back to differences in the frameworks for human association and governance that accompany differences in the character of property in different settings. The economic theory of a market economy is grounded on concord. This is easy to understand, as it is based on exploring economic organization when human governance is based on a clear recognition of the distinction between mine and thine. With that distinction in place, the conditions for concord are simultaneously present.

A variety of Hyatts the hotel can exist concordantly within a market economy because all of those organized human relationships arise out of the same principles of governance. To be sure, utopian fantasies are to be avoided, which requires some recognition that there will always be challenges at the boundaries of mine and thine. There are multiple margins of discord that emerge once property as a natural fact of human nature becomes encumbered as well with grafting from positive, state-directed law.[6] Among other things, society is an arena within which associations relate to one another. Those associations that are formed within the market square all operate under the same rules or principles. But when positive law is imported into the public square, differences can emerge in governance across associations. Those differences alter the performance properties of associations and generate zones of conflict among associations within a society.

In his 19th century treatise *Ancient Law*, Henry Maine (1864) noted that the direction of movement in progressive societies had been one of a continual movement from human relationships grounded on status to relationships grounded on contract. Regardless of the veracity of Maine's claim, the distinction between status-based and contract-based relationships is pertinent to the topic being addressed here. Relationships grounded in contract allow no privileged positions for particular associations within society. Anyone is free to challenge for the position of First Violin. In contrast, relationships grounded in status entail positions of privilege, and in so doing eliminate degeneracy and create particular nodes through which entrepreneurial plans must run. The presence of such status positions generates sources of continuing conflict beyond those that would exist even under natural ordering.

Such discord can arise as a clash between politically-based and market-based enterprises. It can also arise as a politically-generated clash between market-based enterprises. Consider a politically-generated conflict that appears to arise from within the market. It is not a violation of any right of property for people to form an association to create a retail store. That store might generate more patronage than other stores, but the owners of those other stores would not have suffered any violation of their right of property. Within a framework of private property, successful commercial competition is not an offense against other competitors who do not fare so well.

Successful competition can, however, be treated as offensive through positive legislation. There have been a number of occasions where legislation has sought to penalize successful competition. One of the more recent instances concerns proposals to prohibit retail outlets beyond some stipulated size.

Conflict can also result when politically-based and market-based enterprises are established in the same region of enterprise space. In the early 20th century in the United States, there was fairly free and open competition to carry people between their residences and their places of work. Many people who were driving downtown would offer to carry other people who were also going downtown. This jitney service (Eckert and Hilton 1972), as it was called, was a form of unlicensed taxi service that operated only during morning and evening rush hours. At the same time, cities often operated bus lines and trolley lines. There are reasons related to the economics of organization, as explored in Chapter 5, to think that that city-operated services will generally be supplied at higher cost than privately-organized enterprises. To the extent that this differential in cost exists, it raises questions concerning the ability of politically-sponsored enterprises to survive in competition against privately-sponsored enterprises.

One possibility is that the two types of enterprise operate in distinct domains, so that there are no collisions among competitors organized according to different principles. This presumption, for instance, is central to the theory of public goods. In contrast to that theory, politically-sponsored and market-based enterprises often inhabit similar regions of enterprise space. In such cases, a politically-sponsored enterprise exists in the same vicinity as market-based enterprises. The operation of transit services by a municipality is one such example. If a municipal transit enterprise is more costly than a market-based one, we should expect the municipal enterprise to contain some characteristic features that keep the superior market-based enterprises from driving out the politically-based enterprises. Those features would contain fiscal phenomena that would not be found under the institutional and organizational arrangements associated with the governance of enterprises created on the market square.

One set of those phenomena would surely involve restrictions on the ability of privately-organized enterprises to compete with politically-based enterprises. Political enterprise will often set up zones of protection to secure their territory against encroachment from market-based enterprises. The margins along which such restrictions might be inserted are numerous, and perhaps limited only by the extent of the imagination. For instance, private enterprises could be required to operate only along approved routes, and at politically stipulated schedules and frequencies. This would raise the costliness of the service offered, thereby enhancing the competitive position of politically based enterprises.

In many cases, politically-sponsored enterprises offer services to favored customers that are financed in part by particularly high charges imposed on other customers. Those customers who lose through this operation are, of course, particularly likely to shift patronage to private enterprises. The competition of private enterprises in this instance is commonly described as cream skimming. This is a peculiar, politically inspired use of language. What is called cream skimming is an element of a process that if left unchecked would tend to subvert the political enterprise. Hence, political enterprises will seek to establish a variety of restrictions on what otherwise would have been private property to maintain their market presence in the light of their general commercial inferiority. One of the most significant of those restrictions is taxation. Within a theory of political enterprise, taxation amounts to the creation of an alternative system of pricing as Maffeo Pantaleoni (1911) explained, and one that places much of the cost upon people who have low demand for the services of political enterprises, as will be explored in Chapter 6.

## VII.   THE CONSTITUTION OF ORDER FOR PUBLIC SQUARE CATALLAXY

With the demise of feudal patterns and the advent of modern forms of state, the state lost its property and enterprises and gained access to taxation, various features of which are explored by Joseph Schumpeter (1954 [1918]).[7] Private property provides a simple framework through which enterprises can be put together and their commercial merit subsequently tested. With the advent of modern states and democratic forms that transformed princely private property into collective property, new forms of constitutive parliamentary rules were required. The actual conduct and operation of public squares reflects the same underlying principles as always, except that the transformation of princely property into collective property brings into the analytical foreground issues regarding parliamentary procedure and organization.

Individuals can act directly, but groups can take action only in conjunction with some procedural or constitutive framework that orders relationships among the members of the group. With respect to political action, that medium is some structure of procedural rules. Recall the mention of lighthouses in Chapter 2, and imagine what might be involved as people seek to bridge the gap between the expressions of concern over lost cargos and sunken ships and the subsequent activities that eventuate in lighthouses. It is impossible for the members of a parliamentary assembly to have any serious and substantive deliberation. To conduct parliamentary business, various forms of delegation to restrict deliberation will be necessary. Two or perhaps even three or four people can discuss whether they might want to build a lighthouse somewhere, with that discussion covering the various combinatorial possibilities that are relevant. An assembly of 100 or more people, however, can't do this. For business to be done within the public square, deliberation will have to be restricted (de Jouvenal 1961). This restriction will take the form of various institutional rules that govern par- liamentary procedure. While the rules of parliamentary procedure have rarely been part of the theory of public finance, those rules actually provide a substantial part of the constitutive framework within which enterprises come to populate the public square.[8] Those procedural rules will have to operate dramatically to pare down the volume of deliberation toward what would characterize exploration in the private square. Parliamentary assem- blies in democratic regimes would necessarily take on oligarchic character- istics once they reach some size where formal parliamentary rules are required to facilitate conversation and exploration.

At any particular moment, a number of distinct enterprises will be sup- ported through any public square. One enterprise might collect refuse, another might repair roads, and a third might build and maintain play- grounds. At some later time, yet other enterprises might also be supported through the public square. When the state is recognized to be an order and not an organization, its resulting polycentric character means that the pattern of supported enterprises at any particular moment is an emergent outcome of the interaction among interested participants in both the market and public squares. A government's budget is typically portrayed as a product of collective choice, with an emphasis on the chosen-ness of the budget. This portrayal recalls the stylized setting of consumer choice: a government, like a consumer, must choose how to allocate a limited budget among competing desires. The alternative portrayal from a social-theoretic orientation is one of bottom-up emergence, in which the aggregate entity called a budget is generated within the competitive, instituted process that characterizes a public square, taking due account of the connections between public squares and market squares.

## VIII. STATE REDISTRIBUTION AS EMERGENT CATALLAXY

The emergent character of the economic organization of the public square can be considered in more detail by focusing on the subset of state activities that are commonly described as comprising the welfare state. Those activities, moreover, are commonly subdivided between programs of social insurance and programs of public assistance. Whichever version of the welfare state is the object of reference, that reference commonly brings to mind purposeful activity pursued to achieve some goal, with it being meaningful to consider *ex post* how effectively that goal was pursued. For instance, some might claim that public assistance programs are effective in curbing the extent of poverty within a society, while others might claim that those programs might even increase poverty by discouraging individual foresight and initiative. Regardless of these conflicting claims, the set of programs that constitute the abstract construction that is designated as the welfare state are treated as the output of an organization.

The treatment of the state in general, and the welfare state in particular, as an activity of an organization, is conveyed nicely in the contemporary theory of optimal taxation, which expressly describes an optimal fiscal choice in terms of maximizing a social welfare function. This is not to say that it is easy to discover the terms of that choice, and the literature on optimal taxation contains a number of formulations in reflection of this difficulty. Whether the setting for choice is easy or difficult, however, it is still construed as someone's choice. For the classical optimal tax problem, the objective is to maximize some personified social utility function by creating some Robin Hood scheme of redistributive taxation. Redistribution is supported because it is presumed that the marginal utility of income falls as income rises. Redistribution is limited because it is recognized that the incentive to earn income weakens as the marginal rate of tax increases. The amount of redistribution that turns out to be optimal in these models depends on the rate at which people substitute leisure for labor as the rate of tax increases. Many such models conclude in favor of relatively low rates of tax and redistribution, due to presumptions about the elasticity of substitution. Regardless of the details of particular models, what is particularly notable is that this analytical framework unfolds in a top-down direction. This is a model of the phenomena of public finance as arising out of a plan through some planner's allocative choices, with that plan resulting in a single, coherent program of redistribution through the state's budget to revise market-based outcomes.

The standard conceptualizations of redistribution and the welfare state clash directly with the absence of any coherent program of redistribution. Any survey of the actual fiscal landscape would show that there exist hundreds if not thousands of particular programs of redistribution and not some single, global program. Those various programs, moreover, clash with one another and with any simple specification of achieving some redistributive objective. It is conceptually simple to speak in terms of some universal program to redistribute from people with relatively high incomes to people with relatively low incomes. A progressive income tax where the proceeds are used to finance lump sum grants to everyone is one such program, and has provided the archetypical model of optimal taxation.

Actual state budgets, however, contain nothing that resembles this type of program. There are numerous expenditure programs and tax provisions that entail some redistribution in comparison with whatever the alternative to that program or provision might be. But those programs and provisions do not aggregate in any coherent fashion. Just as market outcomes are more aptly modeled as emergent and not planned, so do fiscal outcomes likewise emerge through catallactical processes of exchange and duress and are not derived from some planner's optimizing effort.

Consider the alternative, choice-theoretic explanation. One conclusion that could be reached from contemplating the conflicting and confusing mass of state programs is that they reflect choices made by people with wildly intersecting indifference curves. While such weirdness is not the character that is thought to capture the state when its advocates advocate on its behalf, this is surely the only sensible conclusion that could be maintained so long as the phenomena of public finance are treated as choices that start at the top and filter down. If one were to try to characterize market outcomes as representing choices, they too would seem weird and contradictory, as one would only need to reflect on the simultaneous production of cigarettes and of paraphernalia to prevent smoking. However, we recognize that market outcomes are emergent and not chosen outcomes, so we don't look for coherence in aggregation. Why isn't it the same with political outcomes? They can no more be planned and chosen in comprehensive fashion than can market outcomes.

The alternative approach would treat political outcomes as also emergent, as emanations of a catallactical order of a particular type, one where duress and not just exchange takes place. For instance, a well-placed supporter of an influential politician might succeed in getting the tax code amended to give special treatment to an arena he plans to build. On average, this piece of legislation would transfer wealth in an upward direction, though the recipients of this transfer would be small in number. Some manufacturers of farm machinery might succeed in getting their machinery incorporated into an appropriation for foreign aid. On average, this program too would transfer wealth in a generally upward direction, again to a generally small set of people. Yet again, rules regarding the items to be included within a food stamp program might be altered to shift more business in particular directions, with perhaps questionable distributive impact overall, though with some benefit to a select few.

Perhaps a progressive tax on income might be thought of as constituting a program to redistribute income in a downward direction. Yet the tax code is also replete with provisions that work in the reverse direction. Much legislation that seeks to restrict the domain of market ordering likewise works contrary to the claims commonly made on behalf of a redistributive state, as illustrated by such things as occupational licensing and minimum wage legislation. Universal legislative support for state-operated schooling, though, is perhaps the most substantial expenditure program that works directly opposite to the nominal impact of progressive taxation, especially at the higher grade levels.

If we start with the proposition that people act to remove uneasiness that they sense, we see immediately that there are several avenues they can pursue to remove this uneasiness. For the most part, economic theory assumes that this takes place within the market square. For a theory of public finance, however, its primary material arises within the public square. A state's budget becomes an emergent phenomenon that is generated though interactions among participants, with those interactions being governed by a complex constellation of institutional arrangements and conventions.

## NOTES

1. Instructive treatments of crowds can be gained by comparing Gustave Le Bon (1960 [1895]) and James Surowiecki (2004). Among other things, such a comparison speaks to the importance of context to historical treatment, as distinct from theoretical treatment; this is explained with particular clarity in Ludwig von Mises (1957).
2. Market-based interaction also generates collective outcomes, as illustrated by the emergence of prices. Such emergent outcomes do not, however, originate in the denial of forbearance that establishes the personal–communal boundary that I am trying to indicate here.
3. The Biblical story describes how Esau, the elder son, returned home famished from hunting, and sold his birthright to his twin brother Jacob for a 'mess of pottage' (Genesis 25: 29–34).
4. An outside-in perspective can give the appearance of smoothness in the aggregate. An increasing number of people may agree to commit murder as the price offered to do so increases, even if everyone possesses the threshold implied by lexicographic ordering. This is a case where an outside-in view does not generate the same perspective as an inside-out view.
5. Also noteworthy because it is specifically a treatment of public finance is Robert McGee (2004).
6. The naturalness of property is expounded lucidly in Robert Ardry (1968).
7. Schumpeter's piece was originally published in 1918, and was both preceded and followed by essays by Rudolf Goldscheid that when collected provide a debate regarding the place of property in public finance. For a collection of these essays, see Rudolf Hickel (1976).
8. Notions of agenda control are where such considerations have entered, as illustrated for instance by Plott and Levine (1978) and Romer and Rosenthal (1978).

# 4. Political entrepreneurship within the ecology of enterprises

A society contains a configuration of enterprises, some established through the market square and others established through the public square. The historical record contains instances where these configurations have been relatively static. Indeed, it is possible to imagine a completely static configuration that simply reproduces itself. A society that conformed to this configuration would be a static, caste-based society. The pattern of relationship denoted by caste may not be explicitly recognized and acknowledged by the members of society, but that society would have a caste-like character all the same. A corporate executive whose husband is a physician will be replaced by a daughter and son who subsequently occupy those same positions. If the parents live in a house of 5000 square feet on a hill with a lovely view, their children who replace them will live the same way. An auto mechanic and her husband, a waiter, will be replaced in those capacities by their children. If the parents live in a house of 1200 square feet without a view in a noisy, dusty and congested part of town, so will their children. Parents who associate with people within the environs of a country club will have children who form their associations the same way. Parents who associate on street corners will have children who associate the same way.

Such a static society would be described as one where people accept their place and position within society because that is just the way things are. The historical record provides many instances of such societies, at least as reasonably accurate approximations. But modern and progressive societies are nothing like this. There are still corporate executives and auto mechanics, and large houses on hills with nice views as well as small houses with much noise and no view. Who occupies those positions, however, is not determined in advance by parentage. Someone who grows up in a small house can end up living in a large house. Moreover, houses change. Where small houses without views once stood, condominiums with views and amenities may now stand.

Entrepreneurship is the source of propulsive energy within a society that sets in motion processes of continual transformation in the map of enterprises within a society and, concomitantly, undermines the caste-like quality of societal reproduction. The phenomena of public finance, just as the phenomena of market economies, emerge through the creation of enterprises. Political enterprise and political entrepreneurship thus occupy the core of theorizing about public finance or the public economy. To be sure, the public economy is not formed independently of the market economy, nor is subsequent activity within the two spheres independent of one another. There is continuing interaction among enterprises formed within market and public squares, with that interaction generating both cooperation and conflict. This chapter first describes the enterprise map of a society, for this map is formed and transformed through entrepreneurship. This is followed by a quick examination of entrepreneurship in the market square to provide a benchmark for the subsequent consideration of entrepreneurship in the public square. The chapter then examines tectonic relationships at the various boundaries where politically-based and market-based enterprises meet, with these relationships generating turbulence within a society.

## I.   THE ENTERPRISE MAP AND ITS TRANSFORMATION

Economists make wide use of spatial references with respect to both market and political phenomena. With respect to theorizing about market phenomena, economists refer to 'commodity space', with distinct commodities occupying unique positions in that space. With respect to political competition, economists and other public choice scholars refer to 'issue space', with different candidates seeking to find a location in that space that will yield more votes than other possible locations (Enelow and Hinich 1984, 1990). Here, these two uses of space are joined to form a single 'enterprise space'. This conceptualization represents the realization that market squares and public squares are populated by the same people, who are acting in different capacities or taking on different roles. The members of a society are simultaneously involved in both public and market squares. Just as it is possible to think in terms of locating commodities in commodity space or locating political platforms in issue space, so it is possible to think in terms of locating particular enterprises in enterprise space.

Indeed, the politically organized enterprise is regarded as the basic unit of analysis for the approach to fiscal theorizing taken in this book, and by extension the market-based enterprise would be the basic unit of analysis for market-based theorizing. By 'basic' unit, I mean to identify the source of energy and imagination that drives the enterprise forward, transforming the entrepreneurial map in the process. Any enterprise, whether organized in the market square or the public square, can be thought of as occupying a particular location in enterprise space. Leonard Read in his justly famous essay *I, Pencil* (1958), points out that no single person knows how to make even a simple pencil, let alone the myriad of vastly more complex products that surround us. The ability to produce anything emerges out of a nexus of relationships among those who possess complementary inputs. This recognition of the crucial character of nexus means that any enterprise must have connections as well as location. Indeed, in constructing a map of enterprises, each enterprise will be represented by its location and by its connections to other enterprises.

Figure 4.1 shows two distinct types of enterprise map, and an examination of the construction of these maps can convey the animating ideas for the enterprise-based theory of public finance that this book explores. Both panels show a mixture of market-based and politically-based enterprises. In both panels, market-based enterprises are denoted by circles and politically-based enterprises are denoted by squares; moreover, in each panel there are nine market-based enterprises and six politically-based enterprises. Each enterprise, whether founded within the market square or the public square, occupies a unique location in enterprise space. Since no enterprise can exist independently of all other enterprises, entrepreneurship will also involve the creation of patterns of connection that allow a particular enterprise to thrive.

Obviously, Figure 4.1 is an extreme simplification of any actual enterprise map, as it would be impossible to work with a map that showed the millions of enterprises that actually exist in any society. Indeed, it would be impossible actually to construct such a map in truly accurate fashion, for such an act of construction would run afoul of the overwhelming complexity of the

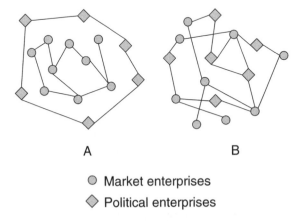

A          B

○ Market enterprises
◇ Political enterprises

*Figure 4.1    Alternative maps of market and political enterprise*

task. Figure 4.1 portrays small-scale enterprise maps to make them easily digestible and yet has a sufficiently large scale to allow the central ideas that govern the generation and transformation of that map to be presented.

The two panels obviously represent very different enterprise maps. The map shown in Panel A illustrates a classically liberal approach to political economy. That enterprise map has several notable features. One is that market enterprises lie at the core of the map while political enterprises exist on the periphery. This pattern of enterprise location conforms to the classically liberal notion that public enterprises exist to maintain the framework for the market economy, but do not participate within the market economy. The political enterprises are fully connected with one another, to indicate that they act as an equilibrated unit to maintain the framework of the market economy.

It is also notable that the market enterprises are not wholly connected with one another, for reasons explained in Jason Potts (2000). It is possible to trace a path from one particular market enterprise to any other market enterprise, but it is impossible to go directly from any one market enterprise to all others. Enterprise space is thus conceptualized as a network and not as a field. This network conceptualization corresponds to the idea of a division of knowledge, where individual actors know a lot about their particular area of expertise and a little about everything else. The operational quality of the overall nexus of relationships is thus a matter of how effectively diffused bits of knowledge are used within and throughout the nexus (Hayek 1945).

Panel B shows a strikingly different enterprise map. Two remarks are in order about this difference.[1] One is that the relative locations of political and market enterprises are dramatically different from those shown in Panel A. In Panel B, political and market enterprises are commingled, in contrast to the core–periphery relationship described by Panel A. Panel B illustrates what has been described as a mixed economy (Littlechild 1978; Ikeda 1997). Furthermore, the political enterprises are no longer fully connected to one another, so do not act as a coordinated entity. The densest connections among enterprises are among collections of subsets of political and market enterprises. This suggests a symbiotic relationship among particular political and market enterprises, where each type of enterprise supports the other. It also suggests that a particular cluster of enterprises, both politically-based and market-based, can be mutually competitive with both political and market enterprises located elsewhere in a society's enterprise map.

In asserting that political enterprises do not act as a fully connected entity, the enterprises that constitute the public economy of a society are conceptualized as an order and not an organization. One public enterprise might supply water and sewage services while another provides parks and playgrounds. There will be a formal connection between the two enterprises due simply to their common formal supervision by a legislative assembly. Yet the legislature does not truly work as a unit unless it contains only a handful of members. Moreover, the most important connections for a public enterprise are to complementary and competitive market enterprises, and not to the other public enterprises. For the water and sewage enterprise, those connections would run to such market enterprises as providers of water purification technologies and septic field maintenance. The public enterprise, moreover, might be complementary to water purification and competitive with septic fields. The public park and recreation enterprise might likewise stand in a complementary relationship to market enterprises that supply concrete and manufacture playground equipment, while standing in a competitive relationship to market enterprises that manufacture recreational equipment that can be used in homes and yards.

A second pertinent remark concerns the distinction between emergent or process-based thinking and thinking in terms of equilibrium and comparative statics. The orthodox interpretation of these two panels would be of alternative systems of equilibrium relationships on which analyses in terms of comparative statics could be performed. The exposition pursued here, however, is one of emergent development of non-equilibrium systems of partially-connected relationships. Hence, Panel B is an entrepreneurially-driven transformation of Panel A: Panel B represents Panel A transformed through time by entrepreneurial action. That transformation, moreover, is a product of both market and political entrepreneurship, and of the interaction among entrepreneurs acting in both market squares and public squares.

Transformation, of course, can be large scale or small scale, and which it is often depends on the length of time involved. The enterprise map is continually undergoing transformation through entrepreneurship. That transformation is propelled by the insertion of entrepreneurial plans into society. Once such a plan is inserted, it becomes a source of stability over some period. Over any small interval of time, much of the entrepreneurial map will remain unchanged, as previously laid entrepreneurial plans are being executed. Change will come from new acts of entrepreneurship, including the entrepreneurial revision of previously laid plans. These entrepreneurial acts will unsettle those previously laid entrepreneurial plans, leading thus to further transformations of the entrepreneurial map (Schumpeter 1934). For a sufficiently short interval of time, thinking in terms of equilibrium relationships can appear to be a reasonable approximation. Within some sufficiently short time interval, the hypothesis that a society's entrepreneurial map represents a static equilibrium might pass muster by standard tests of statistical significance. Nonetheless, processes of transformation are always at work, which means that emergence and process is more fundamental or foundational than equilibrium and statics.

Regardless of the particular configuration of enterprises that may pertain at any moment, entrepreneurship is that part of economic theory that deals with the transformation of the economic landscape. If one particular landscape prevails at $t_0$ and another at $t_1$, entrepreneurship resides at the core of the process by which the economic landscape is transformed from that which existed at $t_0$ to that which exists at $t_1$. The ecology of political enterprises within a society constitutes the macrocosm within which the phenomena of public finance emerge; the micro analytics regarding the generation and the operation of that macrocosm reside inside the individual enterprises that comprise that ecology. Any enterprise, whether it is organized within the public square or through private property, faces three related tasks. One task, the subject of this chapter, is entrepreneurial in nature, and concerns the establishment of a politically-based enterprise, for a public economy is an aggregation across all politically-based enterprises. A second task, which is examined in Chapter 5, is to develop an organizational framework that is suitable for securing entrepreneurial objectives in a context of team production. A third task, which is examined in Chapter 6, entails the generation of revenues to support the activities of political enterprises, which includes rewards for clients and supporters.

## II.    ENTREPRENEURSHIP IN THE MARKET SQUARE

The map of enterprises within a society emerges through the exercise of entrepreneurship, either through private property in the market square or within the public square that is superintended by a legislative body within a democratically organized polity. To be sure, entrepreneurship is a minor topic for conventional theorizing about market phenomena, due to the conventional focus on equilibrium states. Entrepreneurship is centrally concerned with economic change, as is noted in such works as Frank Knight (1921), Joseph Schumpeter (1934), Israel Kirzner (1973, 1979, 1985), Brian Loasby (1982, 1991), Mark Casson (1982) and Frédéric Sautet (2000). To give significant scope for entrepreneurship requires theorizing about processes of continual evolution and development, with entrepreneurship providing the source of that motion. What results is a distinctly emergent and non-equilibrium line of analysis.

With reference to Figure 4.1, an entrepreneurial plan formed within the market square can be described as a combination of location and connection that an entrepreneur seeks to establish. A new entrepreneurial offering is inserted at some particular location within the ecology of enterprises that are present at that particular moment. A new firm might offer services very similar to what other firms are offering, in which case its location would contain a number of close neighbors. Alternatively, the firm's offering might be quite innovative, in which case it would inhabit a low-density part of the economic landscape.

Regardless of where an entrepreneur locates an enterprise within the economic landscape, that enterprise will have to establish connections, perhaps a great number of them, to be successful. The idea of creating a new enterprise starts with the entrepreneur, who forms the belief that a commercially attractive offering can be inserted into the existing ecology of enterprises. For that enterprise to go forward, the entrepreneur will have to convince many kinds of people to support the enterprise, and in many different capacities. For instance, the new enterprise will generally need to attract investors and creditors. It will need to convince other people to support the enterprise with labor and material, with that support financed by investors and creditors. The enterprise will also need to convince customers to support it by buying its products and services. The institutional framework of private property provides a syntax or procedure by which the crafting of those connections can be attempted.

The market square is an arena in which people are free to try to promote their entrepreneurial ideas. Being free to try, of course, is no assurance of being successful. An entrepreneur might not succeed in attracting sufficient investment or credit to drive the enterprise forward, or might attract only an amount sufficient to start an anemic enterprise that fares badly. Even if a new enterprise is well capitalized, it might find that customers are not willing to pay enough for the enterprise's products and services to render it viable. Still, the institutional framework provided by private property provides an arena wherein entrepreneurs are free to experiment in creating new commercial offerings.

The fundamental entrepreneurial choice involves a comparison between an experienced past and a conjectured future (Shackle 1961, 1972). It is impossible simultaneously to compare two experienced pasts, and it is likewise impossible to experience the future. About the future we can only conjecture. An entrepreneurial choice to establish a new enterprise, or, equivalently, to undertake some new direction within an existing enterprise, involves the construction of a conjecture about a proposed course of action, followed by a comparison of the conjectured value of that course with the presumed value of a continuation of the present course of action.

Entrepreneurial plans can thus fail to be realized from two directions: a continuation of the present course of action may work out differently than the entrepreneur thought; the conjecture about the proposed alternative course of action may prove to be wrong.

Entrepreneurial plans bridge time. A plan is laid today but the actual value of that plan won't be revealed until some tomorrow, possibly a relatively remote tomorrow, as when the value of hickory trees planted today aren't revealed until they are harvested 30 years hence. Since all production requires time, inputs are offered contractual terms based on what value the entrepreneur anticipates his commercial plans will realize as today's production plans are brought to market tomorrow. Anticipations are rarely fulfilled in full detail, of course, sometimes for the better and sometimes for the worse. In any case, entrepreneurial profit resides in the ability to bridge time successfully, as Frank Knight (1921) explained.

To characterize an entrepreneurial choice as between an experienced past and an imagined future is not to render such choices unintelligible manifestations of exuberant animal spirits, in which case entrepreneurial profit would be meaningfully described as the result of luck. While entrepreneurial choices are typically made with exuberant spirit, they are not unintelligible and thereby reducible to meaningless randomness. Entrepreneurship is an inside-out activity, and all people by virtue of their humanity enter any situation with a fair amount of knowledge about what other people will like and how they are likely to react to various entrepreneurial offerings. No one is going to offer a new breakfast cereal made of garlic chips roasted in cod liver oil. Someone might overestimate the extent to which people will buy a corn flake coated in chocolate, but that entrepreneurial plan would have been based on recognition that many people like corn flakes and many people like chocolate.

Entrepreneurship has many similar characteristics to the testing of hypotheses, as explained by David Harper (1996). Hypotheses are not tested by random selection among all possible combinatorial options. This might be a suitable framework for exploring biological evolution, but evolutionary processes within human societies are different because of the knowledge we have about each other. This knowledge does not provide recipes that guarantee commercial success, but it does provide clues. So people might reasonably introduce a chocolate-laced breakfast cereal while refraining from doing the same with garlic, and desist even more vigorously from offering a porridge made from cow brains.

Any entrepreneurial plan will involve taking action today based on intelligent conjectures about future conditions. Those conditions include beliefs about future demands for the product and about the entrepreneur's ability to construct the organizational framework that will both produce the product and generate the network of relationships that will connect creditors, distributors and customers so as to render the enterprise profitable. The entrepreneur faces a type of scientific problem, and entrepreneurship proceeds not by random guesswork but by intelligent hunch. Those hunches, moreover, are informed to a large extent by our common humanity and the general knowledge that this allows us to bring to bear on possible lines of entrepreneurial activity.

## III.  PROPERTY AND THE CONNECTION BETWEEN MARKET AND PUBLIC SQUARES

It is easy enough to understand how people can act within the principles of property and contract to form enterprises within the market square. In some cases, an entrepreneur's own property may be sufficient to establish an enterprise. More commonly, though, an entrepreneur will also require the use of property owned by other people. To accomplish this, she will have to convince those property owners to place their property under her direction. The principle of private property entails a grammar and procedure for doing this. In some cases those property owners will become investors, while in other cases they will become creditors. Regardless of the form of their participation, that participation will be agreeable to all participants. Once that enterprise is established, its success will subsequently be governed by its ability to generate revenues from the services it offers to potential customers. If the enterprise succeeds, it will be because it secured sufficient willing support from customers. The resulting enterprise map of the market square emerges and evolves in response to such entrepreneurial effort.

But how is it possible to extend such a conceptualization of entrepreneurship to the formation of enterprises on the public square? At first glance, the difference between enterprise formation in market and public squares is striking. The use of taxation to support political enterprises seems to involve a kind of inversion of market relationships. When a political enterprise acquires capital from taxation, it is surely inaccurate to describe those taxpayers as investors.[2] They might be forced investors, but they are hardly genuine investors. It is the same for the use of taxation to support the operations of a political enterprise. Those taxpayers could be described as being customers of the enterprise who support it with tax payments, but this relationship is not at all of the same kind as the relationship between enterprises and customers in the market square. While it is always possible to assimilate political to market entrepreneurship through the use of a formal language, the substantive content of language is destroyed in the process when taxpayers are described as investors and customers.

While fiscal theorists who work within an exchange paradigm (for instance, Buchanan 1967, 1976) speak of taxes as prices, a tax–price is an intellectual construction and not a genuine market price. This is true, and yet there is also truth in the construction that speaks of tax–prices. If within a society there was no desire to undertake activities in the public square, that square would be empty. A more careful consideration of market and public squares mitigates but does not eliminate the differences between market and public squares.[3] The source of mitigation resides in our natures, which entail interest both in our own activities and projects and in the activities of other people. This interest in others constitutes the bedding ground of a society's public square.

At any instant, there exists a conceptual division of capital within a society between that part to be employed within the market square and that part to be employed within the public square. This division, it should be stressed, is purely conceptual, and is distinct from any such observed distinction between private and public shares in GDP. The mental orientations of the members of a society at any particular time entail some predispositions of mind that can map into varying degrees of willingness to support activities in the market and public squares. Hence, there is some ability for political entrepreneurship to populate the public square that resides within a particular population at any moment. Again, this purely conceptual construction is distinct from actual historical conduct.

Let me give a simple illustration of what I have in mind, one that harks back to an earlier chapter. Suppose a society exists in a marshy area where flooding occurs on occasion and mosquitoes are energetic always. It's easy enough to imagine some of the features of the enterprises that would populate the market square. Some enterprises might manufacture repellants for homeowners to use when they venture outside. Another enterprise might sell bats and bat houses, under the belief that bats will keep mosquitoes in check when bat houses are located nearby. Both of these enterprises founded in the market square will arise out of people's concerns about mosquitoes. With respect to flooding, an enterprise might be established to produce and sell inflatable boats that people could use if they need to escape in the event of particularly high water. Another enterprise might be established to produce waterproofing compounds that would reduce the damage caused by whatever floods happen to occur. Once again, these enterprises would likewise be established in the market square in the light of people's concerns about flooding.

The concerns about mosquitoes and about flooding are held by people in the society. Market-based enterprises emerge as entrepreneurial responses to those concerns. There is, of course, no reason why entrepreneurial proposals should arise only in the market square. The public square is populated in various ways. Most fundamentally, it is populated by the widespread concerns that the members of society have about mosquitoes and flooding. Advertisements for mosquito repellant and waterproofing material appear in the newspaper and on television, and people talk about their concerns and reactions while at work, when going to parties, and when meeting people while shopping. In such a setting, it is only natural to find such concerns seeping into the public square, perhaps being aired in meetings of a town council or whatever kind of legislative assembly might be in place in the public square.

Some people might propose to build levees to reduce flooding. Others might propose to spray bodies of standing water located on property that no one owns, but which is thought to be a breeding ground for mosquitoes. Proposals to develop enterprises to pursue these projects might well garner strong support, sufficiently so that the enterprise goes forward. How such an outcome might compare against standard models from public goods theory is inconclusive and, moreover, is beside the point. For the central point in any case is that the ability of enterprises to populate the public square resides in our own natures, as does the ability to populate the market square. Where the two squares differ is in the syntax according to which enterprises can be established within the two precincts.

## IV.   ENTREPRENEURSHIP IN THE PUBLIC SQUARE

It is easy enough to understand the formation of enterprises through the market square, even if economic theory has not given much attention to market-based entrepreneurship.[4] Political entrepreneurship provides more challenges for an emergent orientation toward fiscal phenomena. The enterprise map described by Figure 4.1 contains both market-based and politically-based enterprises. The market-based enterprises are formed through entrepreneurial choices. It is the same for politically-based enterprises, except that the entrepreneurial process is more translucent than transparent.

In its most generic sense, an enterprise entails an entrepreneurial plan for the creation, production and delivery of a service to customers or clients. There is wide latitude in the organizational arrangements by which enterprises might be constituted. Among all the various enterprises established within the public square, there are distinctions among those enterprises in their constitutive details. Some may operate with appropriations from the legislature, while others operate with revenues paid directly by customers. Some may operate with a mixture of revenue sources. The particular organizational arrangement that pertains to any particular political enterprise is a matter of entrepreneurial choice and is a fit subject for fiscal analysis.

In the theory of public finance, it has been conventional to use the term public enterprise to refer to particular politically-sponsored entities that sell services directly to consumers through market transactions. Many national governments sponsor airlines in this manner. Many cities organize the provision of water in this manner. Most activities that governments undertake are supported by appropriations of tax revenue instead of from direct consumer payments. The organizations that provide such tax-financed services are typically described as bureaus or agencies and not as public enterprises. In this book, all of these various organizations are politically-sponsored enterprises, for their entrepreneurial creation and continuation lies in the public square and not in the market square.

How is the enterprise map populated with political enterprises? The foundation of a political enterprise resides in entrepreneurship just as does the foundation of a market-based enterprise. A political entrepreneur starts with a belief that a profit opportunity exists that can be exploited through the creation of a political enterprise, and then tries to implement a plan of action that will bring about this result. As a purely formal matter, there is no significant difference between political and market entrepreneurship. Both start with a belief that potential opportunities for gain are present to be exploited. Both require the cultivation of investors and sponsors, along with the cultivation of relationships among suppliers and customers. To be sure, political enterprises can contain forced investors and sponsors that are not possible on the market square. Within a democratic polity, however, not all investors and sponsors can be of the forced variety, though a good number of them can be, as will be explored in Chapter 6.

The cardinal presumption of the analysis pursued here is that there is a single underlying approach to explanation that can account for the formation of both market and political enterprises, as well as of the boundaries between the enterprises. In both settings entrepreneurship is initiated by a belief that the entrepreneurial action will prove profitable to the entrepreneur, a condition that in turn means that there are other people in society who also support the enterprise. The boundary between political and market enterprises is governed by the same principle that governs the boundary among various firms within the market economy. This is simply the universal desire to replace something that is desired less highly with something that is desired more highly. This desire is identical as between market-based and political enterprises.[5]

In taking an emergent or generative approach to fiscal phenomena, it is necessary for political enterprises to emerge as particular organizational forms that offer advantages to their entrepreneurs over any alternative entrepreneurial action. Profits, the substitution of higher value for lesser value, are the generating feature of entrepreneurial action. Action starts from the articulation of a belief that some alternative course of action holds out a better future than does a continuation of the present course of action. Political enterprises must offer returns to their creators, and returns, moreover, that can be compared with those that are offered by profit-seeking enterprises. Profit is a universal economic category, the search for which leads to the generation of a tomorrow that differs from what exists today. Profit can take any of several forms, with direct monetary returns being but one category, and possibly the predominant category in the market square. The other two categories of interest here are indirect monetary returns and non-monetary returns.

By indirect monetary returns, I mean monetary returns that accrue through ancillary enterprises that are connected with the particular political enterprise under examination. For instance, a hospital might be organized as a profit-seeking firm or as a political enterprise. Profit from the operation of a politically-organized hospital could not accrue through dividends or capital appreciation, but it could accrue through increased returns to a pharmaceutical company with which the hospital deals heavily (Pauly and Redisch 1973). Alternatively, profit could accrue to a research lab that supports the activities of some staff physicians, and who in turn might appropriate profit through patents they obtain from their research. A particular node in a chain of transactions might be organized so as to offer no dividends or capital appreciation, but this does not mean that such an enterprise offers no return on the capital invested. It means only that the return on investment accrues elsewhere, as what would otherwise be profits are passed through to other nodes to which the political enterprise is connected.

Profit in the public square can also be taken in such non-monetary forms as glory, recognition, esteem, or even calling (La Manna and Slomp 1994; Brennan and Pettit 2004). It is apparent that some people seek positions under the public spotlight while other people prefer positions of greater intimacy and anonymity. Someone who develops a different assembly for delivering ink-jet printing that delivers better quality printing while using less ink will surely do well commercially and will benefit many people. That person, however, is not likely to be the object of much public adulation, which might not be an object of desire anyway. In contrast, someone who had a strong desire for public adulation might well choose to pursue entrepreneurial opportunities in the public square. Someone who promotes a political enterprise to control flooding is likely to receive more public adulation than the inventor of the ink-jet assembly, even if on some cosmic scale of value the inventor was the more significant benefactor to everyone else in the society.

A full approach to economic organization and the ecology of enterprises that populate a society must include the full range of possibilities. Profit simply denotes success in replacing a less valued with a more valued condition. To the extent that the property relationships that are involved entail alienability, profit will be monetized. Should property be inalienable, as with collective property, profit will not be monetized directly, though it can still be monetized if the transactional node that is involved connects directly to some node where property is alienable. Profit can appear in multiple guises, for any action that replaces a less valued with a more valued option yields profit to the actor. There are some analytical principles that can be illuminated nicely by restricting the domain of analysis to profit-seeking enterprises. Yet the world also confronts us with a variety of political enterprises. Their existence must be accounted for, in terms that render sensible the entire ecology of enterprises that populate a society. The material of public finance comes particularly into play with politically-based enterprises, and yet those political enterprises are also embedded within the larger social ecology.

In *As You Like It*, William Shakespeare has his character Jacques observe that 'all the world's a stage, and all the men and women on it merely players'. That stage offers numerous parts for people to play, only there is no director who matches people and parts. This matching of people to parts, as well as the very character of those parts and their place within the overall human drama, is generated through interaction among the participants. Within a pure form of market economy organized wholly through private property, recognizing that this is an ideal type and not a historical type, the leading parts that secure the most prominent positions on stage are occupied by the most successful entrepreneurs. It is successful entrepreneurs who impart the direction of motion to a society organized around private property.

Everyone is free to compete for such leadership positions in a market-based society, even if the results of such competition reflect the skewness of lognormal types of distribution. But the market square is not the only stage in a society. Positions of acclaim and the search for glory can also be pursued in the public square. Furthermore, the characteristic features that govern success in the market square can be influenced through actions taken in the public square. Competition is ubiquitous in social life. It is unavoidable, so there is no point being either in favor or against it. As Frank Knight once remarked, to call something unavoidable is equivalent to calling it ideal, for the unavoidable cannot be avoided. Competition among people can't be avoided. Much of that competition will take place among enterprises organized in the market square. This is what economists ordinarily mean when they speak of market competition. But competition also takes place for position in the public square. Even more, the two forums for competition are not separable, which means that political activity serves as an instrument of market competition, just as market activity serves as an instrument of political competition.

Mancur Olson (1965) argued that the organization of activity on the public square will be thwarted unless some means is found to overcome the free rider problem. This setting is described in standard prisoners' dilemma terms. Each member of society is presumed to be better off if each contributes to support the collective activity, but to the extent that people free-ride, collective action will not be supported. Olson argued that such collective action problems can be overcome by making that action a by-product of the supply of some activity in the market square. This claim is subject to dispute, for if the activity in the market square earns only normal profit, nothing will be left to support the collective activity.

This standard presentation of the problem of collective action and the associated specter of the prisoners' dilemma misconstrues the setting within which the problem is claimed to arise. The standard problem setting is one of a disconnected mass of people, each of whom would gain modestly from collective action. If a sufficient number of such people fail to support collective action, there will be no such action. The problem this formulation depicts is due to the disconnected character of the participants. Once it is recognized that they are typically connected through some structured pattern of relationships, the problem dissolves or at least is transformed considerably. A disconnected mass of people is transformed into a network. Entrepreneurial activity in the public square, moreover, unfolds within this network framework.

The existence of a parliamentary assembly in the public square implies the existence of a network of relationships. The standard formulation of the problem of collective action envisions each person alone at home being plagued by mosquitoes. A message appears anonymously at home, asking for a donation to combat mosquitoes. If enough donations are received, war is declared on them. The trouble with this formulation is that there is no society that proceeds in this manner, nor could there be. People talk with one another, the media carry stories about mosquitoes, and these issues are aired in such public spaces as grocery stores and parliamentary forums. There is no such thing as an entrepreneurial action that aims to energize a disconnected mass of people. Myriad are the particular patterns of connection that can exist, but some such pattern will exist in every case. The organization of entrepreneurial activity will invariably have a networked pattern to it. In some cases this might involve placing stories in newspapers. In other cases it might involve placing advertisements. Yet again, it might involve sponsoring lectures and discussion groups. Part of the entrepreneurial challenge is acting upon the right vision of the appropriate network.[6]

## V.  THE ORGANIZATIONAL ARCHITECTURE OF THE PUBLIC SQUARE

The substantive activities that take place within the public square are generated through interaction among participants, just as are the substantive activities that take place within the market square. There is, however, an apparent position of hierarchy within the public square that is not present in the market square. If a diagram were to be prepared of all the enterprises in the market square and their connections, there would be no node through which all connections ran. Some nodes would have more connections than others, but it would be possible to navigate between any two non-adjacent nodes without passing through any particular node. Such a diagram would epitomize polycentrism and degeneracy.

A graph of the public square would contain a particular node through which all connections pass. The identity of that node would vary with the particular constitutive architecture of the public square. In a democratically organized polity of the parliamentary type, that node would be some type of legislative assembly or forum. For a presidential type of arrangement, a bipolar arrangement might be more accurate than a hierarchical arrangement. A legislative assembly, however, is not an acting being but is a forum or arena that provides a framework for the taking of particular types of action. So, too, for that matter is the position of president, at least within the American context. Where action within the market square is structured according to principles of private property, action within a public square is structured according to principles of collective property. Within a democratically constituted public square, moreover, the syntax of collective property is instantiated through the organizational arrangement of a parliamentary assembly.

While all connections within a particular public square run through the legislature, the legislature itself is not an entity but a structured nexus of relationships. It is, moreover, a nexus that is ill-suited for substantive deliberation, as Bertrand de Jouvenal (1961) explains. It is well recognized that no one could plan the activities that emerge within a market square of a modern society because any effort to do so would be overwhelmed by the complexity of the task. The situation is no different for the activities that emerge within the public square. Any effort to plan those activities would likewise be overwhelmed by the complexity of the task. The activities of the public square, like those of the market square, emerge through a form of free enterprise, as Gordon Tullock (1967) explains crisply in his analysis of bureaucratic free enterprise.

One feature of emergence-based theorizing is the ability to generate what looks like hierarchy when what is really being observed is polycentric processes in action. Consider again the discussion from an earlier chapter of the emerging economic organization of British towns in the 16th century examined in J.H. Thomas (1933). Initially, people were responsible for hauling their rubbish to a site where it was dumped. Rubbish disposal was handled through the market square. Enterprises emerged to haul rubbish to dumping sites. People could choose whether to haul their own rubbish or to hire someone to haul it for them. They could also let it accumulate in their yards. If this happened often, it would be easy enough to imagine a growing volume of complaints about foul odors and pests reaching the public square. Such complaints might have been taken directly to the legislature, but more likely would have been accompanied by such things as public forums and newspaper accounts that prepared the ground by getting the attention of some legislators.

It is also possible, and Thomas reports that it happened, that occasionally a carter would drop his refuse beside the road before arriving at the dump. In those days it might not have been at all easy to ascertain who actually dumped the rubbish. In any case, disgruntlement arising out of rubbish would make it to the public square, which in turn would have prepared the ground for some type of entrepreneurial action. There are, of course, different kinds of action that could be undertaken, which is also a matter of entrepreneurial choice. One type of choice would involve action in the market square, as perhaps illustrated by a lawyer who would hire a detective agency and bring cases on behalf of property owners whose property was littered by wayward carters.

It is also easy to imagine action in the public square. A police chief might seek to add a new line of activity by hiring a deputy to look for wayward carters. Someone else might suggest that the town license carters and assign routes. While carters would no longer compete among themselves, it would be much easier to assign responsibility for rubbish that was deposited short of the town dump. Someone else may suggest that the town council establish its own carting enterprise. There are several considerations that might lead someone to support a town enterprise to haul refuse. Where some might point to the possible higher cost of the town's carting enterprise, others could claim that the town enterprise would reliably dump refuse in the right place. Such people might believe that their share of the added cost associated with the town enterprise would be worthwhile. Yet others might support the town enterprise because they thought they might be in a good position to procure contracts for the maintenance of town carts or town oxen.

However it turns out in particular detail, refuse collection comes to run through the public square. At some later time, events transpire that make street maintenance an object of concern in the public square. Individual property owners are supposed to maintain the condition of streets in front of their properties. Some property owners do this well but some do it badly, allowing potholes to accumulate, which in turn leads to broken axles and even broken legs. Once again, the resulting discontentment can follow any of several paths. One would involve legal actions against property owners who fail to maintain their portions of roads. Another would be the town's sponsorship of an enterprise to maintain streets. If this route is adopted, road maintenance would now join refuse disposal in running through the public square and the town council. The connective geometry of relationships and activities within the town precincts would have changed.

A map of the enterprises involved in hauling refuse and maintaining streets would show many participating enterprises. Many of these would be organized in the market square. They would include the breeding of oxen, the building of carts, manufacturing wheels and quarrying gravel. All of those enterprises, however, would have connections that ran through the town council. The town council would now sponsor two enterprises, one to haul refuse and another to repair streets. If the town council were treated as a person, the town might seem to be an organization that supplies two services. This would be to mischaracterize the situation and its supporting relationships, just as Craig Roberts (1971) showed that it was wrong to characterize the Soviet Union as a planned economy. Both refuse disposal and street maintenance involve a variety of participating enterprises, some organized in the market square and some organized in the public square, as Vincent Ostrom (1962) notes with particular illumination for contemporary arrangements regarding water supply. The town council is simply an arena in which varying mixes of people interact, and through which various activities emerge; legislative assemblies provide a type of brokerage or middleman service, as explained in Robert McCormick and Robert Tollison (1981). The public square in a democratic polity is polycentric in its organizational architecture.

## VI.   EMERGENCE, TELEOLOGY AND POLITICAL ENTREPRENEURSHIP

While the predominance of equilibrium-centered theorizing about market economies has limited the analytical interest in entrepreneurship, any interest in political entrepreneurship has been further limited by the systems design orientation of most fiscal theorizing, wherein the establishment of political enterprises is implicitly portrayed as following an interventionist logic that is independent of the economic categories that are thought to apply to market-based entrepreneurship. In contrast, a social-theoretic orientation toward public finance must seek to explain the emergent organization of public economies in terms of such standard economic categories as utility, cost and profit. One significant entrepreneurial choice, moreover, is the selection of square in which to locate the enterprise.

Contrary to conventional theorizing about public goods, it is common to find market-based and politically-based enterprises providing the same or similar services. For instance, within the past decade or two numerous acts of entrepreneurship have transformed the organizational and technological landscapes on which telecom services are provided. Those telecom enterprises have been organized both through market and political processes. Many have been created to offer broadband services, of which many have been sponsored within the market square. However, such enterprises have also been sponsored within the public square by a number of municipalities.

If a city council decides to sponsor a broadband enterprise, that sponsorship must be explainable in some manner as generating some stream of net benefits that is subject to capture by sponsors, or else the enterprise would not have been sponsored. For a political enterprise to be sponsored, the sponsor must have judged that the success of the enterprise will produce an outcome that the sponsor values more highly than whatever other endeavor the sponsor might have pursued. Such economic categories as utility, cost and profit are as much in play in the emergence of enterprises in the public square as they are at work within the market square. Without profit to be captured, enterprises would not be sponsored in either square.

Within the market square organized through private property, profit opportunities are open for anyone to exploit at will provided only that they adhere to the syntax of human relationships based on private property. People are free to locate enterprises wherever they choose, and to seek to develop networks of connections among suppliers and customers in their efforts to maximize the values of their enterprises. It is the same with political enterprises in the public square. The institutional rules that govern the formation and determine the success of enterprises are different in the public square from those in the market square. But even those differences are constrained by cross-cutting participation in both squares by the members of society.

There are numerous particular reasons why an enterprise might be established in the public square. The enterprise might generate acclaim for its sponsors and officers, giving them a coveted position on the stage of public life that they would not secure, at least not so easily, from establishing an enterprise in the market square. Alternatively, that enterprise might generate business for particular enterprises in the market square, in which the sponsor holds an interest. The enterprise map in a society is changed as entrepreneurs pursue opportunities to replace less desired with more desired circumstances. This is a universal quality of all human action. The public square differs from the market square only in that the search for profit generally takes on less direct forms in the public square. The theoretical challenge is to give an account or explanation of the resulting entrepreneurial map associated with what are called mixed economies, and to do so without resorting to teleology, by remaining within a generative or emergent analytical framework.

Such a call to give an account of entrepreneurial activity based on a universal desire of people to replace what they value less with what they value more is sometimes opposed on the ground that it entails self-interest to the neglect of altruism. This opposition is based on a failure to distinguish between the substance of action and the form of action. For one thing, interest is a property of acting subjects or selves; it is not a property of the objects of interest. All action is unavoidably self-interested. Mother Teresa and Pol Pot were both self-interested creatures, though the objects of their interests differed dramatically. People differ hugely in their objects of interest, but relatively few appear to be like Narcissus, whose only object of interest was his own reflection.

## VII.    BOUNDARY TECTONICS AND ENTREPRENEURIAL TURBULENCE

Within any field of activity, people who are passionate and energetic will tend to dominate the tenor of enterprises relative to people who are enveloped in indifference and lassitude. Thriving enterprises, whether organized in the public or the market square, will be those that are energetically seeking additional lines of profitable business. Such business is acquired by moving location and expanding connections. Panel A of Figure 4.1 illustrates an initial situation where political and market enterprises occupy distinctly different territory and have little connection with one another. In their search for new business, political and market enterprises will each tend to invade territory occupied by the other and to establish connections with those enterprises. Over time, this produces an enterprise map that resembles Panel B of Figure 4.1.

Panel A describes a situation where a market-based enterprise might establish a brewery where it chooses and the only connection with a political enterprise might involve the use of roads produced from within the public square. Panel B describes a situation where the market-based brewery and assorted enterprises from the public square negotiate over such matters as location of the brewery, associated conditions of taxation, and the interpretation of rules regarding workplace safety.

The coalitional structure of a society described by Panel B is sharply different from that described by Panel A. In Panel A the state acts as a unit in intervening in the activities of enterprises in the market square. It is always better to lose less from that intervention than to lose more, and it is reasonable to expect that those who gain from intervention will support a larger state than those who lose. This situation maps directly on to a simple left–right spectrum, with the left denoting supporters of a larger public square and the right denoting supporters of a smaller public square. Even today, this kind of notion dominates political discourse.

This discourse today, however, does not seem terribly accurate – like, for example, the situation in Panel B. Of the enterprises formed within the market square, some will be in close proximity to political enterprises and will have many connections with them. There will be other market-based enterprises that are distant from political enterprises and which possess few connections. The closer a market-based enterprise is to a political enter- prise and the greater the number of connections, the stronger will be the ability of political and market enterprises to influence one another. To be sure, this influence may be either harmful or beneficial to a market-based enterprise.

Panel B shows all enterprises to be of the same size. This makes for sim- plicity in construction, but it is wildly inaccurate. Enterprises differ both in size and in age, and both are important. Size is important because the amount of wealth involved can be used by market-based enterprises to secure more favorable treatment from political enterprises. At the same time, increased wealth makes such enterprises particularly valuable targets for rent extraction, as Fred McChesney (1997) explains. Age is also important because many connections take time to craft. Those who belong to the nouveau riche lack the density of connections that the long-time rich possess.

At a deeper level of enterprise mapping, a distinction could be made between established and incipient enterprises. Incipient enterprises would generally find they have limited connection to political enterprises, both because they are new and because they are small. Established enterprises are in the reverse position. Public relations become an important activity for established enterprises because they operate with multiple connections to enterprises located in the public square. Incipient enterprises tend to make little effort at public relations, as distinct from customer relations.

Disputes between enterprises across the two squares work out differently from disputes between enterprises located within the market square. Collisions will occur among market-based firms. When they do, they can generally be negotiated peacefully through such things as mergers and joint agreements. For instance, a brewery might think that its prospect for growth warrants some expansion in its present facility. This urge to expand collides with the dairy that is currently using the land that would be suitable for the brewery's expansion. Whether the dairy's land is more valuable as a dairy or as a brewery is easily answerable. If the brewery is able to buy the land from the dairy, the owner of the dairy has agreed that the land is more valuable when used to support the expansion of the brewery.

What makes such disputes as that between the brewery and the dairy relatively easy to resolve peacefully is the presence of private property and residual claimacy. It is different when one party to a dispute is a political enterprise because residual claimacy is absent. This absence changes commercial calculations in several ways that increase turbulence within the enterprise map.[7] The situation now might involve the same brewery, only with the adjacent land used as a garage for repairing county vehicles. The brewery might make the same offer to buy as before, but the county garage has no owner who bears the value consequence for the response. If anything, the administrator of the garage will bear a cost and receive no gain. The administrator's salary will remain the same in the new location should the sale be made; however, the administrator will bear the inconvenience of having to move locations.

Commercial disputes where one party is a political enterprise also play out differently from disputes between enterprises established on the market square. For market-based enterprises, the expenses of litigation reduce their net worth, which give them good reason to settle disputes, provided only that they have similar outlooks about the probable resolution of the case should it go to trial. This simple calculus in favor of settlement does not apply when one party to a dispute is a political enterprise. For a political enterprise, a reduction in litigation expense through settlement does not increase net worth that anyone can claim. Indeed, it could well impose an inconvenience cost on the official who is handling the case. After all, the official has already borne a fixed cost of getting familiar with the case. If the case is settled, she will have to move on to another case. By refusing to settle, she can avoid doing that, her salary remains the same, and there is no increase in net worth to be distributed.

## VIII.   VOTING AND PARLIAMENTARY ACTION

To this point nothing has been said about voting and its impact on activities within the public square. A common formulation in the literature on public choice holds that the competition for office is a competition to design policies that have the strongest appeal to voters. The most prevalent formulations in this respect treat democratic electoral outcomes as reflecting the policy mix that maximizes utility for the median voter in the society, or alternatively, maximizes some average of utilities in a probabilistic voting model. Whatever the analytical details, the central argument is that people choose policies through elections, with elected officials more-or-less delivering on their promises to maintain electoral credibility.

This is one of those warm and fuzzy metaphysical metaphors that might not do a great deal of harm. There is competition for political office, with votes being cast and counted. To treat elections seriously as a means by which voters choose policy measures indirectly by choosing among candidates is to encounter De Jouvenal's problem of the chairman once again. The earlier example of the lighthouse contained a policy space that contained ten billion options. It would be impossible even for a legislative assembly to have a genuine discussion about these options, and so parliamentary assemblies necessarily use various parliamentary rules to restrict such discussion in numerous ways. If a legislative assembly does not discuss the full range of options, a rational deliberation and choice can be said to have been made in only a formalistic and tautological sense. What holds within a legislative assembly would surely hold within the society at large.

An election is a device that selects a candidate to occupy a node within a network of relationships. It is quite reasonable to think that different occupants of that node will act differently for any of many reasons. To occupy a parliamentary node, however, is not to choose the outcomes of parliamentary deliberations. It is only to become a participant in those deliberations. Moreover, it is not just members of the parliamentary assembly who participate in those deliberations. Each member of a parliament is embedded within a particular pattern of connections within the parliamentary assembly, as well as embedded within networks of connections that run elsewhere throughout the society. Much of the activity in the public square surely emerges through the nexus of relationships that has been generated, which to a large extent operates independently of particular electoral outcomes.

This is not to deny that policy outcomes can change with electoral outcomes. It is only to claim that the most significant work is independent of electoral outcomes, and is an emergent property of the nexus of relationships that is in place. To the extent that electoral outcomes matter, it is more through changes in the patterns of network connection that are subsequently established than in changes in the identity of the person who happens to occupy a particular node in a previously established network.[8]

Consider a simple allegory. Standing on the 20th floor of a commercial building, you look out of a window on to a park below. You see a crowd running across the grass. One man is in front, with the rest following. When the man changes direction, so does the following crowd. This spectacle continues for several minutes until they all vanish from sight. What have you seen? These were adults, and you think that perhaps they were trying to recover glimpses of their childhoods, when they played follow-the-leader. You realize, of course, that you really couldn't tell without asking the participants. You further realize that the pack might have been savagely in pursuit of the lead runner, perhaps because he had maliciously stabbed the guide dog of the blind woman who sold cotton candy at the entrance to the park over which you were looking. Again, there is no way to tell from simple observation.

When we leave the 20th floor and return to the public square, the issue is whether elections are instruments by which policies are chosen or whether policies are emergent outcomes of some constitutive nexus of relationships. To be sure, these options are not antagonistic to one another. Elections can change the occupants of particular nodes within a nexus, and this can bring about changes in the public square. The types of changes and how they come about, however, would be generated in networked fashion through subsequent changes in the nexus of relationships. Within any network, moreover, some nodes possess greater scope for injecting change than other nodes. A presidential system, for instance, contains a node that offers greater scope for introducing change, both good and bad, however evaluated, than does a parliamentary system.

## NOTES

1. Jonathan Hughes (1977) shows that such an enterprise map is a conceptual idealization that should not be confused with actual history for even the early period in American history.
2. Jonathan Macey (2006) develops an imaginative conceptualization of government as an investor in the economic activities of everyone, and examines some of the resulting implications for taxation.
3. For a careful effort to bridge the two squares by recognizing the bivalent character of taxes as both prices and impositions, see Attilio Da Empoli (1941, pp. 91–136).
4. For a fascinating portrayal of the entrepreneurial activities of eight major personalities in American history, see Jonathan Hughes (1965).
5. For some examinations of political entrepreneurship in this vein, see Doig and Hargrove (1987), Eisinger (1988), Frohlich, Oppenheimer and Young (1971), Lewis (1980), Osborne and Gaebler (1992) and Schneider and Teske (1995).
6. Schneider and Teske (1995) emphasize the network pattern of entrepreneurship.
7. This turbulence is similar to what Roger Koppl (2002) characterizes as Big Player effects.
8. For related examinations of voting as expressive and not instrumental acts, see Fiorina (1976), Brennan and Hamlin (1985), Brennan and Lomasky (1993) and Brennan and Hamlin (2000).

# 5.  The economic organization of political enterprises

Political enterprises are established in the public square with legislative approval.[1] To speak of legislative approval, however, is not to speak of some acting person making a choice, but rather to speak of the outcome of a polycentric process that involves a transitory set of participants whose actions are structured by parliamentary rules. While the various members of a legislative assembly typically differ in details concerning the structure of enterprises they would prefer to see operate in the public square, it is also reasonable to presume that those members are in general agreement that a robust public square is better than an anemic one. While there can be intense controversy among members of a legislative assembly over which particular enterprises to support and how fully, underlying this disagreement will reside a general desire to be part of an expanding rather than a contracting legislature. There is no genuine option to be part of a static legislature. A failure to attempt to expand is a choice to contract by losing out to competitors who are seeking to expand. Someone who wants to see the legislature do less business in general is unlikely to be attracted to seek a legislative seat in the first place, is unlikely to find investors and other supporters in the effort to seek such a seat in the second place, and thirdly, is unlikely to be successful within the legislature even if elected to it.

All enterprises entail team production. The effectiveness of any team depends on how well the varying talents of different people are combined and managed, as well as on the congruence between those talents and the objectives at which the team is directed. Some enterprises may operate more effectively than others for any number of reasons, including differences in the capabilities of personnel and differences in the managerial guidance of team production. To provide a benchmark for the examination of political enterprises, this chapter first considers briefly the organization of enterprises in the market square. For the most part, effective team production in the market square is promoted through various practices that are connected with the existence of freely transferable ownership shares in those enterprises. When it comes to enterprises organized on the public square, however, shares of ownership are not freely transferable, so the effectiveness of team production must be accounted for differently. The remainder of this chapter explores the organization of team production in enterprises organized in the public square, for the persistence of such enterprises shows that they are able to organize and conduct their activities effectively even if differently from enterprises organized on the market square.

Political enterprises are not organized as profit-seeking firms, nor are the revenues to support those enterprises typically secured directly from customers through contractual arrangements. Yet the search for profit and the exploitation of opportunities for profit is a universal quality of human action. The challenge for a social-theoretic public finance is to reveal the underlying economic sense of observed public sector supply arrangements. The treatment pursued here fits within the general rubric of the firm as a governance structure for securing complementary competencies, except that the institutional framework for governance that pertains to politically organized enterprises differs from that which pertains to market-based enterprises, and this difference both contributes to enterprise success and accounts for differences in conduct between the two forms of enterprise.

## I.   TEAM PRODUCTION ON THE MARKET SQUARE

To say that people seek individually to be effective in their chosen activities does not imply that any aggregation of individuals will likewise generate effectiveness or coherence. While many people with musical instruments may have the ability to produce a symphony, cacophony is also possible. Which alternative actually results depends on the effectiveness with which the capabilities of the individual participants are combined so as to form a coherent team.

The coherent team in economic theory is conveyed by the model of the profit-maximizing firm. What is perhaps most notable about this model is that its accuracy is never examined directly. The profit-maximizing firm is represented by the condition that the firm acts to maximize the difference between total revenue and total cost, which in some cases can be reduced to equating marginal revenue and marginal cost. The claim that market-based firms can be treated as profit-maximizing entities is not subject directly to empirical verification or refutation. A firm's cost function is defined as a locus of input combinations, along which inputs are combined at each point so as to equalize the ratio of marginal products to prices across inputs. A cost function is thus a boundary between possibility and impossibility. For any level of output, it is always possible to produce at higher cost but it is never possible to produce at lower cost.

It is reasonable to wonder why the purely theoretical construct of a boundary condition should be taken as being empirically accurate. There does not exist anywhere a library shelf of studies of independent measures of marginal products, with those measures compared with prices for inputs. Those shelves contain numerous assertions that marginal products are revealed by input prices, which is simply a restatement of the initial assumption of profit maximization. This model is widely accepted not because of empirical observation but because its inner logic fits with our understanding of human conduct within an institutional framework grounded on private property and residual claimacy.

What gives cogency to that model is not direct empirical observation but the congruence between the logic of that model and our knowledge of ourselves and our conduct, as conveyed by the universal principle that in action we seek to replace conditions and circumstances that we value less highly with those that we value more highly. Any such gain in value is profit, so to make a loss is to sacrifice higher value for lower value. An enterprise that is not maximizing its profit is thus failing to cover its cost, as explained by James Buchanan (1969) as well as by the essays of Ronald Coase and Jack Wiseman in Buchanan and Thirlby (1973). It is the institutional framework of a market economy that gives compelling power to the model of the profit-maximizing firm, wherein a proprietorship and a large corporation are treated as acting identically. There is no independent gauge of how effectively team production is organized within market-based firms, and there never could be without independently generated observations on marginal products. What we have instead is an appreciation of the logic of economizing action in the presence of transferable ownership, and it is this institutionally-grounded logic that gives general credence to treating firms as profit-maximizing teams. Modeling from the inside out arrives at the same destination as modeling from the outside in.

Nonprofit forms of organization, including political enterprises, present substantive but not formal challenges to profit maximization (this is discussed further in section III of this chapter). The search for profit is universal, but its specific manifestations differ across organizational forms. At the same time, the generation of different organizational forms must also be capable of explanation in terms of the universal search for profit. Before moving to a consideration of team production within politically-based enterprises, it will be helpful to explore a bit more fully the institutional framework for team production within market-based enterprises.

## II. AGENCY, CAPABILITY AND MARKET-BASED GOVERNANCE

For a theory of market equilibrium, a treatment of the firm as a production function or profit-maximizing entity is sufficient for purposes of that theoretical construction because it yields two of the four required ingredients: input demand functions and output supply functions. (The other two ingredients, input supply functions and output demand functions, are yielded by the construction of a utility-maximizing consumer.) For emergence-based theorizing, where aggregate formations are generated from the inside out, the assembly and coordination of team production require analytical examination.

There are several options to treating the firm as a production function. While there are significant differences among these options that would be pertinent to theorizing about business firms, they are less significant for theorizing about political enterprises than are the similarities. One line of thought treats a firm as a nexus of contracts (Alchian and Demsetz 1972; Fama 1980; Fama and Jensen 1983; and Meckling and Jensen 1976). The performance of a firm will depend on the manner in which that contractual nexus is put together. While this is a reasonable belief to hold, one feature of this treatment is that the firm actually loses its identity and dissolves into its spontaneous order background. A second line of thought treats the firm as an arrangement for dealing with asset specificity by controlling post-contractual opportunism (Williamson 1985, 1996). Yet a third line of thought treats firms in terms of their competencies and capabilities (Penrose 1959; Nelson and Winter 1982; Foss 1993; and Loasby 1998).

Putting aside differences among these approaches, they all recognize that the extent to which the members of a team act in coordinated fashion is not something to be assumed but is something to be explained. A firm contains a complex web of institutionalized practices and procedures that have been crafted to overcome problems of discoordination that would otherwise result. As with any team, success is not a simple addition over the performance of individual members. In various ways, the quality of the patterns of interaction among team members matters. The value of the contribution that any particular member makes will depend on the types of contributions that other members make.

There are several main places where issues of coordination arise, starting with the attraction of capital to the firm and continuing with the organizational arrangements that govern the operational conduct of the firm. Any firm will have to attract capital, either equity or debt. In either case, for a firm to attract capital it will need to provide its investors and creditors with assurances that the capital will be put to proper use, as against, say, being transferred into the personal accounts of corporate managers. Independent auditing is one institutionalized practice that operates to provide such assurance. As Ross Watts and Jerold Zimmerman (1983) explain, independent auditing emerged within the market square in response to the efforts of entrepreneurs to convince investors to participate in the enterprise.

Nine investors each provide $1 million, along with the entrepreneur who also provides $1 million. Five years later, the enterprise is liquidated for $1 million, with each investor receiving ten cents on the dollar for his investment. This situation could have arisen despite the firm's best effort, perhaps because the market for the product evaporated through technological change introduced by other firms. It could also have arisen because the entrepreneur paid himself $1 million per year while dissipating some $800 000 per year traveling first class throughout the world pretending to gather information for subsequent commercial use. Independent auditing can provide some assurance that corporate funds have been used as corporate officials claim they have been used, although there is no assurance of perfection. Even if the funds have been used as promised, the commercial results might not have been very good. The firm might still end up liquidating for ten cents on the dollar, even though managerial pay was reasonable and the firm actually made an effort to produce and market products.

This possibility speaks to more subtle issues regarding the quality of managerial efforts. Auditing may reveal whether funds went into production or into on-the-job consumption by executives, but it cannot reveal the quality of the effort that went into managing production within the firm. An executive may sit at his desk playing video games rather than searching relevant data bases. Several forms of institutionalized practice speak to these more subtle issues. One deals with the structure of corporate boards of directors. Those boards typically include large equity holders, substantial creditors and major input suppliers. These are people who tend to possess both strong interest in preventing opportunistic behavior among managers and who have both knowledge and organizational position that would facilitate the attainment of that interest.

Furthermore, ownership shares are transferable, and the market for equity shares likewise operates in several ways to restrict though not to eliminate opportunistic conduct. For one thing, corporate managers are paid only partly by salary. They are also paid through bonuses and stock options. Bonuses are typically based on some accounting measure that is thought to relate monotonically to corporate profit. The value of stock options varies directly with the extent of the increase in share prices subsequent to the granting of options. There is a market for executive talent, much of it populated by firms known as headhunters that search for such talent. Good managerial performance in a subordinate position in one firm can thus lead to a higher position in another firm (Fama 1980). Executives who shirk in their current position could thus lose the present value of future increases in compensation because they become less attractive in the market for managerial talent.

The transferability of ownership also creates an arena within which the control of corporations may be contested. The market valuation of corporate assets depends on the valuation that market participants place on anticipated future net cash flows. A corporation whose assets is managed in such a manner as to generate a net income of $10 million when potentially those assets could have been managed so as to generate $20 million offers a capital gain to someone who can acquire control and change the operation of the firm. With a discount rate of 10 per cent, for instance, that potential capital gain is $100 million. To be sure, life is never as simple as arithmetic illustrations seem to imply. While the net income of $10 million can be observed, the potential income cannot be observed. That potential exists only in someone's imagination, as a belief or hunch about what those assets could accomplish if managed differently. Still, someone who believes that a corporation could be managed in such a way as to increase those net cash flows will perceive an opportunity for a potential capital gain because the firm will presently appear to be under-valued (Manne 1965).

Competition among corporations has stimulated the development of a wide variety of institutionalized practices that connect the members of the corporate team so as to facilitate productive coordination among the members. This is not to say that corporations are operated according to some notion of perfect efficiency, but is only to say that the complex pattern of governance arrangements that connect those who participate within a corporate enterprise can be rendered intelligible as a means of restraining opportunistic conduct that would impair overall team performance. An institutional regime based on property and contract entails an operating logic wherein the transferability of ownership tends to promote effective team production by creating a common focal point of value maximization for all team members. However, it should also be noted that life is never so simple as blackboard exercises make it seem, so that at any moment there are differences in effectiveness among the commercial teams in existence; it is only that there is an institutionally-grounded tendency for less effective teams and management to give way to more effective teams and management.

For enterprises organized on the public square there is no transferability of ownership. Yet such enterprises are engaged in team production, with some of the teams being quite large. Before considering how team effectiveness might be secured for politically-sponsored enterprises, some brief consideration will be given to the operation of nonprofit enterprises organized in the market square, for these provide a form of intermediate way-station: they are organized in the market square but they lack transferable ownership.

## III. NONPROFIT FIRMS IN THE MARKET SQUARE

With respect to the organization of governance, nonprofit firms face the same organizational problems as do profit-seeking firms. Nonprofit firms have assets, generate contractual relationships and provide services. Such firms make plans to pursue objectives, and are engaged in a team production process that is guided by some set of managers. Whether the result is a symphony or a cacophony will depend on how effectively the team works together, which in turn depends importantly but not exclusively on managerial guidance and supervision. Nonprofit firms involve processes of team production just as fully as do profit-seeking firms, only those firms lack the capital-market tools that are available to profit-seeking firms.

Problems of agency arise at several points within the organizational logic of the nonprofit firm. Firm managers control assets that have been supplied by others, and in many cases the suppliers of assets are deceased. The potential is present for managers to transfer firm assets into their own accounts in several ways, many of which involve the substitution of leisure for effort through managerial shirking. With nonprofit firms, however, there is no market for ownership shares, which means in turn that executive compensation cannot be based upon changes in the market value of the firm. While mergers do occur among nonprofit firms, the absence of transferable ownership removes one significant tool that operates to limit agency costs among profit-seeking firms.

Net worth cannot serve as an organizational focal point whose power of attraction is strengthened through the various capital market tools that are used by profit-seeking firms. This raises issues regarding coordination within nonprofit firms. For instance, a museum may have one executive in charge of painting, another in charge of sculpture and a third in charge of lectures and special exhibits. Even within a profit-seeking museum, differences of opinion may exist about how much space to devote to each type of activity. Those differences of opinion, however, are capable of being narrowed if not resolved through the common orientation toward the value of the enterprise that is reinforced through arrangements for executive compensation. Thus, a supervisory board may decide to support an expansion in the amount of space devoted to sculpture, based on a finding that sculpting generates 30 per cent more revenue per dollar of capital than does painting. This type of calculation, and ones like it, could not be made so readily or so precisely for a nonprofit museum. Surveys might be taken, perhaps, but this is a weak replacement for a comparison of revenues actually generated.

Yet nonprofit firms are thriving, so they must be able to deal with these agency problems and situations in some fashion. When there is no market value for the enterprise, the museum requires some alternative focal point to guide such enterprise choices as the allocation of space among activities. One thing this suggests is that an underlying homogeneity of value or preference among managers is more important for nonprofit governance than it is for profit-seeking governance. So too is the articulation of what is called 'vision', for the vision that orients economic calculation by nonprofit firms is expressible only as a vector of characteristics or attributes that cannot be reduced to a scalar measure of net worth. Organizational coherence cannot be established by a common interest in value maximization, and is established instead by shared values concerning the structural pattern of the firm's activities. This situation surely places a greater burden on the members of the supervisory board with respect to their substantive orientations towards the firm's activities, for coherence in the enterprise's activities resides in vision and not in net worth, as explored in Auteri and Wagner (2007).

When vision replaces net worth as a focal point for organizational navigation, the organization will typically develop points of contact with activities on the market square to secure additional navigational guidance. In this respect, nonprofit firms have the same parasitical relationship with market-based firms as do political enterprises, as befits their intermediate position between market-based enterprises and political enterprises. For instance, a museum might not charge admission separately for painting and sculpture, and might not even charge admission at all. Nonetheless, museum officials can get some indication of the contribution of various components through such things as sales of merchandise in gift stores and attendance at lectures and special events for which tickets may be required even if admission is not charged, as these serve as proxy indicators of market demand.

## IV.   OPPORTUNISM, GOVERNANCE AND POLITICAL ENTERPRISE

Political enterprises face the same formal setting of team production as do market-based enterprises. As with large corporations, the management of a political enterprise is concentrated among a small set of people while the capital with which the enterprise operates is supplied by all those people whose taxes are used by those who can gain control of them within the legislature to support the enterprise. The same types of issues regarding agency, competence and team production that scholars have addressed with respect to large corporations pertain as well to political enterprises. Opportunism, whereby those who control the operation of enterprises convert investor wealth into the service of their personal interests, is a potential feature of large-scale enterprises of all forms. Problems of agency, opportunism and competence arise in all enterprises as their scale expands.

There are two significant differences between political and market enterprises. One is that shareholders are compelled and not contractual investors, in that capital for political enterprises is typically secured through taxation. The other is that there is no transferability of ownership in political enterprises; therefore, no market value is established for political enterprises and the capital market tools that have been developed to promote effective team production in market-based enterprises are not available to political enterprises. To be sure, it is possible to imagine circumstances, including some that have been realized historically, where this divergence in ownership has had little or no significance.

The earlier comparison between Hyatt the city and Hyatt the hotel provided such a framework of similarity. Hyatt the city might sponsor a few enterprises on its public square. For instance, one enterprise might maintain streets, another might provide police protection, and a third might supply fire control. These enterprises secure their capital from a tax on the value of property within the city, with the franchise limited to the owners of property. Within this institutional arrangement, an owner of property within the city is simultaneously an owner of the political enterprises organized within the city. The two types of ownership form a tied package, wherein the value of any piece of transferable real estate includes the value of the nontransferable ownership in city-sponsored enterprises that accompanies the ownership of real estate. Within this type of institutional setting, team production would seem to proceed similarly in Hyatt the city as it would in Hyatt the hotel.

To point to the similarity that is created through the tied relationship is not to acknowledge an identity. The two forms of ownership are nonseparable, and this situation creates scope for using managerial discretion over political enterprises to influence the value of particular landholdings, thereby redistributing the value of market-based enterprises. For instance, street maintenance might favor property in part of the city, as might police and fire protection. The value of property located throughout the city will still be a tied combination of private and public ownership, except that the differential provision of service by political enterprises influences the distribution of values across market-based enterprises, including residences.

The potential divergence between Hyatt the city and Hyatt the hotel that is created by forced investment in city enterprises is surely intensified by the historical institutional transformation whereby the franchise is no longer limited to property owners and the property tax is no longer the predominant source of capital for political enterprises. Capital market tools are surely less applicable now than they once were to securing effective team production within enterprises organized within the public square. The setting of team production, however, remains in place, and the operating characteristics of political enterprises remains to be examined, for the persistence of political enterprises shows that those enterprises are able to secure effective team production.[2] So what are the tools by which political enterprises achieve this?

Within commercial corporations, transferable ownership acts to create something approaching unanimity in orientation among shareholders (De Angelo 1981; Makowksi 1983). This does not deny that shareholders might not have differences of opinion in the choices that managers make. The value of any choice today will be revealed only in the future, so the present value of any choice is at the moment a matter of conjecture, about which there can be many possibilities. With transferable ownership, however, shareholders will generally agree that desirable choices will increase share prices while undesirable choices will lower them. There is plenty of scope for differences of opinion about the future consequences of present choices, but transferable ownership tends to promote unanimity regarding the ultimate desideratum. Whatever particular choices are made on behalf of a corporation with transferable ownership, the ultimate value consequences of those choices are diffused across shareholders through changes in the market value of the firm. It is thus meaningful to speak substantively of the relationship between shareholders and managers as one of principals to agents.

Once transferable ownership disappears, ultimate unanimity about value consequences disappears as well. The formality of the principal–agent relationship remains, but the substance changes, possibly dramatically. Principals need no longer speak with the same voice, because they no longer share in the value consequences of corporate choices according to their shareholdings. Transferable ownership provides a means of aggregating the value consequences of a set of preceding managerial choices. Without transferable ownership, those same value consequences remain diffused among the individual principals, with each principal being primarily concerned with his or her particular consequences.

Hyatt the hotel might eliminate a few rooms to provide daycare facilities for employees and guests. At the time that decision was being deliberated, shareholders might well have held different appraisals of the commercial consequence of this decision, as well as varying appraisals about various sizes of daycare facility. Nonetheless, all will share in the commercial result of that decision, and so have every reason to be soberly realistic in their judgments and appraisals. It is different for Hyatt the city. Since there will never be any ultimate concentration of value consequences, people can appraise the choice based on their conjectures about the consequences to them, for there is no aggregate value that is apportioned among those people by their relative shareholdings. Modeling from the inside out does not lead to the same destination as modeling from the outside in.

One potentially interesting feature of the elimination of a substantive agency relationship is the suppression of honesty in personal and public expression (Kuran 1995). This is a topic that is surely worth more consideration than can be given here, where only a few remarks can be offered. Ultimately, this topic speaks to the quality of life on the public square. With substantive agency, people may honestly and openly hold different conjectures about the future value consequences of present actions. In this setting, people can engage in an open process of conjecture and refutation (Popper 1962) as best they can, realizing always the inescapable difficulty involved in seeking to compare some past experience with some future that is created as an act of imagination. For one thing, there is no guarantee that the future will follow the past even if no change is made. Moreover, since the option of change to the status quo always involves an act of imagination, people can differ about the results of such imaginative acts and thus evaluate differently a proposed course of action, even if they act with reference to some such common focal point as maximizing the value of the enterprise. Where some might think the conversion of some rooms to a daycare facility might increase the value of the enterprise, others can honestly hold the opposite conjecture. Regardless of the particular conjecture held, the value of the enterprise provides a focal point around which the discussion can be organized, as well as providing some subsequent test of past conjectures.

When substantive agency is replaced by the formal shell of agency, honest and truthful deliberation disappears as well, or at least its scope is diminished. No one is going to say that they support the conversion of rooms to a daycare facility because they will secure personal gain that exceeds their share of the fall in the aggregate value of the enterprise. For one thing, there is no aggregate value of the enterprise because there is no transferable ownership. Furthermore, the speaker would doubtless feel embarrassed about advancing such an argument. It would be the same thing if a speaker were to announce support for such a program because he would then grant a contract to one of his political associates to operate the program. Normal morality requires that such claims do not proceed in terms of personal interest but in terms of some aggregation across the set of participants.

Yet there is no institutionalized means by which that aggregation is ever actually performed. Hence, participants become involved in a dialog of discourse that can easily become dishonest and fraudulent, or at least self-deceptive (Cowen 2005). With respect to Pareto's (1935) formulation, the gap between derivations and residues with respect to the actions to which they are purportedly linked would surely widen. For Pareto, residues were the true foundational sentiments that guide action. Derivations were the superstructure of intellectualized justifications that were presented in public to rationalize observed actions in the world. We observe action and we observe derivations, but we do not observe residues. It would seem plausible that the gap between residues and derivations is larger within the public square than within the market square.

## V.  PARLIAMENTARY ASSEMBLIES AS UNUSUAL INVESTMENT BANKS

A parliamentary assembly is a particular organization within a democratic polity. Since fiscal phenomena are connected to a parliamentary assembly within a democratic polity, it might seem as though a democratically constituted state should be described as an organization and not as an order; however, the order that is the public square supervenes on the organization that is the parliamentary assembly. A parliamentary assembly is an *unusual* form of investment bank, and it is the peculiarity that elicits the supervention.

Like an ordinary investment bank, a parliamentary assembly is an intermediary that connects people who have enterprises for which they are seeking support with people who have the means available to support those enterprises.[3] With respect to being an intermediary whose service is one of offering connections, a parliamentary assembly is in the same position as an investment bank or any other type of market-based intermediary. What allows the order of the public square to supervene on the parliamentary assembly resides in those institutional features that transform the parliamentary assembly into an unusual form of investment bank.

Whether an investment bank is organized as a partnership or as a corporation, there will be a value to the enterprise, and rights to the enterprise's cash flow will be apportioned among the owners or partners. With a partnership, moreover, membership can change only with the permission of existing partners. Parliamentary assemblies do not apportion cash flow among the members, for organizationally they have a nonprofit format. Whatever cash flows a parliamentary assembly generates are distributed through other channels. Existing members, moreover, have no say over who enters the enterprise. The parliamentary assembly is simply a network of nodes that people within the society are free to fill, the procedures for doing so being through electoral processes.

The suppliers of capital bear a different relationship to the parliamentary assembly than they do to an ordinary investment bank. For the latter, that relationship is contractual, though investors may not receive the returns they expected because the enterprise they supported did not perform according to initial anticipations. For a parliamentary assembly, the relationship is not expressly contractual, though as noted earlier there are some institutional settings wherein something close to a contractual relationship is in play. Furthermore, the individual members of parliamentary assemblies receive electoral support from various subsets of the population, which surely leads to the formation of some nexus of expectation in at least some suppliers of capital.

As noted earlier, parliamentary assemblies have weaker incentives to consider and explore options for support than they would have if they were investing on their own account, or if, equivalently, they were compensated with rights to the net cash flow generated by the enterprise. The time required for genuine deliberation imposes strong limits on the quality of deliberation, as Bertrand de Jouvenal (1961) explains. A parliamentary assembly that engaged in genuine deliberation could not do much business. This can be illustrated with some simple arithmetic. Suppose a parliamentary assembly contains 100 members, and it operates as a committee-of-the-whole, as a genuinely deliberative assembly must. Any issue to be deliberated is of a scientific character, in that it involves an effort to probe alternative conjectures about future conditions contingent upon whether some proposed measure is adopted, rejected, or possibly amended. In this idealized setting, the 100 members independently form their initial conjectures, and then engage in a process of discussion and probing with an eye toward clarifying their beliefs about the likelihood of different conjectures. Suppose it takes two days for all the members of the assembly to articulate an initial conjecture. Even this is but a short matter of time for a serious effort on any matter of much complexity, as any researcher would attest. Each member's conjecture is examined for two hours, much like a university seminar. This again is not a lot of time to devote to a complex topic, but even doing this will require 25 days, assuming a working day of eight hours.

After these 27 days have passed, the members revise their initial conjectures, and engage in further though abbreviated discussion. Perhaps the revision requires only half a day, with the subsequent discussion requiring one hour per member. This period of revision will thus require 13 days, meaning that 40 working days of deliberation have passed before this issue can be considered in an informed manner before the assembly. Suppose parliamentary action on the matter takes ten days to negotiate and work out. With an issue taking 50 days to resolve in a careful parliamentary manner, and with roughly 200 working days available in a year, it is easy to see that a serious but careful parliament would also be one that did not do a lot of business. For instance, it might do something with mosquito abatement, decide what to do about internet access in libraries, decide whether to offer martial arts in schools, and decide about the location of trails and bike paths. It would have been a busy year, but the scale of accomplishment would have been miniscule by contemporary standards.

The modern scale of accomplishment is possible only by replacing genuine deliberation with the appearance of deliberation. Rather than operating as a committee-of-the-whole, the legislature divides into 11 committees of nine members each (with the presiding officer being an *ex officio* member of each committee). Using the same time requirement as assumed earlier, each committee will now require 47 hours to deliberate an issue, which can be reasonably rounded to six days. Such a committee could thus deliberate 33 issues over a year, while leaving two hours for an end-of-session celebration. Provided that committee members agree to exchange support across committees, the legislature can now do 90 times as much business as it formerly could (Leibowitz and Tollison 1980). This 90 fold increase, moreover, is a lower bound, in that it is based on a presumption that committees replace the full assembly as places of deliberation. The same intensity of deliberation occurs, but it is conducted among subsets of particularly interested parties, due to the assignment of members to committees based on their special interests and talents (Crain and Muris 1995; Crain and Tollison 1990).

How much business a legislative assembly can support depends on how fast it can operate. Partly, this is a matter of its internal organization, with an organization based on committees and sub-committees increasing the amount of business that can be done. It is also a matter of the amount of genuine deliberation that actually takes place. While many clubs and civic associations seem to use Robert's Rules of Order (Robert 2000) or something similar, parliamentary assemblies don't seem to follow such a format. Robert's Rules is a parliamentary procedure that facilitates a good deal of deliberation, as illustrated by the ease with which items can be placed on an agenda and by which various motions can be amended. Parliamentary assemblies often operate with parliamentary rules that restrict the avenues of deliberation, as compared with Robert's Rules.

It is easy enough to understand why a parliamentary assembly would operate with a reduced standard of deliberation. The members of a parliament, unlike the partners in a venture capital firm, do not trade on their own account. If they were investing their own money in the various projects they decided to support, it would be reasonable to expect parliamentary assemblies to operate with a level of care similar to what might be observed in a venture capital firm. Within a venture capital firm, the partners bear the cost of deliberation but also reap the gains, both positive and negative. Within a parliamentary assembly, the legislative partners also bear the costs of deliberation, but reap only a minor part of the gains, whether these are positive or negative. With respect to reaping the gains, legislative partners are in much the same position as ordinary citizens, for whom the gains accrue in such forms as programmatic benefits and tax consequences.

There are respects in which the internal organization of legislatures is similar to those of profit-seeking investment banks. While political investment bankers are not paid with stock options, they are rewarded with bonuses, though again of an unusual form. Politicians who bring more business to the legislature rise into such leadership positions as committee chairmanships, which in turn are positions that offer rewards through the ability to restrict access to the legislative agenda. The absence of an equity market, however, leads also to a number of differences in conduct between political enterprises and market-based enterprises.

## VI. EQUITY STRUCTURE OF POLITICAL ENTERPRISES

It is a truism to say that people who direct capital to political enterprises do so because they anticipate that they will receive a higher return than they would receive from an alternative use of that capital. There is also a large literature that seeks to compare aspects of technical efficiency between political and market-based enterprises, with this literature finding generally that market-based enterprises have greater technical efficiency.[4] While this finding about technical efficiency is not universal (see, for instance, Caves and Christensen 1980; Pescatrice and Trapani 1980; Gouyette and Pestieau 1999; and Schlesinger, Mitchell and Gray 2004), it does suggest that to a considerable extent market-based enterprises would dominate politically-based enterprises in head-to-head competition where both meet each other in free and open competition. These enterprises do not, of course, engage in such free and open competition, and differences in conduct emerge out of the different competitive environments the two categories of enterprise face.

While the two types of enterprise face different competitive environments, it is nonetheless the case that political enterprises are supported because their sponsors anticipate that they will receive at least comparable returns to those they could have received had they devoted the same energy and capital to the sponsorship of market-based enterprises. People who direct capital to political enterprises do not direct it from their personal accounts, but from the accounts of other people, acquired through taxation. The creation of political enterprises allows the sponsors of those enterprises to leverage their own supply through their share of taxation, with capital provided by other taxpayers who would not have chosen to invest in the political enterprise.

We should always remember that aggregates don't act, whatever the form of the aggregate. Only people can act, and what matters for their action is their belief about the value consequences of interest to them of alternative actions among which they choose. Whether the aggregate of individual actions constitutes some such coherent outcome as is conveyed by notions of value maximization depends on the properties of institutionally-mediated relationships among participants. Market-based enterprises have a strong tendency to pursue aggregate value maximization because the employment of capital market tools tends to harmonize individual interests to this aggregate focal point. To be sure, this harmonization is only a strong tendency and most certainly not a universal quality of all action.

Political enterprises are created in the anticipation that they will generate returns to their controlling investors, and those investors comprise just a subset of the entire set of tax-induced investors. Political enterprises must generate returns for investors or else they would not be supported in the public square. Some of those returns might speak to such non-marketed qualities as a belief that participation in politically-sponsored enterprises is socially more significant or meaningful than participation in profit-seeking enterprises.[5] Moreover, since political enterprises do not have transferable ownership, the returns they generate cannot accrue as capital appreciation or as dividends. They can, however, offer indirect forms of dividend, both as lower prices to favored buyers and as higher prices to favored input suppliers.

Whether the political enterprise is a school, a hospital or a highway department, profits are appropriated in some fashion, for such appropriation is a necessary element in the generation of support for the enterprise. For market-based enterprises, the appropriation takes place directly through monetary payments and is simple to see. For political enterprises, the appropriation is indirect, and can follow different channels in different cases. How can a politically-organized hospital return profits to its supporters? One obvious question this raises is the identity of the hospital's supporters, both in the legislature and outside of it. Outside the legislature, that support can be separated between support among input suppliers and support among output demanders. On the demand side, the hospital might offer low-cost services to particular groups of demanders. Since the political hospital cannot truly offer lower costs across the board, assuming that it cannot truly operate in a technically more efficient manner than profit-seeking firms, that low cost must entail the imposition of higher costs on some people. Discriminatory pricing is a standard tool of political enterprises. Much of that higher cost is imposed through taxation, which is itself a form of price discrimination, what Maffeo Pantaleoni (1911) called a political price system. One of the things that taxation accomplishes is that it allows political enterprises to charge people who do not consume the enterprise's services, thereby making possible price reductions to those who do consume those services. As a result of this form of political price discrimination, political enterprises are able to gain standing in the commercial marketplace amidst profit-seeking firms.

Profits can also be appropriated on the factor supply side of the market, with the specific channels of appropriation again depending on details about the service in question. For a political hospital, profits might be appropriated by the physicians who practice there. They could also be appropriated by the manufacturers of medical equipment who supply state of the art equipment to the enterprise. Pharmaceutical manufactures might gain also, through increased sales of patented drugs. Perhaps the hospital uses a unionized labor force, at least in some parts of its operation, with politically organized hospitals receiving strong union support. The central point in any case is that the appropriation of profit is not abolished by the creation of a political enterprise, for without profit to be appropriated there would not have been any interest in creating the enterprise. The shift from market-based to political enterprise changes only the form that appropriation takes, and envelops that appropriation in a fog of indirect transactions, which is something that Amilcare Puviani (1903) would surely have appreciated in the light of his perceptive treatment of fiscal illusion.

While the comparison of cost across enterprise forms has generated a substantial literature, that literature necessarily contains a good deal of ambiguity because such things as cost differences are part of the returns captured by supporters of the political enterprise. Think about the market for alcoholic beverages across different environments. Within the United States, some states have some form of free competition subject to taxation and age restrictions while other states allow retail sales only in state-operated stores. It is easy to imagine that a comparison between states with market-based and states with political stores would show that political stores were less costly than market stores, using the methodology found in this literature. That methodology would take some such standardized product unit as a proof-gallon, and compare the expenses incurred in providing proof-gallons across the two types of enterprise.

This same methodology can be applied to refuse collection, fire protection, hospitals, campgrounds, or any service that is supplied under different organizational arrangements. What limits the meaningfulness of all such comparisons is that such observed cost differences are generally one facet of the different ways that returns to supporters are transmitted to them.

Consider further the comparison between politically-based and market-based retail outlets for alcoholic beverages. Where political stores are used, a much narrower range of product options is available. Hours of operation are more limited. Political stores will often not allow the use of credit cards or debit cards. They will be more sparsely located, which means that most customers will have to travel longer distances to make their purchases. All of these considerations operate in the direction of lowering the observed cost of political enterprises relative to market enterprises, which is made possible by imposing higher costs on consumers.

Those differences are also part of the means by which the return from a political enterprise is transferred to supporters, and without those differences there would have been no return to the political enterprise and hence, no political enterprise would have been established in the first place. With respect to alcoholic beverages in particular, there seem to be at least four distinguishable sources of return. One source is return to enterprise managers and staff. Keeping a smaller inventory, shorter hours and operating fewer stores, releases managers and staff from having to be solicitous of consumer desires, and allows leisure to be substituted for what otherwise would have been effort. Second, the limited offering available in stores represents the imposition of a quota on potential suppliers of alcoholic beverages. This limitation gives a privileged position to those who occupy prominent positions in the awarding of slots within that quota arrangement. Secondary transactions of some sort will arise as producers compete for entry into the limited market. The direct form of such competition is, of course, bribes. A substitute for bribes is the offering of samples of products. Yet a third substitute channel is through public relations efforts, wherein a producer seeks to generate heightened support, perhaps by encouraging customers to make phone calls and write letters. A fourth difference is that the limited availability of political enterprise is a type of return for prohibitionists, who prefer full prohibition but who find restriction preferable to open competition.[6] In other words, the difference in organizational form cannot be addressed by the standard techniques of *ceteris paribus* because the organizational change will both entail and generate changes in conduct throughout the entire nexus of relevant commercial relationships.

## VII.  PRICING, REFORM AND THE PUBLIC SQUARE

Much legislation speaks of reform in some fashion. But what is the object that is being reformed? Some reforms are small and confined, as illustrated by telecom reform or banking reform. Other references to reform have a wider scope, as illustrated by electoral, economic or social reform. Whatever the type of reform that someone has in mind, there is one inescapable feature of every reform that has ever been proposed or ever will be: it must involve a change in the structure of prices generated within the market square. If there is no change in the structure of prices, there is no reform. Some reforms seek to change product prices, as illustrated by the prices of prescription drugs purchased by retired people. Other reforms seek to change factor prices, while others seek to operate on both sides of the market. Whatever the type of reform, however, it will change the structure of prices. After reform, some people will pay lower prices for the things they buy and others will necessarily pay higher prices. Similarly, some people will receive higher prices for the things they sell and others will receive lower prices.

That any program of reform that emerges from the public square must be directed at prices within the market square and not at prices within the public square stems from the inability of the public square to generate prices. Prices are phenomena that emerge out of exchange relationships which themselves operate within an institutional framework of property and contract. A public square that truly existed independently of a market square would not generate market prices because the necessary institutional framework that enables prices to emerge would be absent. While programs that call for reform are an activity that is pursued on the public square, the object of efforts at reform must be prices within the market square.

In all kinds of ways, enterprises that are established in the public square borrow and act upon price information that is generated within the market square. In this manner, enterprises established within the public square bear a parasitical relationship to enterprises established within the market square. Political enterprises use price information in numerous ways in conducting their activities. They compete for inputs with market-based enterprises. The services that political enterprises offer can likewise be compared to similar services offered by market-based enterprises, with prices facilitating such comparisons. Prices are generated by market-based enterprises acting within the market square, so we can say that the market square is the host that supplies prices to enterprises that are organized within the public square, recognizing that this relationship of host to parasite is a matter of technical description and not normative evaluation.

## VIII.   THE LEGISLATIVE CREATION OF BUREAUCRATIC ORGANIZATION

Collective property is instantiated through legislative action within a democratically-constituted public square. Political entrepreneurs bring their ideas for enterprises before the legislature, although the exact manner of doing this varies with the various constitutive and parliamentary rules within which the legislature operates. Typically, such ideas will be brought before particular legislators and then to particular committees. When that idea appears before the full legislature for final approval, this will typically be in a pro forma and not a substantive manner. Legislatures are unusual investment banks and not deliberative assemblies.

At the level of initial entrepreneurial activity, a legislature faces a choice of what kind of organizational arrangement to create in response to the efforts of legislative partners to generate business. In this respect, there are two forms of business plan the legislature can follow. One form involves the legislature in contracting with enterprises organized on the market square. The other form involves the legislature in establishing an enterprise on the public square that deals exclusively with the legislature. The condition of roads might be of sufficient generalized concern to reach the public square. One option would be for the legislature to contract with a paving company organized on the market square to repair roads as one of its lines of business. The other option would be for the legislature to create an enterprise on the public square that would operate under exclusive contract with the legislature to repair roads.

Much of the previously mentioned literature about the comparative cost-liness of private and public provision has sought to establish that over a wide range of services, private provision is less costly than public provision. In many cases parliamentary assemblies do contract with private firms to provide services, though it can be debated whether this is because of the evidence offered by the aforementioned studies or in spite of it. Whatever the reason why a parliament might contract with market-based firms, there are also understandable reasons for the limited reach of such contractual arrangements, which supports the prevalence of bureaucratic forms of enterprise.

For one thing, contracting with a parliament can be costly, as governments often impose conditions and standards on the general activities of such firms, which reduces the profitability of such contracts relative to similar contracts with other enterprises organized within the market square (Epstein 1993). Furthermore, and surely more significantly, contracting with enterprises on the market square makes it difficult for parliaments to provide returns for entrepreneurial sponsors of the activity and enterprise. If road maintenance is hired from market-based pavers, that relationship cannot be used to provide returns to legislative supporters and sponsors. The creation of a paving bureau in the public square offers a vehicle for returns to accrue to supporters through the contractual relationship between the legislature and the bureau. What is often treated as the higher cost of public production can be the vehicle by which returns to capital are appropriated within the nominally nonprofit form that public bureaus exemplify.

To say that there is a general congruence of interest between bureaus and their legislative sponsors is not to claim that relationships between the two are fully concordant. The relationship creates rents for sponsors, and there is plenty of room for conflict over the division of that rent between legislative sponsors and political entrepreneurs within the public square enterprises. In this respect a considerable literature has arisen concerning the relationship between legislatures and the various bureaus they create. This literature contains two polar claims. One is that the legislature dominates the bureau, so that the bureau responds to legislative desires.[7] The other is that the bureau has private information that allows it to follow its desires independently of legislative desires.[8] As with many such polarities, both poles have merit, with the relative merit of the two being a variable to be explored.[9]

To speak of a legislature dominating a bureau or a bureau dominating a legislature involves an act of reification whereby the bureau or the legislature is treated as an individual unit within an equilibrated entity. For the most part, this literature has been formulated from an outside-in perspective. Hence, activities of bureaus and legislatures are treated as equilibrium states in a setting of asymmetric information, and the question becomes one of in whose favor the asymmetry resides.

The situation appears differently from an inside-out perspective, as can be seen in the contributions of Ludwig von Mises (1944), Gordon Tullock (1965), Anthony Downs (1967), Vincent Ostrom (1973) and James Wilson (1989), all of which take an inside-out orientation toward the organization of activity within bureaus. Such an orientation starts with particular members of bureaus and legislatures, namely those members who are able to exercise collective authority over the matter in question. With respect to a legislature, this would be the leading members of the committee that sponsors the bureau or agency. With respect to bureaus and agencies, this would be the leading executives.

A legislature delegates authority to a bureau, but what happens then? One problem with simple economic models is that they can obscure important matters that are hidden in the complexity that is simplified out of sight. Hence, the complex combinatorics that are involved in creating packages of educational offerings is reduced to a simple scalar designated as $X. Suppose the issue is kindergarten to grade 12 education. It is possible to construe this situation in the aggregate by taking an outside-in orientation. Thus, the legislature might tell the bureau to educate 3000 students with a budget of $300 million, based on some presumption that per pupil cost is $10 000. If life were this simple, this might be possible. If so, bureaus would be like puppets manipulated by their legislative masters. This is the essential orientation of legislative dominance.

Such simplicity, however, is a property more of classroom blackboards than of reality. How costly it is actually, is a complex matter that depends on many structural details. That one school spends $300 million for 3000 students does not determine the matter for another school, even if the standard of comparison is that idealized construction of a cost function as a least-cost boundary. The second school might have a larger number of disabled children. Perhaps its school buses must travel longer routes. Once it is recognized that an aggregate cost figure is built up from a large number of particular choices and objects of action, cost comparisons necessarily become enshrouded in a fog of probably variable density. While there are tools and techniques for peering through that fog, as illustrated by comparisons of averages across similar enterprises and activities, such techniques can never substitute fully for the residual claimancy that is absent.

It is always possible to compare expenditures on particular objects. A legislator might think a school is spending too much on buses, and so hold a hearing and conduct an investigation on buses across schools. That legislator might well conclude that the school keeps too new a fleet of buses, and orders it to spend less on buses by increasing the average age of its fleet. In this the legislator will probably be successful, because he has selected an attribute that he cares about and is subject to relatively easy measurement. A form can be submitted that contains the ages of buses, and this form can be audited. There is, however, a limit on the amount of monitoring that a legislator will pursue because of its costliness. Legislators bear the cost of monitoring but don't reap the benefits, save to the extent that those benefits are captured by programmatic supporters and investors. Thus, bureaus also possess margins of inside or personal knowledge that gives them some independence from legislative oversight.

Suppose a school were organized in the market square. One could always examine the school's accounts at the end of the year, construct a figure for per pupil cost, and even compare that figure with comparable figures for other schools. That aggregate cost figure would, of course, be comprised of many items, and for a school organized within the market square it is reasonable to presume that the firm's managers make reasonable efforts to ensure that its various expenses contribute to rather than detract from the firm's profitability. Running a business, of course, bears only a faint family resemblance to following a recipe, so success is not assured in commerce even though it is in the kitchen (provided only that the recipe is truly followed).

For a school organized in the public square, cost takes on different significance because of the absence of residual claimants. Legislators are unusual and not genuine investment bankers because they cannot directly compare the profitability of their various objects of sponsorship. All enterprises organized on the public square have a nonprofit form of organization. Within such an organizational framework, expenses are the means by which profit is appropriated. Moreover, practically any item of expense can be a conduit for the appropriation of profit. A school might contain 1000 such items. A legislator who concentrates on bus expenses leaves 999 other paths for the appropriation of profit.

Granted, not every item of expenditure might be appropriate for the appropriation of profit, but many of them surely will be. Perhaps newer buses were used to reward drivers for their support, with a reward through compensation being unavailable due to a fixed wage scale. It is easy enough to imagine that with older buses, overtime hours for drivers would increase as well, which would illustrate a different channel for the appropriation of profit. A legislator could also seek to monitor the work schedules of bus drivers. Doing this, however, would lead to yet another shift in the channel of appropriation. For instance, a cafeteria-style dining room might be replaced by a dining room with table service, possibly even with tablecloths, crystal and china. There are really only two options for preventing the appropriation of profit. One is to shift the enterprise to the market square. The other is for the legislator to become the CEO of the firm. This latter option would be a full-time job that would prevent the sponsorship of other legislation, and yet would still present problems of achieving coherent action among subordinates because of the absence of a genuine position of residual claimancy.

## IX. PEOPLE MAKE CONNECTIONS, ORGANIZATIONS DON'T

It is linguistically convenient to speak of firms as developing connections. Thus a manufacturer of computers would develop connections forward to retail outlets and backward to input suppliers. However, firms cannot develop connections, for only people can do this. To the extent that agency relationships work sufficiently well to generate well-coordinated teamwork within a firm, nothing of significance would seem to be lost by treating the connections as generated by firms, as against being developed by individual participants within those firms.

The situation seems somewhat different for enterprises established in the public square. The enterprise no longer has a market value that can serve as a focal point against which people can orient their activities, with those activities rendered incentive-compatible by various capital market tools.

Within political enterprises, the connections that are created must be attributed ultimately to the promotion of something of interest to those who construct the connection. In usual commercial transactions, those connections are created and severed based on anticipations of organizational profit, as amended by the opportunistic possibilities examined within the literature on agency. Organizational profitability can likewise be used to explain the generation of connections from profit-seeking firms to political enterprises.

Organizational profitability cannot, however, be used to explain or generate the connections that emerge from political enterprises. Those connections must be explained in terms of the interest of particular people associated with the political enterprise. It has often been noted that there are career patterns whereby people move between political and market-based enterprises, perhaps with service in a political enterprise enhancing subsequent standing in a market-based enterprise. This point about people making connections raises some issues of executive recruitment that are absent from the public finance literature.

Before considering this, however, one further point should be made about the difference between a focus on the enterprise and a focus on individual participants within the enterprise, for this is a difference that surely becomes wider as relationships of agency become more ambiguous. We typically view enterprises externally, from the outside looking in. A school superintendent who supervises several schools might announce a curriculum change that would replace penmanship with martial arts, perhaps out of recognition that self-defense has higher value than penmanship these days. If the school were a market-based enterprise and the superintendent were the CEO, we would expect to see the curriculum change enacted quickly.

It would be different if the enterprise were operated in the public square. For one thing, there is no market valuation for the firm that would provide a point of orientation for generating support for the change. There are no bonuses or stock options, and most employees have tenure under civil service rules. To examine the reaction of the enterprise to the new initiative, it will be necessary to employ an inside-out orientation. A district official may well receive a memo from the superintendent detailing desired changes. The district official may well not object to the changes, but not be personally excited about them either. Overseeing their implementation, moreover, will require added effort that could be saved by sticking with the status quo, or even by making just a half-hearted effort to push the change. And it would be the same at lower levels within the organization. How the overall organization looks after the superintendent's initiative depends on actions taken by each node within the organization, and does so in an environment where the various administrative tools that are present for market-based firms are absent, or exist in highly attenuated fashion.

Suppose we were to follow a cohort of young executives through their careers, starting from their receipts of their MBAs or whatever other degrees they possessed upon entering corporate life in the market square. As the years passed, some would move into higher-paying positions, some with the same firm and others with different firms. A process of filtering and winnowing would clearly seem to be at work. The literature on agency and corporate governance provides a reasonable basis for thinking that this filtering and winnowing maps reasonably well into a process that tends to maximize the value of the assets which those different managers manage. There are even specialized headhunting firms that participate in this process.

Now turn to a cohort of young executives who select employment with enterprises organized in the public square. As the years pass, the same filtering and winnowing results. Some police officers make lieutenant, others captain, and a few chief. A few school principals become superintendents of school districts, and some superintendents of smaller districts move to larger districts. While a process of filtering and winnowing is clearly at work, it cannot be mapped directly into a model of maximizing the value of the enterprises being managed. But what kind of model might it map into?[10] Imagine a candidate who tried to act pursuant to some vision of maximizing the aggregate value of the enterprise, realizing that this can be only hypothetical. Such a police chief, for instance, might allocate officers so as to achieve equal anticipated reductions in the loss from crime across various police activities and precincts of activity. An appropriately done cost–benefit analysis, realizing that such a thing could not actually be constructed without controversy because of its hypothetical character, would show that this police chief operated with Kaldor–Hicks efficiency.

It is unlikely, however, that such qualities displayed at an earlier stage in a career would have brought such a person to a position of becoming considered for a police chief. Such a person would have shown no sympathy or attentiveness to the politically expressed concerns that are surely used by appointing officials as indicators of a candidate's suitability.[11] Performance evaluation within political enterprises has not been a topic of interest within public finance, probably because such matters are of no interest within the orthodox teleological orientation. Within the explanatory orientation pursued here, however, performance evaluation is a topic of interest because the market for executive personnel is one point of similarity, though not congruence, between market-based and political enterprises. The similarity arises because current performance maps into future opportunities; congruence is absent because there is no enterprise value to provide either a focal point or a means of compensation.

## NOTES

1. Executive approval is also required in presidential forms of democracy, though a president in such a system can always be analyzed as another legislative chamber.
2. This reference to effective, it should perhaps be noted, has nothing to do with usual references to efficiency. Efficiency is a technical condition of equilibrium modeling, and equilibrium is treated here not as a condition of reality but only as a mental tool that might be useful on occasion. Effective team production is that which allows an enterprise to survive and even thrive, but this concept is of a distinct analytical category from efficient.
3. In a similar vein see McCormick and Tollison (1981), Becker (1983) and Denzau and Munger (1986).
4. Much of the subsequent literature was initiated by Davies (1971). A conceptual framework for much of the subsequent literature was provided by Migué and Bélanger (1974) and Niskanen (1975). More recently, see Savas (1987) and Peirce (1999).
5. For an insightful treatment of meaningfulness in an economic context, see Loewenstein (1999).
6. In this regard, Barnett and Yandle (2004) describe this as a coalition between bootleggers and Baptists.
7. Perhaps the canonical exposition of this theme is Weingast and Moran (1983). A sample of other relevant work includes Bessley and Coate (1997), Breton (1996), Denzau and Munger (1986), Weingast (1984) and Wittman (1989).
8. Probably the canonical exposition of this theme is Niskanen (1971). A sample of other relevant work includes Benson (1995), Breton and Wintrobe (1975, 1982), Hammond (1986) and Mitchell and Simmons (1994).
9. This orientation is expressed in Bendor, Taylor and van Gaalen (1985) and Moe (1984, 1991).
10. For treatments of some pertinent issues, see Ammons and Glass (1988), Pfiffner (1987) and Sherwood and Breyer (1987).
11. For perceptive recognition that effective bureaucrats are engaged in politics and not just administration, see Kato (1994), Ostrom (1973) and Tullock (1965).

# 6. Revenue extraction: crossing the tax–expenditure divide

Any enterprise, whether organized in the market square or in the public square, originates in an entrepreneurial vision. For that enterprise to be successful, it must develop organizational arrangements that facilitate effective team production. A vital component of this is the ability to generate revenues sufficient to keep the team intact when resource owners are free to shift their resources to other teams. Political enterprises must generate sufficient revenues to cover the cost of providing their services. That cost, moreover, includes both the cost of labor and capital inputs and also a return to entrepreneurial sponsors. After all, covering cost and maximizing profit are just two ways of saying the same thing, for enterprises organized on the public square as well as for those organized on the market square.

Much of the revenue to support political enterprises comes from taxation, whereas market-based enterprises mostly derive their revenues directly from consumers through prices. This distinction concerning sources of revenue and forms of enterprise, however, is a matter of degree and not something categorical. Many political enterprises derive some of their revenues directly from prices that customers pay. For instance, a politically organized park might charge admission fees; alternatively, a governmental agency might sell its publications. Moreover, a good number of market-based enterprises derive significant revenue from taxation: any market-based enterprise that contracts with a political enterprise does so. For most revenues, however, the appropriation of tax revenue is the prime source for political enterprises while it is mostly a minor source for market-based enterprises.[1]

In many respects, individual political enterprises are in a position similar to that occupied by the various individual organizations that belong to the United Way.[2] Each individual member of United Way has its own administrative organization and may receive revenues directly from its own supporters. To a large extent, however, those organizations are supported by appropriations from United Way's general fund. There is a similar relationship between the individual political enterprises that are organized on the public square and the parliamentary assembly; the parliamentary assembly is to individual political enterprises as the Executive Board of

United Way is to the individual charities that it supports. Those enterprises may generate revenues on their own from their customers and clients. Appropriations from a parliamentary assembly, however, are generally the major source of revenue. That parliamentary assembly, moreover, typically derives its revenues from a large number of sources. Pursuing the analogy with United Way, appropriation from the parliamentary assembly is the primary source of revenue for the various enterprises that are organized within the public square. Those individual enterprises, however, have their own governing boards. They also have organizational interests that in some cases are antagonistic to those of other political enterprises while in other cases those interests are complementary. This duality of relationship is not surprising, for the public square is an order and not an organization.

This chapter is concerned primarily with the generation of revenue for legislative appropriation, though this concern necessarily extends as well to the appropriation of that revenue among politically sponsored enterprises. It is conventional in the theory of public finance to separate analytically the two sides of the budgetary operation, and then to add the two sides to derive the full picture. In contrast, this chapter, and this book as well, is based on the presumption that the two sides of the budget are not independent, although, of course, different activities can always be separated into accounts and then added to form aggregates. The amount of support that a parliamentary assembly can direct in the aggregate to the enterprises its members sponsor, recognizing that almost never do all members support all enterprises, depends on the distribution of appropriation across enterprises. Some patterns of expenditure will make possible greater legislative support for political enterprises than other patterns of expenditure. Again, there is an instructive analogy with United Way. If the two sides of the budget were truly separable, the pattern of appropriations that United Way made would have no effect on the contributions it received. This is surely an implausible situation, and so it seems with parliamentary assemblies as well.

## I.   THE CONSTITUTIONAL ORGANIZATION OF PARLIAMENTARY BUDGETING

In any domain of human activity, people who are inventive, imaginative and energetic tend to rise relative to people who are dull, unimaginative and lethargic. This is as true within the public square as it is within the market square. Democratically organized polities feature parliamentary assemblies on their public squares. We may reasonably expect that people who are attracted to serve in such assemblies, particularly those who do well there, will bring invention, imagination and energy to bear on their activities. While those members will typically differ in the particular political enterprises that they would like to see promoted, they will be generally united in preferring a densely-populated to a sparsely-populated public square. Only rarely will someone seek to operate in the public square so as to shrink the aggregate volume of its activity, and then almost surely without significant effect on that volume of activity.

The internal organization of parliamentary assemblies will generally reflect both this common interest in promoting an expansion in the aggregate size of the public square and differences among members regarding their particular interests about types of enterprise to promote. For instance, parliamentary assemblies beyond some modest scale will operate with a division of labor among its members according to areas of interest and competence. Thus political entrepreneurs seeking support for their enterprises will deal with those members of the parliamentary assembly who have special interest in and knowledge about the probable value of different enterprises in that part of the enterprise landscape.

Large parliamentary assemblies operate with a division of labor wherein some members specialize in acquiring revenue while others specialize in finding enterprises to support. It is unlikely, however, that a legislature would be organized so as to feature a total separation between these two tasks. Total separation might make sense if decisions concerning which enterprises to support, and to what extent to do so, had no impact upon the revenues that the legislature could generate. While this condition is imaginable, it is highly unlikely to hold. To the extent that there is complementarity between decisions about the support of enterprises and the ability of legislatures to generate revenue, some explicit connection between the two sides of the fiscal account will find organizational expression within legislative assemblies, provided only that people who are attracted into the legislative form of investment banking prefer to do more business rather than to do less.

Competition is ubiquitous in society. It exists among enterprises organized in the market square. It also exists among enterprises organized in the public square, as well as among enterprises across both squares. The appropriation of tax revenue may be affirmed by a legislative assembly, but the source of that observed appropriation lies beneath the surface appearance, and resides in the competitive activities of the various political enterprises. Political enterprises are no different from market enterprises in having to compete for support. Market-based enterprises must cultivate support; they don't wait for support to come to the enterprise. That old aphorism about building a better mousetrap and the world will beat a path to your doorstep is not quite right, for it will be necessary to spread word of your mousetrap before any path will appear. Among other things, those enterprises undertake the sales activity we associate with advertising and public relations. It is the same with political enterprises. Each such enterprise is competing with other political enterprises for appropriations, and each uses the tools of advertising and public relations to do this.[3]

Taxes appear on one side of a ledger and expenditures on the other, but the two sides of the ledger are always connected by a budgetary bridge. Just as there are many kinds of bridges in the world of engineering, so are there many forms of budgetary bridges in the organization of public squares. Some of those bridges are simple, and feature a source of revenue that is connected directly to an object of expenditure. For instance, a special district for mosquito abatement will provide only mosquito control and might be financed by revenue derived from a tax on assessed property value within its boundary. Other budgetary bridges are elaborate and ornate, with many revenue sources being pooled and then apportioned among objects of expenditure through some process of appropriation.[4]

The construction of a budgetary bridge is guided by the constitutional framework that shapes the relationship between market squares and public squares. Such constitutive frameworks have many components, and this analysis will focus on two features of that constitutive framework, which can be described as political rules and fiscal rules.[5] Political rules govern the selection of people to staff a parliamentary assembly, as well as the internal organization and operation of that assembly. Fiscal rules govern the assignment of tax liabilities and decisions about appropriations of tax revenue. This distinction between types of constitutive rules is, of course, just an analytical device for organizing thought, for the political and the fiscal do not denote disjunctive realms of practice but only distinctions to help organize thought.

One simple political rule is that a legislative assembly requires majority approval to take action, though the particular action such an assembly may take will depend on the fiscal rules by which it operates. Majority rule will typically yield a different budgetary outcome when the fiscal rule requires head taxation than when it imposes some other form of taxation.[6] Other political rules would pertain to the structure of committees and to assignments of members to committees. The procedural rules followed by parliamentary assemblies are also political rules, and so are the rules governing the process by which people acquire seats in a parliamentary assembly.

Fiscal rules speak directly to the substantive content of legislative action, as illustrated by the assignment of tax liability and the awarding of appropriations. One simple fiscal rule is that any legislative appropriation is financed by an equal charge on each member of the society. This would constitute a head tax, and would be the public square counterpart to a market price. Other forms of taxation would represent different fiscal rules, as they would change the assignment of tax liability. Changes in fiscal rules will also typically entail changes in the structure of tax administration. A head tax, for instance, will require much less by way of tax administration than an income tax. Other fiscal rules pertain to the processes by which political enterprises receive revenues from the legislature. For instance, a requirement that politically-sponsored enterprises engage in program evaluation within a benefit–cost framework would be a fiscal rule.

Any public square will contain some structure of political and fiscal rules that provide the components by which budgetary bridges are constructed within it. In modern public squares, moreover, that structure of rules is truly complex. This is as it must be, for collective bodies cannot take actions independently of such rules that organize and structure deliberation and action. There is no position of social planner where decisions are made to allocate resources on the public square. It is not even accurate to treat a leg-islator from that orientation. Legislators do not allocate resources. They participate in processes out of which allocative decisions emerge. Such emergent outcomes are not properly described as maximizing or optimiz-ing anything, at least in a substantive as distinct from a purely formal, *ex post* manner.

## II. A SIMPLE BUDGETARY BRIDGE

The simplest budgetary bridge is one that connects one source of revenue with one object of expenditure. Continuing with an illustration pursued in an earlier chapter, suppose marshland adjacent to a town is a source of mosquitoes that plague town residents. In response, residents might well spray themselves with repellent and sleep under mosquito netting. It is also highly likely that mosquitoes will become an object of discussion in the public square. It is easy to imagine that such discussion leads to proposals to undertake some town sponsorship of mosquito spraying on the marsh-land. It should not, however, be thought that such proposals just happen as some kind of spontaneous ignition, as it were. What is commonly described as spontaneous order is really the result of intersecting intentions and the resultant interactions that are set in motion. A proposal to establish an enterprise to combat mosquitoes in the public square will be the result of entrepreneurial sponsorship, and a careful examination of the organiza-tional details of any such enterprise will surely reveal its origins.

To start in the simplest possible fashion, suppose the town operates with a fiscal constitution that requires head taxation and a political constitution that requires majority approval among all residents. Further suppose the town contains only three residents, or, alternatively, three households headed by Primo, Secunda and Terzo. Figure 6.1 provides a straightforward illustration of the organization of mosquito control on the public square, under the postulated fiscal and political rules. To simplify the construction, Figure 6.1 assumes that the three households have equal incomes, so that a head tax is equivalent to a flat tax on income. The three residents differ in their preferences for mosquito control, with Primo desiring the least amount of protection and Terzo the most. Under the postulated fiscal and political arrangements, the collective choice will tend to be the amount of protection that is preferred by the median voter, Secunda.

This collective choice fits the median voter result, and it is difficult to see how any coherent alternative could be advanced under this institutional setting. Different rules governing either taxing or voting, however, may well generate different budgetary outcomes. For instance, suppose majority approval is maintained, only now the head tax is replaced by any of a number of tax options. No general statement can be advanced about the resulting implications for budgetary choice, because those implications will depend on how the particular tax changes influence both the identity and desire of the median voter. For instance, a different tax might raise the price to Secunda,

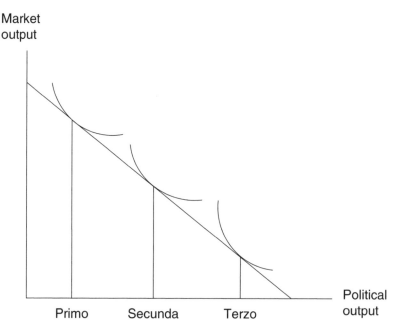

*Figure 6.1    Simple model of budgetary choice*

in which case she would choose less. But that alternative tax could also lower the price to her. Furthermore, the change in tax could also change the identity of the median voter. For instance, suppose the alternative tax lowers the price for Primo and raises it for Secunda. With a sufficient shift in prices between the two, Primo can become the median voter. How much this shift in identity of the median voter changes the collective outcome depends, of course, on a comparison between what Primo wants under the new tax rule with what Secunda wanted under the old tax rule.

Changes in political rules can likewise change budgetary outcomes, even without changes in either tax rules or voter preferences. It is easy enough to imagine a political rule that delegates to one member the ability to study the issue and to make a recommendation for action, with that recommendation to be either accepted or rejected under majority rule. If either Terzo or Primo were to be the recipient of this delegated position of agenda formation, either of them could advance a proposal that would move in their favor and away from what Secunda preferred, and yet Secunda would favor it over the option of having no collective involvement in mosquito control.[7]

The public square described here operates as a direct democracy. With only three people, nothing else is plausible. With three people, moreover, parliamentary rules are likewise implausible. This public square would almost surely operate by consensus and not by majority rule, although consensual operation in these settings will often contain some duress that is reflected by the sense of 'going along to get along'. To provide space for the phenomena we recognize as budgeting and taxation, more than three people must be involved. This number must be sufficiently large so that formalized procedures of some form will replace the informal discussion and negotiation that is possible among three people. If the town contained, say, 100 people, informal negotiation would give way to formal rules and procedures. The parliament could still be organized as a direct democracy, though it would have to have structured rules to bring closure to discussions and to elicit action.

The procedural framework by which enterprises are put together in the public square is necessarily more complex than that followed in the market square. Collective property must be encased within some procedural framework before it can accommodate organized patterns of societal activity. Suppose initially that that fiscal rule requires the cost of all collectively sponsored activities to be shared equally among all town residents. The town thus raises its revenues from a head tax. Further suppose that after due deliberation, the town decides upon action by majority vote. In this setting, the town choice will be the amount of protection that is the highest preference of the median voter.

It should be noted that the simple construction described by Figure 6.1 buries a lot of institutional detail. For one thing, it assumes that parliamentary outcomes yield the same outcome as the constituents would have generated had their deliberations been governed by some such parliamentary framework as Robert's Rules of Order, which provides open access to the agenda for taking collective action. It also assumes not only that an enforceable constitutional requirement for equal taxation of equal incomes is possible, but also that the definition of income for tax purposes is unproblematic. Had a different form of taxation been used to generate revenue, a different collective outcome would probably have resulted, as will be explored momentarily.

In actual societies, we observe some people clamoring for increased political spending while other people are clamoring for reduced taxes. All that clamoring, moreover, has a structural dimension that cannot exist when a single political output is financed by either a head tax or a flat tax on a comprehensive tax base. But reality presents us with a plethora of political enterprises whose financing runs to a significant extent through the legislature. Reality also confronts us with no sign of head taxes or flat taxes comprehensively applied. What reality does confront us with is a complex structure of enterprises on the one side of the legislature and connecting streams of revenue on the other side. In this setting, whether any person picked at random would prefer to see expenditures increased or taxes reduced is likely to depend critically on the precise content of those expenditure increases or tax reductions.

Some probing into that complexity will come later. To give a start, and in a manner that maps into the types of functions that economists like to work with, Figure 6.2 presents a transformation of the information provided by Figure 6.1. The function MPC denotes the marginal political cost from expanding political output. The source of that cost and at whom it is directed will be considered momentarily. So long as political output is less than Primo's most desired output in Figure 6.1, there will be no resistance to increased political output. It is only beyond Primo's preferred output that resistance comes into play. This situation is shown by the origin of MPC at that point in Figure 6.2. It should be noted that Figure 6.1 maps into a set of discrete stages of support and opposition, while Figure 6.2 expresses the same idea in continuous fashion, primarily because continuity will be employed later.

Initially, the opposition to increased political output comes from Primo alone. The valuational axis is described as 'pressure', and the quotation marks are significant, for a model of an auction market is being used to characterize a process that actually proceeds quite differently. Several simple indicators of the amount of loss that Primo would suffer from

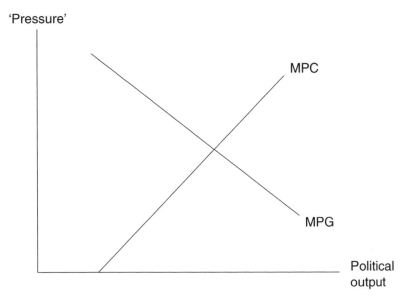

'Pressure'

MPC

MPG

Political
output

*Note:*    MPC = marginal political cost;
            MPG = marginal political gain.

*Figure 6.2    Market-like model of budgetary choice*

expansions beyond his preferred rate of output can be developed from the
various compensating and equivalent variation measures of consumer
surplus. As output expands beyond what Primo most prefers, his utility
level falls, and the amount of this fall can be stated monetarily as some
measure of lost consumer surplus. Once output gets beyond the rate most
preferred by Secunda, she too becomes an opponent of further expansion
and contributes to the marginal political cost of expansion, whereas previously she contributed to the marginal gain.

The marginal political gain from output expansion is constructed in the
same manner. So long as actual output is less than the output most preferred,
that person will gain by expansion and the weight of that gain will appear in
MPG. The model of discrete choice presented in Figure 6.1 can thus be transformed into a model of continuous choice, in similar fashion to that presented in Figure 6.2. We should realize though that such modeling efforts are
perhaps more metaphorical than real. A merchant in deciding whether to
keep longer hours faces genuine pressure, as he must compare the added cost
of staying open longer against the additional revenue that he thinks will
result. There is a simple and direct connection between choice and consequence. It is not so simple in legislative settings, although small-number

illustrations tend to conceal the extent of the differences between market and fiscal settings. In a market setting, pressure is transmitted directly through the buying choices people make. The legislative equivalent would probably require instantaneous referenda on whether legislators would be allowed to continue in office after each issue is decided. Nothing of the sort exists, of course, so the pressure denoted by Figure 6.2 is a metaphorical construction whose relation to actuality remains open for discussion.

## III.   ADDING COMPLEXITY TO BUDGETARY BRIDGING

Even in the simplest possible case where one source of revenue is directed to one political enterprise, political outcomes can vary with the particular political and fiscal rules that constitute the public square. In this simple setting, however, it is reasonable to construe rational voter conduct in a substantive fashion, quite similar to rational conduct in market settings. As complexity expands on the public square, this substantive feature of rational conduct dissolves within the complexity that accompanies budgetary bridging. To be sure, the formal appearance of rationality can be maintained as a feature of equilibrium-based modeling from the outside looking in. Substantively, however, the source of rationality shifts away from individual citizens to the nexus of relationships that pass through the legislature in all directions. In the simple setting described above, it is reasonable to treat fiscal outcomes much as if they were products of voter choice. In the complex settings of contemporary life, such treatment is surely a metaphorical fiction. The source of rationality in substantive conduct, as distinct from some statement of formalized conditions of equilibrium, resides within the nexus of competitively- and cooperatively-organized relationships.

Figure 6.3 presents a schematic illustration of a more complex process of budgetary bridging. There, six enterprises receive legislative sponsorship and appropriations and nine people pay taxes to provide those appropriations. The impact of increasing budgetary complexity can be seen even by considering what happens when just one other enterprise is added to the three-person setting described above. Once the second enterprise receives parliamentary support, an individual citizen can no longer compare an increased tax burden with some valuation of the increased political output that results. The same tax extraction can be evaluated differently by any citizen, depending on the particular enterprises to which those taxes are directed. Someone who values output from the first enterprise but not the second will evaluate a tax change differently depending on his belief about the subsequent flow to his preferred enterprise.

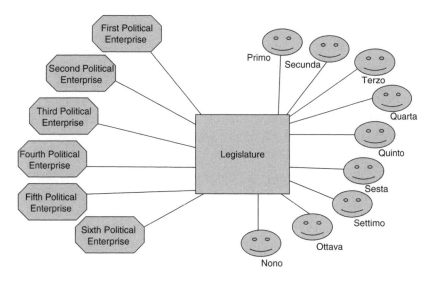

*Figure 6.3    Budgetary intermediation*

As the number of enterprises and the number of citizens continue to expand, it quickly becomes impossible to attribute tax changes to changes in support for particular enterprises. Any semblance of market-like rationality dissolves. To be sure, some resemblance to rationality could be maintained by adopting the posture of outside-in equilibrium modeling. By taking this approach, some composite good theorem could be applied in hedonic fashion under some such presumption as revenues being selected so as to maximize the expected votes of the governing party. This kind of set-up could be assimilated readily to a model of probabilistic voting, which in turn would generate a nice center-of-mass type of outcome, and would map well into such efficient democracy constructions as those presented by Donald Wittman (1989, 1995), Walter Hettich and Stanley Winer (1999) and Albert Breton (1996).

This type of approach brings a good dose of analytical tractability, though that comes at the price of leaving many knotty questions buried deeply within a black box that is nailed shut by assumptions about maximizing equilibria. This can be illustrated nicely by Gary Becker's (1983, p. 386) widely-cited claim that 'competition among pressure groups supports efficient tax methods'. Becker constructs a model where people are divided into two groups, and compares two institutional arrangements. One arrangement is a pure market economy, where each group receives the value of its marginal product. Aggregate real income is the sum of what each group earns. The alternative arrangement involves a contest over the receipt of transfers. The winner of that contest will receive transfers while the loser will supply those transfers. The transfer is lump sum, and so itself has no effect on aggregate income. However, there are two sources of pure loss from the transfer. One source is what Becker calls the lobbying costs in either supporting or opposing the program. The other is the deadweight loss associated with the taxes required to finance the program. Becker's argument is that taxes that have lower deadweight loss allow greater transfers, so winners would support taxes with low deadweight costs. Similarly, for any given size of transfer, losers would prefer to pay taxes with low deadweight costs. In the aggregate, wealth is destroyed, though in a relatively efficient manner when measured against other methods for achieving that same transfer.

The two-sided nature of any transaction, including involuntary ones, guarantees that a bridge will exist to connect sources of revenue provided by citizens to sources of service provided by political enterprises. To be sure, political enterprises do not operate by the same rules that govern market-based enterprises, but the connection between revenue and service must be there all the same. It would always be possible to make that connection as direct as it is with ordinary commercial transactions. Knut Wicksell's ([1896] 1958) well-cited formulation articulated one particular approach to doing just this. Wicksell's fundamental interest was to make explicit the connection between revenue and service, and to do so at the individual level because he recognized that it was nonsensical to speak of this being done at the aggregate level without it having been accomplished through aggregation across individuals. What resulted in Wicksell's formulation was a procedure whereby any proposal for expenditure would be accompanied by a statement of how the cost would be covered. In principle, Wicksell joined this procedure to a requirement of unanimous consent, which would place political enterprises on exactly the same footing as market-based enterprises. Hyatt the city would have been transformed into Hyatt the hotel. While principle suggested unanimity for Wicksell, the prudent part of his judgment led him to advocate something short of unanimity but well beyond majority approval.

Regardless of what one might think about this gap between principle and practice, Wicksell was proposing to make explicit the institutional recognition of the inescapable bridge between revenue generated and service provided. In the Wicksellian formulation, the legislature would serve explicitly as an intermediary to connect those who supply services with those who demand them. The present organization of legislatures along non-Wicksellian lines does not deny the connection between service and revenue, but it does render that connection complex and ambiguous, and something to be explored and illuminated. A good deal of that complexity comes about because of the large number of political enterprises that run some of their financing though the legislature, along with the large number of revenue sources that legislatures tap.

With respect to Figure 6.3, it is easy to see that a person's experience of an increased tax liability does not translate into any particular pattern of output expansion within the set of political enterprises. So long as tax revenues enter a general fund for subsequent appropriation, as against being earmarked for particular enterprises and purposes, the organization of activity in the public square does not follow the simple logic of organization in the market square, at least when the effort at explanation starts from inside the world as experienced by individuals and from here moves outside to the world of societal formations.

In considering that complex expansion of Figure 6.3, moreover, it is misleading to think of the legislature as a simple intermediary that connects two sets of people who have no direct contact with one another. If a complete map of the pattern of connections were drawn, connections would run from particular political enterprises to particular citizens. These connections are particularly significant because those enterprises are competitive with one another. A particular enterprise is able to acquire increased support within the legislature through a combination of its own activities and complementary activities among sufficiently interested citizens. It is those connections between particular people on the right-hand side of Figure 6.3 and particular enterprises on the left-hand side that become the medium through which the 'pressure' portrayed in Figure 6.2 is generated and transmitted. It is through channels such as this that demand is articulated and support conveyed.

## IV.    EXPLAINING AGGREGATE TAX BURDENS

How might the aggregate tax burden within a society be explained? In contemporary, western-style democracies, those burdens generally range between 30 and 50 percent of measured economic output. The formal categories of the theory of markets can be used to account for the relative amounts of activity devoted to different activities such as raising turkeys, growing turnips and manufacturing pesticides. It is reasonable to seek to apply those same categories to the place of politically-based enterprises within the overall social economy. Equilibrium-based theorizing would approach this challenge by postulating a societal equilibrium where the relative size of political output is an equilibrium based on vote maximization, as illustrated by Hettich and Winer (1988, 1999).

An aggregate version of Figure 6.2 can be used to characterize the size of government by incorporating fiscal processes into the conventional rubric of aggregate equilibrium theorizing. Hence, the aggregate size of government will expand so long as the additional support generated by that expansion exceeds the support that is lost by the taxes necessary to finance that expansion. Such a formulation can be assimilated readily to a presumption that a politician seeks to produce a vote maximizing bundle of policies, particularly when this presumption is developed within a framework of probabilistic voting that generates nice center-of-mass properties. Within this framework, political output would be evaluated by voters as a composite good, thereby eliminating by assumption the complexity portrayed by Figure 6.3.

This approach to explanation has the advantage of resting comfortably within the contours of equilibrium-based theorizing about market allocations. The size structure of political enterprises can also be incorporated into the same explanatory rubric through some disaggregated version of Figure 6.2. This would be a form of generalized marginal productivity approach to explanation. Each political enterprise would expand so long as that expansion gained more political support than it lost, with that loss of support having two components: one is the opposition to taxation and the other is opposing claims from proponents of other objects of expenditure. In any case, it would be possible to conceptualize political outcomes as a part of a general equilibrium within a society.

An advantage of this kind of approach is that it brings a look of precision to what is presented. Equilibrium, after all, is a precise condition. The size of government and the sizes of its various activities can be accounted for by the same formal precision. The disadvantage of this approach is that it is incapable of yielding insight into the processes that generate the world in which we live. It is possible to describe equilibrium conditions for a world where everyone takes prices as given data, but it is impossible for prices to arise or to change in such a world. An equilibrium-based model is incapable of generating what it purports to explain, and so is confined to describing conditions for consistency because it is not amenable to explaining emergence and change.[8]

Even the presumption of vote maximization is not as innocent as it might sound. If competition occurs over support for a median voter, the electoral success of incumbents would seem plausibly to hover around 50 per cent, and certainly not in the vicinity of 90 per cent. When rates of re-election rise toward 90 per cent, moreover, vote maximization surely loses some of its intuitive cogency as an indicator of competitiveness. To rescue vote maximization, it could be asserted that it is better to win by larger over smaller margins. Yet it is not apparent why this should be so. Whether a representative gets elected to a parliamentary assembly with 51 percent or 71 percent support, that person simply has one vote among many within the assembly. Only in some parliamentary settings can excess votes from a larger margin of victory be transferred to transform otherwise losing candidates into winning candidates, which is an action that might increase influence within a parliamentary assembly. If there is any advantage to winning by a large amount, it is through its effects on longevity, which generally translate in turn into more influential positions within a parliamentary assembly. How much this might be worth depends on the particular parliamentary rules in place, as its value would increase the more strongly those rules reward longevity.

The approach that lies behind Figure 6.3 suggests a different way of explaining the relative volume of economic activity conducted through political enterprises. In the first place, people seek seats in a parliamentary assembly for the same kinds of reasons that people seek positions in a regular investment bank: the net rewards that such a position offers exceeds that offered by other relevant prospects. The substantive character of those rewards has many components: salary and expense allowances are certainly fine, even if perhaps not lavish by some private-sector comparisons; post-legislative employment can be even more rewarding with respect to compensation; many people are fascinated with politics and the use of power; and some doubtless bring a sense of vocation and service to their activities. The relative significance of material and non-material considerations surely varies among people who seek legislative office just as it varies among everyone else. Whatever the substantive character of the rewards associated with holding a partnership in the legislative form of investment bank, success in that activity will depend on the ability of those partners to satisfy clients who are sponsoring enterprises in the public square and who are seeking legislative support.

A legislative assembly is a type of bazaar where the aggregate budget is generated in bottom-up fashion. Each political enterprise must have champions within the parliamentary assembly. Some champions will carry more weight than others. That weight is partly a matter of place within the nexus of legislative arrangements, as illustrated by seniority and committee assignments. It is also a matter of the supporting connections a political enterprise is able to establish to enterprises located in the market square. For instance, the First Political Enterprise depicted in Figure 6.3 might establish supporting connections to enterprises owned by Nono and Ottava, and so secure their support within the legislature. Nono and Ottava might thus support a three-part tax program that would (1) increase aggregate collections, (2) earmark some appropriations for the First Political Enterprise, and (3) include special depreciation provisions that apply particularly heavily to the enterprises owned by Nono and Ottava, even though those provisions are universal in their applicability. For instance, immediate expensing might be allowed for all expenses associated with constructing domed stadiums that were completed within some stipulated period. Only one stadium in the land might quality for this treatment, but the legislation would be general and not particular in its application. Otto von Bismarck doubtlessly knew what he was talking about when he observed: 'Laws are like sausages. It's better not to see them being made.'[9]

## V.  TAX PHILOSOPHERS, POLITICAL REALISTS AND FISCAL CONSTITUTIONS

The history of fiscal theorizing contains numerous efforts to state principles of good or sound fiscal conduct. One of the most cited formulations occurs in Adam Smith's mini-treatise on public finance in the fifth book of the *Wealth of Nations* (1991 [1776]). There, Smith laid down four canons of good taxation: (1) taxes should be levied in proportion to property, (2) taxes should be certain and not arbitrary, (3) taxes should be convenient to pay, and (4) taxes should be economical to administer, for both the taxpayer and the government. Smith's canons have certainly been influential in subsequent fiscal scholarship, as they have been cited continuously in it. Whether those canons are effective in practice is a different matter, and one whose truth is not so easy to discern.

A few years before Smith, the cameralist scholar Johan Heinrich Gottlob von Justi (1969 [1771]) described six canons in his treatise on *Natur und Wesen der Staaten*. Justi's formulation of tax canons ran thus: (1) taxes should be in proportion to property, while bearing equally upon all those who possess the same amount of property, (2) tax obligations should be transparently clear to everyone, (3) taxes should be convenient and economical, for both taxpayers and the state, (4) a tax should not deprive a taxpayer of necessaries or cause him to reduce his capital to pay the tax, (5) a tax should neither harm the welfare of the state and its subjects nor violate the civil liberties of the subjects, and (6) a tax should be compatible with the form of government, as illustrated by tax farming being suitable only for absolute monarchies.

The first three of Justi's canons are similar to Smith's four canons, while Justi's final three canons cover territory not articulated by Smith. Justi's canons would seem clearly to place more constraints on the use of taxation than would Smith's. But more than tax canons are involved in a comparison between Smith and Justi. For Smith, taxation was ideally to be the exclusive source of revenue to support activities in the public square. Were Smith to have his way, the state would divest itself of such non-tax sources of revenue as lands and enterprises, and rely wholly upon taxes imposed upon market-based commercial activity. For Smith, the state was treated as existing and operating outside the framework of the market economy and intervening into the market economy to procure its revenues. The canons of taxation were to provide guidance for keeping the subsequent disturbances to the market economy in check.

In sharp contrast, Justi argued that ideally a state would not tax at all, because the enterprises organized within the public square could use their property to generate the revenues necessary for their support. For Justi, a prince who resorted to taxation was verging on being a failure at his princely tasks. The state was envisioned ideally as participating within the market economy on an equal basis with all other participants. To be sure, ideals are rarely found mirrored in practice, and the relationship between tax philosophers and political realists seems to have current running in each direction, with any measure of their ratio being subject to a good deal of imprecision.

Justi's canon that a tax, if it is to exist at all, should be compatible with the form of government treats the material of public finance from the standpoint of a theory of social order and organization, as against treating it from the standpoint of a theory of resource allocation. Knut Wicksell's articulation of the problem of just taxation (1958 [1896]) exhibits directly this same treatment, particularly in his lament that most writing in public finance reflected a presumption that political absolutism ruled the day. Wicksell's approach to just taxation reflects Justi's sixth canon nicely. So, too, did the subsequent formulations of *Ordnungstheorie*, ranging from the early articulation by Walter Eucken (1990 [1952]) to such more recent articulations as those contained in Helmut Leipold and Ingo Pies (2000), and also the comparison between Walter Eucken and Max Weber in Corinna Rath (1998). The formulations from *Ordnungstheorie* have sought to articulate canons that would generate a broad consistency between the operating principles of enterprises established on the public square and those established on the market square.

The distinction between these two approaches can be illustrated alternatively by considering the model of leviathan developed in Geoffrey Brennan and James Buchanan (1980). While the leviathan of the Bible lived in the sea, it is easy enough to imagine that it could have been a land-based creature. The question at issue concerns what it takes to live in the neighborhood of this roaming beast. The approach associated with Smith and carried forward by Brennan and Buchanan would be to seek to do such things as clip its claws and pull its teeth. The approach associated with Justi, and carried forward by such scholars as Wicksell and the contributors to *Ordnungstheorie* would look toward domesticating the beast. Whether that beast can be domesticated, or to what extent, is a different matter, but the difference in approach is apparent in any case.

Regardless of approach, a significant issue arises concerning the relation between the various fiscal norms asserted by tax philosophers and actual fiscal conduct, which lies within the province of what are surely political realists. Over the years, tax philosophers have articulated several norms that are cited regularly in the fiscal literature. These norms, moreover, do not harmonize with one another. One common norm is the benefit principle of public finance, where ideally people pay taxes according to their evaluation of the services those taxes provide. This norm seeks to place government on the same footing as all other organizations in society. Wicksell's principle of just taxation is one particular expression of the benefit principle.

While the benefit principle is often described as a principle of efficiency, another principle of efficiency looks to the tax side alone. Lump sum taxes, for instance, are widely regarded as efficient on the grounds that they do not distort market prices and choices. To be sure, the idea of non-distortion is a purely mental construct that finds no counterpart in reality, just as the idea of a risk-free investment is a construct of the mental imagination with no referent in life. For instance, the actual imposition of a head tax would require a process for identifying taxpayers, and we may be sure that the higher the tax the smaller would be the identified set of taxpayers. The higher the tax, moreover, the greater would be the effort devoted to tax administration to collect the tax.

For the most part, tax philosophers have plied their trade in a teleological manner, seeking to lay down principles that good fiscal administration should follow. One question that can be asked is whether those formulations shape actual fiscal conduct, or whether fiscal conduct proceeds independently of the efforts of the fiscal philosophers. Natural morality does seem to provide some limit on actual fiscal conduct, though perhaps not much of a limit. There would probably be nearly universal agreement that the best tax is always one that someone else pays. There would surely be equally strong agreement that it would be wrong for two diners in a restaurant to force a third diner to pay part of their bill. But where does taxation come into this? Suppose we start with a uniform tax. A measure that grants a tax credit to one particular person is equivalent to one diner sending part of his bill to the other diners in the restaurant. These things happen all the time in legislation, but even here some modicum of generality is preserved. For instance, a tax credit might be offered to all firms whose exports exceed $5 million annually. Alternatively, a credit might be offered for all athletic arenas whose construction was finished during 1994 and which cost more than $50 million. Yet again, a credit might be offered for all assisted living facilities that treat more than 20 dementia patients or, alternatively, less than five. In all of these cases, and the millions more like them, some people secure tax reductions, which in turn means higher taxes for those who don't secure those reductions.

## VI.   FISCAL POLITICS AND THE GENERATION OF TAX COMPLEXITY

While the tax philosophers do not speak with one voice, there is a preponderant choral group that displays a strong preference for broad-based over narrow-based taxation. This preponderance begins to break down once the concern with general principle gives way to specific detail concerning tax codes. Where some tax philosophers support a degressive rate schedule where a flat rate is combined with some uniform exemption from the base, others support a progressive structure. There are also differences between those who favor a tax on income and those who favor one on consumption.

Regardless of the philosophical writings, actual fiscal conduct seems to display only modest evidence of having been influenced by those writings. Suppose we start from the presumption that people who inhabit the legislature tend overwhelmingly to support an expansion in the amount of custom that passes through it. There can be huge differences among legislators in the types of custom they would like to see sponsored more heavily, but in any case they would be generally agreed on an expansion in custom in the aggregate. To accomplish this requires, in turn, more revenue. A simple system of broad-based taxation conflicts with the nearly universal desire for expansion held by members of legislative assemblies. A good deal of the phenomena of public finance can be characterized in terms of a process of interaction that unfolds in the presence of this conflict.

Suppose initially that some comprehensive and uniform income tax is the sole source of revenue that legislators can use to support political enterprises. This tax might well accommodate the postcard return promised in Robert Hall and Alan Rabushka's *Low Tax, Simple Tax, Flat Tax* (1983). There are practically countless ways that increasing complexity can be added to this simple tax structure. Whether such complexity will be added, and in what particular manner it will be added, will depend primarily on the amount of custom that different measures are anticipated to bring to the legislature. In any case, what would result would be an evolutionary process by which a simple and transparent tax came to be replaced by a complex and opaque structure of taxation. The question at issue is whether added complexity in any of numerous dimensions can generate more revenue than the postcard tax. If so, the postcard, along with the one-page revenue code, will surely end up in the archives.[10]

In thinking of tax legislation, it is helpful to think of tax policy as arising in the context of some given aggregate amount of revenue to collect. What this means is that provisions that lower tax liability for some people raise it concomitantly for everyone else. This presents a simple framework. Suppose that the broad-based tax is initially 10 percent. Tax discrimination can be incorporated into a flat rate tax by introducing such things as exclusions and exemptions from the tax base. Initially, everyone still pays 10 percent on their respective bases, only now the bases differ among people who would earlier have had the same base. Since the tax base was initially comprehensive, the introduction of exemptions and exclusions would reduce total political revenue. This is an unlikely event, which means that the general rate would be increased above 10 percent to finance the exclusions and exemptions.

That rate might be increased to, say, 12 percent at the same time that various exemptions and exclusions were enacted. The amount of revenue collected would rise, though by less than it would have risen had the 12 percent rate been applied to the previous base. Moreover, take a look at the politics of so-called tax cuts. There is never a simple reduction in tax rates, keeping the base the same. Rates may be reduced, but the cuts in taxes are targeted at particular sets of recipients. One proposal might include a tax credit for tuition, perhaps with that credit being phased out above a stipulated income level. Another might allow expensing of investment made in export industries that employ at least 300 people at above-average compensation, and hence perhaps unionized.

In addition to such points of controversy among those fiscal philosophers who support the idea of a broad-based tax, there are also others who support narrow tax bases. In many cases this support for narrow-based taxation is tied to arguments about the use of taxation to correct alleged market failure. For instance, taxes on alcoholic beverages are often advocated based on claims that such taxes are necessary to correct what would otherwise be market failures. The idea behind these claims is that the price of alcohol reflects the cost of the inputs that are needed to produce the product, but don't reflect the damage done to third parties through vehicular accidents and the like. For example, Cook and Moore (1994) argued that the external cost of drinking alcoholic beverages was 63 cents per drink when they did their study, which was about double the tax at the time.

The economic logic of such corrective tax claims is generally quite weak. It makes no sense to say that the market price of alcohol net of tax reflects the price of inputs to produce the product but not the external damage. People are liable for the damages they impose on others through drunken driving, as well as facing penalties. Figure 6.4 illustrates the situation. The functions $D_M$ and $S_M$ illustrate the demand and supply conditions in the

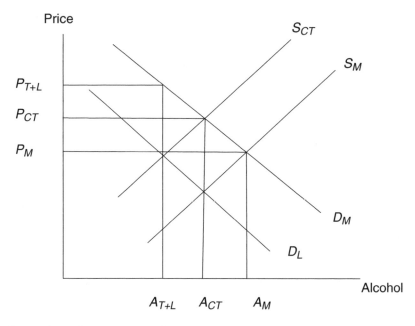

*Figure 6.4    Corrective tax claims*

market for alcoholic beverages without taxation or personal liability. The
amount sold would be $A_M$ and the price would be $P_M$. The insertion of an
excise tax shifts the supply function to $S_{CT}$, which raises price to $P_{CT}$ and
lowers output to $A_{CT}$.

This line of analysis ignores the operation of civil and criminal liability,
which reduces the demand for alcoholic beverages relative to what they
would be without such liability. This reduced demand is illustrated by $D_L$,
which also reduces the amount sold to $A_{CT}$ and raises the price to $P_{CT}$.
The presence of liability, in other words, accomplishes the same thing on
average as does the so-called corrective tax. When the tax is joined to civil
and criminal liability, the full price rises to $P_{T+L}$ and the amount consumed
falls to $A_{T+L}$. The corrective tax is a form of double taxation that actually
creates a welfare loss, as this is appraised by the usual methods.

There is one big difference between the tax and liability approaches. The
tax approach treats each ounce of alcoholic beverage as equally implicated
in the imposition of damage on third parties. Yet only a relatively small
share of alcohol consumption has this effect. It is more likely that so-called
corrective taxation has little to do with somehow seeking to correct market
failures, and has much more to do with probing for revenues. Taxation is
never written explicitly in a manner to identify particular people, but a

sufficiently complex tax code could probably come to resemble a setting where tax liabilities are specified almost by individual. That individuals are not identified explicitly probably reflects a belief in some type of equal treatment condition that in turn is part of natural morality. A head tax is a form of equal treatment. As other tax forms are developed, the scope for arbitrariness in taxation necessarily enters because tax liability becomes a matter subject to legislative stipulation.

It is plausible to think of taxation proceeding in a two-stage process. The first stage features a belief in generality or uniformity. This stage yields the first draft of a tax measure, so to speak. The second stage allows for amendment for 'good reason'. That good reason, moreover, cannot be stated quite so baldly as to assert that it is always better to tax someone else. What thus results is a variety of exclusions from tax liability for various types of articulated reasons. Many of these are what Fred McChesney (1997) describes as rent extraction.

## VII.    HEARINGS, STUDY COMMISSIONS AND TAX LEGISLATION

Democratic procedures are replete with hearings and the formation of study commissions, many of these organized within the executive branch in a presidential system or a revenue committee within a parliamentary system. A question arises about what such activities accomplish. Within a model of an interventionist state, such activities would represent the decision process of the intervening agent. For instance, a monarch of a relatively benevolent sort might be interested in testimony about the excess burdens of different forms of taxation. While such a monarch will surely demand his revenue, he may desire to soften the excess burdens attendant to raising them. A monarch inspired to pad his personal account who might have advisers familiar with concepts from the theory of fiscal illusion might seek to articulate a program of illusion-fostering tax reform along the lines sketched by Amilcare Puviani (1903). Whatever the particular form of advice, that advice would be directed at some action-taking agent who is able to act on it.

No such position exists in a democratic polity. Many people participate in generating collective outcomes, but those outcomes result from interaction among participants and are not some person's choices. Such hearings and studies can still inform various people who are involved in legislative processes, but to what effect and in what manner depends as well on the types of interest different participants have. There are some ways in which the process is similar to processes of scientific inquiry, but there are also differences that arise out of the collective nature of the process, within which personal liability and residual claimancy is absent.

Consider Jerzzy Neyman's (1950, pp. 272–89) treatment of 'the problem of the lady tasting tea'. The problem arises in response to a lady's claim that she can distinguish between two ways of making tea. One way is to put tea into the cup first and then add milk. The other way is to put the milk in first and then add the tea. Much of Neyman's discussion and analysis concerns different experimental settings for generating the evidence that will be used to reach a judgment about the lady's ability to discriminate between the two methods for making tea. For instance, the lady could be given ten pairs of cups and asked to distinguish between the two methods. Alternatively, the lady could be given one pair on each of ten consecutive days. Yet again, the lady could be given one cup and asked to declare by which method it was made, with this experiment perhaps continued for 20 days.

Besides discussing various experimental settings and the power of those experiments to allow for accurate discrimination, Neyman also discussed the standard to be used in reaching a judgment. As he noted, there would probably be a conflict between the jury and the lady. Moreover, there are differences between a strict jury and a benevolent jury. Whether one false assignment from ten pairs is sufficient to reject the lady's claim or whether it might take three miscues is not a matter of science but of the standard of judgment. Neyman's hypothetical setting was that of a parlor game.

The setting for tax legislation is different. For instance, the lady might be a constituent of some member of the legislative assembly, with a history of strong past support. Alternatively, she could be a vocal supporter of activities that are strongly opposed by some members of the legislative assembly. A legislative assembly is infused with interests that are outside the spirit of the parlor game that Neyman described. It thus seems likely that a good part of what study commissions and hearings accomplish is to gauge the intensity of various desires about potential legislation (McCormick and Tollison 1981), which is a necessary activity in the absence of genuine markets.

Consider, for instance, some issues surrounding eligibility under various kinds of welfare programs. It is obvious that some people support easier eligibility and stronger support for welfare recipients than others do. That difference in support could be ascribed to differences in generosity, though generosity is a difficult concept to apply when people are talking about spending other people's money. Still, it would be within the framework of economic analysis to describe some people as being relatively generous of spirit (when it comes to legislative appropriation anyway) while others are relatively miserly. In this setting, people with the same incomes would support different welfare measures due to their differences in spirit. The resulting structure of welfare programs would thus depend on the relative influence of generous and miserly sentiments over the relevant budgetary processes.

It is also possible that people of equal generosity could support different welfare measures due to differing beliefs about the relevant parameters of human nature. Where some might believe people to be naturally provident and hard working, others might believe the reverse and believe instead that the road to success runs through the fear of failure. The former belief could be captured by the hypothesis that changes in welfare payments would have little effect on such variables as the supply of effort, whereas the latter belief would support a hypothesis that increased support through welfare induces significant reductions in personal responsibility for self-support. In this case, equally generous spirits would generate different degrees of support for various welfare measures.

Such issues as these might be discussed in academic seminars, but legislative hearings are not academic seminars even though academics offer testimony at such hearings. But testimony is also offered by many other people as well, with many of these actually representing various governmental agencies. Among the remaining suppliers of testimony, many of those represent various agencies and organizations with specific interests in the legislation being discussed. Indeed, such agencies and organizations often contribute much to the writing of the very legislation being considered. Hearings and testimony are dominated by people who plausibly have relatively high demands for the object of the hearing. This is not surprising. To register opposition does not yield any kind of anticipated appropriable return, and so the process operates in an asymmetrical fashion that is quite unlike that which informs the spirit of a parlor game. Making legislation has features that bear some resemblance to a parlor game, but it surely bears a much fuller resemblance to a sausage factory.

## VIII.   SOME AGONISTICS ABOUT EXCESS BURDEN

Conventional fiscal analysis makes heavy use of the excess burden of taxation. Excess burden is part of the conventional public finance program of taxes being uncaused insertions from outside the society. A fiscal despot seeks to rearrange people's economic lives, and to do so in a kindly fashion. This is the problem setting for optimal taxation. Taxes have burdens represented by the amount of revenue that is transferred from market to political use, but they also have excess burdens that are represented by the utility losses people experience as they respond to tax-induced changes in market prices. In such a framework, it seems perhaps only natural to think in terms of trying to minimize the excess burdens that accompany quasi-divine intervention into a society.

The question that must be asked, however, is how does a tax come to arise in the first place? A tax cannot simply be imposed, it must be chosen, and there are two categories of process through which a tax might be chosen, with each holding different implications for excess burden. In terms of Figure 6.1, Primo, Secunda and Terzo might support a political enterprise to construct a project to eradicate mosquitoes from a nearby swamp. Doing this represents a distinct improvement over the alternative. There is a burden associated with the tax, and this burden is represented by the reduced volume of market output that can be purchased because mosquito protection is being purchased instead. But there is certainly no excess burden. If anything, there is an excess benefit to the extent that the mosquito protection allows people to attain utility gains.

An alternative setting for taxation would be one where a majority is able to impose costs on a minority. Primo and Secunda might own property in a low-lying area that is prone to flooding, while Terzo lives securely on higher ground. Rather than Primo and Secunda forming a joint venture to protect their property, they use the legislature to force Terzo to contribute to the support of their project. It still makes no sense to speak of the tax as possessing an excess burden for Primo and Secunda, for it is one side of a transaction by which they achieve a more highly desired state of affairs. Terzo, of course, is helping to support a project that he would veto if he could, and so could be thought to bear an excess burden as well. Still, there would be no excess burden in the aggregate, though without unanimity it is impossible to say whether in the aggregate the project represented some type of improvement. It was an improvement for Primo and Secunda, and was not for Terzo, and that is about all there is to be said about the situation.

Once it is recognized that a tax arises out of participation and not out of intervention, claims about excess burden become dubious. A monarch may stand outside the system over which she rules, but there is no such outside position in a democratic polity. A tax cannot be imposed on everyone. At least some people must choose the tax, and must do so because the combination of less market output and more political output generates a higher level of utility for them. Without doubt, taxation also generally involves a good number of people in paying for output they do not value, or value less than the sacrificed market output the tax makes necessary. Those people are burdened directly by the tax, and are burdened again as they rearrange their market conduct in response to the tax extractions imposed on them. Still, there is no readily sensible procedure of aggregation that can yield excess burden. Recalling Dennis Robertson's (1940, p. 25) portrayal of

John Maynard Keynes's liquidity preference formulation of a theory of interest, excess burden is like a grin without a cat.

Excess burden is an artifact of the conventional presumption that the state is some outside agent that intervenes at will into market-based relationships. What is now called the 'Laffer Curve' reflects the same orientation of an alien state that intervenes in an economy. Figure 6.5 describes a simple Laffer relationship. So long as the tax rate is less than $T_{MAX}$, such as illustrated in the vicinity of A, an increase in the tax rate will generate increased revenue. If the tax rate exceeds $T_{MAX}$, however, as illustrated by region B, a further increase in the tax rate will reduce the amount of revenue collected. The conceptual experiment to which Figure 6.5 pertains is one where government arbitrarily intervenes in the market square by increasing the tax rate. Market participants subsequently respond to the tax increase. Revenues may either rise or fall, depending on whether the initial situation was more like A or more like B in Figure 6.5. The tax increase is an uncaused cause of subsequent market reaction.

This formulation, along with its excess burden cousin, is surely dubious once it is recognized that taxes are not exogenous shocks from outside the economy but rather emerge from inside it. Once the emergent character of taxation is acknowledged, it seems clear that tax rates are always at what is portrayed as $T_{MAX}$ in Figure 6.5. The members of the legislature seek to do as much profitable business as they can, and to do that business they must

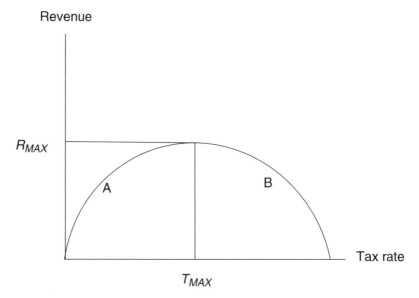

*Figure 6.5    Revenue–rate relationship*

generate complex connections between political enterprises and sources of revenue. The legislature and its programs is the size it is and not some larger size because the members of the legislature were not able to generate any additional profitable business connections. And it is not of smaller size because to reach that smaller size would require members of the legislature to fail to respond to profit-seeking opportunities. What keeps taxes from rising still higher is the politically generated force of opposition to yet higher taxes. What keeps the legislature from doing yet more business is competition from other enterprises within society.

## IX. PUBLIC DEBT AND THE INTERMEDIARY STATE

To this point, the treatment of budgetary bridging has assumed that the revenues that are transferred to political enterprises are raised from taxes extracted currently from the population. While taxation is the prevalent method of public finance, loans are used as well. The standard treatment of public debt in the theory of public finance likewise follows the presumption that the state exists outside the economy and intervenes in it. The state is thus conceptualized as an acting entity whose tax interventions impose excess burdens and whose appetite sometimes requires it to borrow to finance its wants. Indeed, there is a literature on sovereign debt that construes public debt from the standpoint of reputation and credibility.[11] The questions raised in this literature concern such things as how a sovereign might make credible commitments to creditors when she can always choose to default on her debt obligations.

Yet public debt within a democratically-organized polity does not represent a liability to some particular entity called the state. A monarch of old could become indebted but a modern democratic state cannot, for it simply occupies an intermediary position within a complex of debtor–creditor relationships, with the precise nature of those relationships to be worked out in future years. Once we recognize that the state is not an acting entity but an intermediary that bridges people who have enterprises for which they are seeking support on one side of the budget and people who have the means to support those enterprises on the other side, public debt takes on a different character. A legislature whose appropriations exceed the amount of taxes collected authorizes an issue of debt to meet the gap between appropriations and revenues, thus generating public debt. But who is it that is indebted?

To speak of a monarch's debt is a truth that is equivalent to speaking of personal debt. To speak of a democratic state as being indebted, however, is to speak metaphorically. There are two ways that this relationship whereby public debt is created can be construed, neither of which involves the state as some indebted entity. One way approaches public debt from the perspective of politically sponsored enterprises. Those enterprises receive in the aggregate more appropriations from the legislature than current legislative commitments regarding current tax liability warrant. Those enterprises are thus borrowing against future revenues, which they will repay to the legislature in future years by effectively accepting lower appropriations. In those future years, part of the legislature's appropriation to political enterprises would thus be returned to the legislature to allow debt redemption.

The alternative orientation is that taxpayers support higher appropriations to political enterprises, except that many of them would rather borrow to finance those payments than reduce their current consumption or liquidate assets. Once again, the legislature acts as an intermediary, in this case to organize loans to taxpayers rather than to political enterprises. The net result is the same in either case: the state is simply acting as a financial intermediary and is not itself an entity that is incurring debt.

With respect to aggregate accounting, public debt necessarily conforms to Ricardian equivalence (Barro 1974). This equivalence is a matter of the simple arithmetic of double-entry accounting. Hence, as an accounting identity at the aggregate level, the amount of debt incurred is equal to the present value of the future taxes required to amortize the debt. An identity that pertains to aggregate accounting, however, has no particular significance for actual budgetary processes. It would be different if at the time public debt was created people were given specific liabilities for their future taxes. Under such an arrangement, each individual taxpayer would both pay tax liability for the current year and receive an assignment of future liabilities to repay debt that was also incurred in the current year.

Under such an illusion-free regime, the cost of public debt would rise because it would be riskier for people to buy public debt. Issues of public debt sell at lower interest rates than issues of corporate debt, and this would surely change if debt liability was made explicit by assigning it expressly as it was incurred. The lower rate of interest on public debt does not indicate less uncertainty in the returns of political enterprises, but rather represents the shift in the locus of uncertainty to taxpayers under unlimited liability. A project sponsored by a political enterprise might have been supported under conditions that involved cost projections of $2 billion. Should that cost subsequently rise to $3 billion, it is not the sponsors of the enterprise who bear this loss, in contrast to the situation with market-based enterprises. That loss is rather borne by taxpayers, as distributed by existing tax institutions, since taxpayers ultimately stand in the capacity of being forced investors under conditions of unlimited liability.

To speak of taxpayers is to speak in aggregative terms, but aggregates can't act. Within the United States, for instance, over 90 percent of collections of personal income tax by the federal government come from the top 50 percent of taxpayers. When this observation is added to the exemption from tax liability of millions of eligible voters, it is easy to see that a majority of the voting age population could be nearly free from income tax liability. Even among those who do bear tax liability, public debt can affect different people differently. One margin of consideration is age. Consider a comparison between bearing a $1000 tax liability now and supporting a debt issue that incurs an annual liability in perpetuity of $100, assuming a discount rate of 10 percent. In this example, the arithmetic of Ricardian equivalence holds. For someone who expects to pay taxes for only ten years, the present value of borrowing is only $614, whereas it is $978 for someone who expects to pay taxes for 40 years. Differences in age can thus promote different orientations toward public debt. To be sure, one can always posit intergenerational altruism to restore Ricardian equivalence. But there are many people without heirs and many others who clearly don't care much for their heirs. And what matters in any case is how interactions among differently situated people play out.

## NOTES

1. Military contracting to provide major weapons systems is a major exception, and in the American context at least, officials from the Department of Defense participate heavily in firm management with respect to those systems.
2. United Way is a national network of locally governed organizations that work to create positive change in local communities. Common focus areas are helping children and youth succeed, improving access to health care, promoting self-sufficiency and strengthening families. See http://national.unitedway.org.
3. See, for instance, the essays collected in David Tuerck (1978).
4. With respect to budgetary bridges, the United Way's budgetary process stands somewhere between these two poles. Its revenues come from individual donations and are appropriated typically among a hundred or so charitable enterprises.
5. For a formulation in terms of political and fiscal rules and the trade-off between them, see Buchanan (1967). For a treatment of budgetary bridges, see Marlow and Orzechowski (1997), and for a related analysis of parliamentary appropriation see Kraan (1996).
6. I have used majority rule simply because of its practical prominence. Buchanan and Tullock (1962) advanced a strong argument in support of unanimity as a benchmark, and in so doing extended Knut Wicksell's (1958 [1896]) argument in this respect. The relationship between Wicksell and Buchanan and Tullock is examined in Wagner (1988).
7. On agenda control in particular, see Shepsle and Weingast (1981). On more general issues concerning the ability of fiscal institutions to affect budgetary outcomes, see Poterba (1996) and Crain and Crain (1998).

8.   Susan Hansen (1983) examines tax politics from a similar orientation.
9.   Bismarck also once observed that 'Politics is the art of preventing people from taking part in affairs that properly concern them'.
10.  For some perceptive treatments of fiscal history in a generally similar vein, see Sidney Ratner (1942), Elliot Brownlee (1996, 2006), Charles Adams (1993), Margaret Levi (1988) and Carolyn Webber and Aaron Wildavsky (1986).
11.  For a sample, see Bulow and Rogoff (1989), Calvo (1988) and Grossman and Van Huyck (1988).

# 7. Federalism, polycentric polities and open societies

Up to this point in the book, a democratically constituted public square has been treated as containing a single parliamentary assembly wherein politically-sponsored intermediation occurs between political entrepreneurs and citizens. This formulation, however, does not identify the parliamentary assembly as the public square. Rather, that assembly resides within the public square, with participation within the public square, as with the market square, being open to everyone. The public square simply represents our non-solipsistic nature, which leads in various ways to interests in each other's activities, for worse as well as for better. The parliamentary assembly is embedded within the public square but is not itself the public square.[1]

This formulation maps into a world of experience where people are connected with one parliamentary assembly; however, most people in democratically-organized polities experience the world through connections with multiple parliamentary assemblies. People typically face multiple units of fragmented and overlapping governments, each of which has some ability to act without direction from other governments. For instance, within the territory covered by any particular national government, a number of provincial or state governments may also exist, as may more local units of government as counties, cities and prefectures. There are also numerous governments that have been constituted for particular purposes, and yet operate independently of all other units of government. In the United States, for instance, the most significant of these other units of government are school districts. But there also exist units of government to deal with flood control, transportation planning, parks, urban redevelopment, mosquito control and subdivision governance, among numerous other types of specialized forms of government.

The institutional organization of public squares has a polycentric character. This chapter starts by comparing compound republics and simple republics as ideal types. The public square in a simple republic contains a single parliamentary assembly. A compound republic (Ostrom 1987) contains multiple parliamentary assemblies, each of which has spheres of independent action over budgetary and regulatory matters. A compound republic thus entails what might be called double (or even multiple) jeopardy in taxation and regulation. In the face of this double jeopardy, it might seem paradoxical that federalism is typically characterized as an organizational arrangement that promotes liberty over servitude (Dye 2001). If Mark Twain was right in asserting that 'no man is safe when the legislature is in session', it is reasonable to wonder what basis there is for thinking that safety is strengthened by multiplying the number of legislatures that a person faces. Whether federalism's form of double jeopardy is a blessing or a curse, and to whom, is surely a topic that requires examination. Competition is a process of securing coordination, but it also produces conflict, and this chapter explores the operation of competition and conflict within a federated public square. In pursuing these matters, particular attention is given to the institutional environment within which participants within the various parliamentary assemblies inside a federalist polity pursue their plans, for it is through the pursuit of such plans that the actual patterns of federalist governance emerge. The federalist form of double jeopardy can work in different ways, depending on those institutional arrangements.

## I. COMPOUND REPUBLICS AND SIMPLE REPUBLICS AS IDEAL TYPES

Up to this point I have worked with a simple conceptualization in terms of a market square and a public square to denote two arenas for the organization of enterprises within a society, with the public square serving as the source for the phenomena of public finance. Within this conceptualization, someone who wants to secure support for some enterprise within the public square must look to the duly constituted parliamentary assembly for support. The particular configuration of enterprises within the public square will emerge out of the budgetary processes that pertain to that parliamentary assembly. This situation where a single parliamentary assembly is the locus for organization within the public square comprises a simple republic.

A simple republic represents a point of monopoly within the public square. To be sure, a simple republic presents a different form of monopoly from a monarchy because a parliamentary assembly is a network of relationships and not a person. There can be plenty of competition among people who are attempting to secure support for politically sponsored enterprises (Breton 1996). The success of those competitive efforts, however, will be adjudicated within a single parliamentary assembly that will itself necessarily have an oligarchic character (De Jouvenal 1961). The working properties of this assembly will be conditioned by several features of its network of relationships and connections. For one thing, the size of the assembly matters. An assembly with five members can plausibly act in concert; an assembly with 500 members cannot. When assemblies reach the size where formal rules of parliamentary procedure are necessary to conduct business, parliamentary outcomes become decreasingly likely to reflect the coherence associated with an organization and take on the characteristic features of an order.

The manner in which people acquire membership in a parliament will also matter, and in several respects. A parliament where all members are selected in a single at-large election will tend to yield less diversity in orientation among members than in one where selection is through subsets within the society. The use of subsets is most commonly done by geography through creating distinct electoral districts for selecting members. There are, however, many other ways that such selection among subsets could be achieved: occupation, age, gender, religion and wealth are five such examples among many that could be used and have been used historically. A parliament where all members are selected in the same election will likewise tend to generate more commonality in orientation than one where the membership is staggered across multiple elections, because with staggered elections there will be some variation across elections in the identities of voters and in the sentiments that happen to be in play at the time. It also matters whether the electoral system tends to generate two parties or multiple parties. Furthermore, a system that has such an independently elected executive as a president will have yet different operating characteristics (Moe and Caldwell 1994).

However a parliamentary assembly might be selected for a simple republic, that assembly still possesses some position of monopoly over the organization of activity within the public square. Within the market square, someone who has an idea for an enterprise can take that idea to a multiple number of independent possible sponsors. In this setting, an initial negative response might be followed subsequently by a positive response from someone else. There is no particular person within the market square whose participation is necessary for an enterprise to go forward. Within a simple republic, however, some such veto points may exist, depending on the parliamentary rules that operate within the assembly. An arrangement where legislation must pass through a committee and where the Chair of the committee can set the agenda for action possesses such a veto point. In contrast, an assembly that is guided by some open-access process of agenda formation, whereby any member of the legislature can introduce a proposal, will not contain any such veto point. Large-scale parliamentary assemblies work with veto points.

An entrepreneur might seek to sponsor an educational enterprise that would teach martial arts and self-defense in schools. This proposed enterprise is advanced as a new offering within the educational activities currently being sponsored by the parliamentary assembly. Had that idea been taken to schools organized within the market square, there would exist no veto point, so that some schools might accept the proposal while others reject it. Within the market square, the new idea will tend to gain acceptance if the managers of schools think that the value of their enterprises will increase, which means that they think in turn that parents and students will value this offering more highly than they valued whatever would be displaced by this new offering.

The situation is not so simple and direct in the public square of a simple republic. Most significantly, monetary calculation is not directly possible. There is no net worth for the enterprise, so there is no way that reasoning can occur to compare some current net worth with some projected net worth subsequent to the entrepreneurial change. Economic calculation is limited to that of a barter-type economy. Some people might say they like the proposal, while others say they don't. Moreover, a veto point might exist within the parliamentary assembly, in which case the entrepreneurial idea might never be given a test. If access to the committee agenda is restricted by the Chair, she will decide the fate of the proposal because she commands a veto point. The fate of the proposal will depend on the rigidity of the overall parliamentary framework. If committees have exclusive jurisdiction and if committee Chairs have something like veto authority, the fate of the proposal will be sealed. This may not be the case if the legislature is more competitively organized or partitioned. In this case, a proposal that was rejected by the Chair of the committee that controls the education agenda might be taken to the Chair of the committee that controls matters dealing with parks and recreation. The Chair there might be interested in the proposal because it offers the prospect of increasing demand outside of school hours. In this case, there are competitive sources of organized activity within the parliamentary assembly that resides in the public square.

In contrast, the public square of a compound republic contains multiple parliamentary assemblies that are able independently to sponsor activity. This describes a situation where any individual receives services from enterprises sponsored by at least two parliamentary assemblies, and perhaps several such assemblies, as well as paying taxes to multiple assemblies. In this instance, an exercise of a veto point within one parliamentary assembly need not end the matter, as the proposal can be taken to a different parliamentary assembly. Hence, a proposal to add martial arts might be supported by some parliamentary assemblies while being rejected by others. A compound republic injects some features of open competition into the organization of enterprises on the public square.

To be sure, the impact of the qualifier 'some' with respect to the openness of competition depends on the ability of some parliamentary assemblies to set conditions for other assemblies. Suppose some schools incorporate martial arts into their curriculums while others reject it. This existence of multiple experiments could set in motion discovery processes for the acquisition of knowledge, as explored in Martti Vihanto (1992). It could also set in motion an effort by some more encompassing unit of government to prevent that experiment. That prevention, moreover, could occur either by refusing to allow any school to introduce martial arts or by requiring all schools to introduce martial arts. Either way, that more encompassing government would have prevented competition on the public square.[2] Furthermore, this restriction on competition can occur through contract as well as through regulation. Suppose, for instance, that the alternative to martial arts is penmanship. By offering grants conditional on penmanship, the encompassing government could achieve an outcome similar to the prohibition of martial arts. A good deal of the revenue to support that grant program, moreover, would undoubtedly have been extracted from people who preferred martial arts to penmanship. That encompassing government, moreover, could also achieve the reverse outcome by offering grant support for martial arts but not penmanship.[3]

## II.   OPEN COMPETITION AND THE FEDERATED PUBLIC SQUARE

Federalism potentially injects competition into the organization of enterprises on the public square, and it does so in two ways. One way is through subdivision. This occurs when a national unit is subdivided into states or provinces, and when states or provinces are subdivided into counties and cities. Competition can also occur through the overlapping of public squares. Cities and states might both provide policing services, with citizens potentially having contact with both categories of policing activity and having the ability along some margins to substitute one source of service for the other.

For federalism to offer the potential for open competition does not imply that federalist arrangements will actually entail such open competition, as the preceding illustration about martial arts and penmanship illustrates. The potential gain that open competition offers, moreover, contains two dimensions. One pertains to the ability of multiple public squares to accommodate different preferences among people. It is possible that the controversy between advocates of martial arts and advocates of penmanship is simply a matter of which type of talent people would like their children to possess. Multiple jurisdictions that are able to act independently of one another will increase the extent to which people are able to secure the curriculum they desire, as noted initially by Charles Tiebout (1956) and as amplified, extended or critiqued in such works as David Bradford and Wallace Oates (1974), Albert Breton and Anthony Scott (1978), Richard Cornes and Todd Sandler (1986), Vernon Henderson (1985) and Wallace Oates (1997).

The other potential gain that open competition offers is the generation of knowledge through experimentation (Bish 1999). To some extent evidence could be collected that would not be available under a uniform curriculum. Even more, the mere ability to introduce local experiments would probably promote innovative effort relative to what would happen if an innovation could not be implemented without some central approval. Some approaches to teaching reading may be more effective than others. While a fair amount of controversy has been framed in terms of such dichotomies as phonics and look-see approaches, the particular materials that are used for teaching reading may also matter for judgments about effectiveness. Once this possibility is recognized, it is easy to see that effectiveness is a concept that entails numerous dimensions. Open competition makes it possible to construct multiple experiments and potentially acquire evidence that would be lost with imposed uniformity. While the evidence collected might not always be easy to distill and discern, no such evidence is collected with imposed uniformity.

Once the public square is organized in compound fashion, questions arise concerning the organization of relationships among enterprises sponsored through different public squares. Enterprises created within the market square generate a vast and dense network of contractual relationships, and we should expect to see the same thing among enterprises established within the public square, as well as among enterprises across the two squares. Yet economic calculation does not proceed so directly and immediately within the public square as it proceeds within the market square. This difference regarding the conditions for calculation creates various differences in the operating characteristics of the two categories of enterprise. Some of these differences relate to economies of scale and scope, while others relate to inter-jurisdictional spillovers.

**Economies of Scale and Scope**

It is often claimed that there is some efficient size for a unit for the provision of some particular service, as reflected by the presumption that average cost is U-shaped. This situation might mean that ordinary policing services are best provided in units that serve between 50 000 and 100 000 people. For smaller or larger jurisdictions, it would be more costly on a per capita basis to provide those police services than it would be for jurisdictions in the efficient size range. If so, it might seem as though smaller jurisdictions should merge and larger jurisdictions should fragment, provided that efficiency is desired. If a police department that served 20 000 residents required $1000 per resident to provide the same service that a police department that served 100 000 residents could provide for $800, there would seem to be mutual gains to be secured by combining jurisdictions.

To secure police services at $800 per resident, however, does not require that the five towns combine to form a single city. This outcome could also be achieved through contractual arrangements whereby some towns purchased a police service from another town (Bish 1971; Bish and Ostrom 1973). A town that would have to pay $1000 per resident for a police service would be able to get that service at lower cost by contracting with another town to provide that service. In this setting, the town would operate as a form of buyers' cooperative that made its purchases from an outside producer rather than producing the service itself.

To be sure, contracting might play out differently in the public square than in the market square. It is easy enough to understand the logic by which four firms in the market square might buy some service from a fifth firm rather than produce that service themselves: they would do so if managers thought this would increase the net worths of their firms. For enterprises organized within the public square, there is no net worth in any but a possibly virtual sense. There are five police chiefs when each town provides its own service, but only one chief is left standing if four of the towns choose to buy a police service from the fifth town. These four former chiefs might now be lieutenants at the same salary as before. Yet their social standing might have fallen, as a lieutenant simply does not command the notice that a chief commands. With typical civil service compensation packages, under which compensation is not tied to any notion of even virtual net worth, these police chiefs might resist such use of contract to attain economies of scale.

It could, of course, be objected that some citizens who are aware of the cost differential might press their case before the town council and successfully overcome resistance by the police chief. As a matter of arithmetic, this possibility is implied by the presumption of a U-shaped cost function. But this is to take the blackboard exercise all too literally. The phenomena of reality rarely appear so starkly clear as to lead everyone to recognize that a police chief is maintaining a force for which residents pay $1000 annually when they could get the same service for $800. For one thing, people have limited capacity for attention and most people wouldn't get involved in such matters. For another thing, the options would rarely be so clear and the magnitudes so large, but would rather involve some range of ambiguity. Perhaps most significantly, the best source of information pertaining to policing services is professionals who work in the area. Whether a police department can secure services more cheaply by buying them from another police department is something that a police professional is in a better position to evaluate than is an ordinary citizen. With residual claimancy, such police professionals have a direct incentive to propose changes in operation that increase net worth, but residual claimancy is absent, or at least greatly weakened, on the public square. The generation of contractual relationships obviously occurs within the public square, but the absence of residual claimacy seems likely to retard the extent of those relationships.

## Inter-jurisdictional Spillovers

An externality arises among some set of enterprises whenever independent action by those individual enterprises generates less aggregate value for them than they could secure through some form of cooperative action. In such a setting we would generally expect to find those enterprises developing various cooperative relationships to secure that additional net worth. For instance, a set of retail enterprises located in proximity to one another might each rely only on metered parking, because by providing free parking for its customers some of that benefit would redound to other stores as customers parked once and visited several stores. The provision of more parking by one store would provide benefits to neighboring stores.

Yet all enterprises might gain by supplying more parking to accommodate customers. There are several ways they might do this in the market square. They could, for instance, form a consortium to provide a parking garage, with participating stores sharing in the cost according to their share in the total volume of validations for parking given to shoppers. Alternatively, they might incorporate that parking garage as a distinct enterprise. Yet again, they might seek to promote an enterprise in the public square that would be constituted as a Civic Development District. This special district would cover a limited, clearly defined territory, and would be chartered to provide parking and related services. It would be financed by a charge on businesses in the area, and would be governed by a Board that was selected by votes weighted by tax payments. Under any of these settings, economic calculation operates pretty directly to promote commercial organization on the market square.

The principle of the matter doesn't change when the enterprise is organized on the public square, though the practice might differ in some instances because of the limits on economic calculation. For example, consider an arrangement whereby several neighboring towns contain parks, with those parks having been established under two distinct institutional arrangements. In one case, these parks have been provided commercially, perhaps as illustrated by a set of Chucky Cheeses[4] that also had outdoor facilities and equipment attached. In the other case, those parks were provided by the town with access open to all comers without charge. Initially, we can assume that each town acts independently in deciding how many parks to create, how to equip them and where to locate them. Those decisions will emerge out of each town's budgetary process. It is reasonable to say that the primary factors that will be reflected in this process will be the valuations residents place on parks, which in turn might include the perceived impact on property values if parks are located nearby.

Within this common formulation, what will not be considered is the value that outside residents place on the parks. For market-based parks of the Chucky Cheese variety, the interest of users is taken into account regardless of the residence of those users. But if a town decision reflects only the interest of town residents, as these are intermediated through the town's budgetary process, the interest of non-residents will be ignored (Oates 1972, 1999). According to normal efficiency standards, the amount of park provision might be too low. According to the standard Paretian conditions, each town will expand its provision of parks until the marginal cost of such provision, as refracted through the town's budgetary process, is equal to the marginal value that town residents place on that provision, as this value is again refracted through the town's budgetary process. What is ignored, by assumption, is the value placed on town parks by residents who live elsewhere, whose valuations would be incorporated in parks of the Chucky Cheese variety.

To describe the setting in this manner sets the stage for asking just why the system of towns doesn't have the same properties as the network of Chucky Cheeses, even in the presence of open access without direct pricing. To a large degree, internet service providers (ISPs) use pairing agreements which have the effect of expanding network capacity without transferring revenues among ISPs. In this case, someone who connects with one ISP, and who pays a fee to that ISP, will sometimes end up traveling over a network provided by another ISP. This is the same situation as a resident of one town making use of a park provided by another town. The provision of parks through the public square is not formally any different from the provision of internet connections. If there is any difference, it resides in the different institutional and organizational arrangements within which the different services are provided. When parks are organized in the public square, in contrast to their being organized in Chucky Cheese fashion, the monetary basis for economic calculation is restricted even though such economic categories as value and profit remain. If the officers of park enterprises are paid through the civil service without any connection to enterprise net worth, agreements among governments are less likely to be concluded. This doesn't mean that agreements will never be concluded, only that the infirmities of economic calculation on the public square make those agreements less likely to be reached.

On the market square, a park executive will generally be alert to opportunities for increasing the net worth of the enterprise. On the public square, there is no net worth to be increased, at least in any direct fashion. In place of monetary calculation, the currencies that are present include such things as acclaim and blame. A manager might receive acclaim for innovation in the provision of equipment or services. Or he might receive blame for uninspired services and poorly maintained equipment. While these reputational effects can influence the human capital of park managers, they involve a level of ambiguity that is not present in the market square.[5] To claim that fragmentation creates problems of coordination, as exemplified by claims about externality, is not so much an indictment of fragmentation as it is an indictment of the absence of transferable ownership and the weakened or ambiguous calculative powers that this brings in its wake.

## III.   GENERATING MAPS VERSUS ASSIGNING FUNCTIONS

It is common for economists to approach a federalist form of government through some notion of optimal or efficient assignment of functions. In this literature, federalism is taken to be roughly a synonym for administrative decentralization. Consider a simple two-layer model of government, as illustrated by a national–provincial framework, though it would be easy enough to incorporate additional layers as well. The customary approach would ask which functions should be provided at the national level and which at the provincial level.

One significant consideration in this literature has been economies of scale. Indeed, a substantial literature has been generated through efforts to do such things as estimate cost functions for various governmental services as part of an effort to arrive at some empirically relevant notion of an optimal city size. This concern with cost and size is joined in the literature with a concern about the geographical range over which a service provided by a particular jurisdiction exerts its effects. What results in this literature is a series of relatively straightforward applications of externality theory. For instance, a locality might provide education for its resident children. One simple economic calculus that could be brought to bear on this situation is a median voter model, wherein the amount of education supplied is that where the median voter's marginal valuation equals marginal cost. The literature on education, at least since Burton Weisbrod (1964), claims that an undersupply of local education will result. Not everyone who is educated in a local jurisdiction will remain there. Some of the benefits from local spending will spill over to other jurisdictions. Even in a model where there is no net migration and so no net income effects, substitution effects will remain to drive the conclusion of undersupply.

This type of argument is widely used to support programs whereby higher levels of government offer various forms of grants in aid to lower levels. What results in any case is dissolution of the separation of functions that came out of formulations in terms of economies of scale, and its replacement by a framework whereby multiple units of government are involved in the provision of the same service. This entire analytical program has developed with reference to underlying notions of optimal assignments or allocations of activities and functions. One line of questioning, driven primarily by considerations of cost, would ask such questions as whether schools should be provided by localities, provinces or nations. Another line of questioning, driven primarily by considerations of externality, would ask how the responsibility for schooling should be divided and distributed among local, provincial and national governments. In either case, the theoretical effort envisions some monopoly-like assignment problem to be solved. The map that might be drawn to describe the provision of services would thus be constructed through some effort at systems design. This brings us back once again to hierarchical governance.

What would a social-theoretic approach to governance look like when it comes to mapping the activities of the various governments that populate our societal landscape? This alternative analytical enterprise would seek to explain the actual patterns of activity among the various public squares. There is no planning office that assigns activities to particular units of government. Actual patterns of activity emerge spontaneously through the budgetary processes of the various jurisdictions, and are not assigned by anyone.[6] One thing to be said about economies of scale is that they are largely irrelevant to the size of jurisdictions, as was noted above. Three units of government that are each one-third the size of some reputed optimum size can gain the advantages of larger size through cooperative action in any number of ways. One jurisdiction may produce the service, and the other two jurisdictions might contract with the first jurisdiction to purchase the service. Economies of scale should generally be irrelevant to the size of governments, once it is recognized that it is possible to distinguish between two capacities of governments: one is their capacity as articulators of demand for services; the other is their capacity as producers of services. Once the possibility of contracting among governments is opened up, the production of a service and the articulation of demands for that service can be separated among enterprises within the public square.

One interesting feature of the cost-based claims about a generally optimal size range for governments is that population growth should bring about an increase in the number of governments. If an efficient size serves 100 000 people, an area with one million people would be fragmented into ten governments, if the requirements of efficiency prevailed. Should that population subsequently increase to two million, the number of governments should increase to 20. For this to happen, procedures would have to exist that would allow part of an existing government to secede and form a new government. We should expect to find increasing numbers of governments just as we find increasing numbers of firms. The historical record, however, has mostly been a decrease in the number of governments, at least within national boundaries, as distinct from the proliferation of nations within the United Nations. Within the market square, firms are continually spinning off part of their activities into new firms. These decisions are governed by conjectures about value under alternative organizational arrangements. The fiscal literature on economies of scale would seem thereby to predict that growing cities would occasionally subdivide to secure economies in production.

That we do not observe such subdivision suggests two possible directions of inquiry. One direction entails the possibility that the literature on economies of scale is wrong. Yet numerous people have contributed to this literature, and the general character of its findings seems robust. To be sure, the U-shape might be relatively asymmetrical, with the declining portion being steeper than the rising portion. This possibility would not deny the puzzle about the failure to observe any fragmentation of cities, but it would suggest that the gain to taxpayers from the fragmentation of large cities is less than the gain from the consolidation of small cities. Still, a puzzle remains to be uncovered. The number of governmental units, at least within the United States, has been undergoing continual decline for the past century. All the while, the number of commercial enterprises has been increasing steadily.

The other direction of inquiry would seek to explain and characterize the operation of the processes that generate the underlying map of governments, seeking to locate the features of those processes that operate so differently from the way they operate for commercial enterprises. Consider the sharply contrasting differences in the scale of governments between Switzerland and the United States. Switzerland has 26 cantons and a population of around seven million. The United States in 1790, in the first census after its founding, had 14 states and four million people. The governmental scale of Switzerland today is about the same as that of the United States in 1790. To restore that scale for today's population would require the United States to contain nearly 1000 states. Moreover,

Switzerland has procedures that enable the splitting of cantons through secession, which occurred within the canton of Jura in the 1970s.

An increase in the scale of governments must confer advantages on some people that exceed their share of the rising per capita costs that accompanies such increases in scale. Otherwise, we would observe increases and not decreases in the number of governments. With respect to cities, for instance, expansions in city size beyond 250 000 or so must confer advantages to subsets of people who are politically influential that exceed their share of the rising costs that accompany that expansion. There are a variety of considerations relating to bureaucracy and agency that might be brought to bear on an effort to do this. To reside on the upward part of an average cost function implies the collection of rents somewhere, rents that would be lost through subdivision. There seems to be very little effort to achieve subdivision among governments, though it does happen from time to time. Such subdivision seems more common when ethnic, linguistic or religious separation is involved.

The economic forces that govern the sizes of commercial enterprises clearly do not apply to political enterprises. For commercial enterprises, those forces are grounded in residual claimacy and transferable ownership. A failure by a commercial enterprise to spin off an operation that would have a higher market value if organized as an independent firm would cause direct pecuniary losses for all owners. Secession within a commercial enterprise is a form of divorce that involves gains from separation. Rents that are generated through separation are captured through changes in the aggregate share prices of the affected enterprises.

There are no direct share prices for cities and other governmental units. Consider a simple illustration where a city of 500 000 could be operated less expensively by $100 per resident if it subdivided into two cities of 250 000. The aggregate cost saving would be $50 million per year. If this setting pertained to a commercial enterprise and if the market rate of capitalization were 10 percent, the aggregate value of the enterprise would rise by $500 million. This amount is the limiting value of the capital gain that subdivision would generate, with the distribution of that gain being proportioned according to relative shareholdings.

With cities, there is no direct capitalization into share prices, though there is an indirect capitalization into real estate prices. Transactions in real estate, however, are orders of magnitude more costly than transactions in corporate ownership. The direct cost of transferring ownership in real estate runs in the range of 6 or 7 percent of the value transferred. An additional element of cost comes about through the differential tax treatment of mortgage interest and rental payments, particularly if becoming a tenant is the alternative to a transfer of housing ownership. Furthermore, voting rights cannot be sold separately from the rights to cash flow with respect to the ownership of city assets, whereas such separation is possible for corporate ownership.

There is a quite striking difference in economic organization between commercial and industrial real estate on the one hand and residential real estate on the other. For commercial and industrial real estate, unified ownership of large parcels is the rule, with most occupants being tenants. For residential real estate, fragmented ownership is the rule, with there being relatively few tenants in most cities. Moreover, residential tenants maintain their voting rights to participate in decision making, whereas commercial and industrial tenants do not have voting rights. These various differences all seem to operate to create a sharper focal point on aggregate value maximization for both commercial firms and the operation of commercial and industrial real estate than they create for cities and residential real estate.

The numerical illustration given above might well play out differently with changes in the mix of commercial, industrial and residential property, as well as the composition of residential property between owner occupancy and rental occupancy. Capitalization operates directly on commercial and industrial property, works only indirectly on owner-occupied residential property, and works practically not at all on renter-occupied residential property because the owner of that property does not control the aggregate voting rights of its inhabitants. Where some people face an economic calculation based on a comparison of capital values, others face one based on rental streams. Even the capitalized component is easily exaggerated. It is a conjectured gain, based upon some hypothesis that the city could be operated less expensively after subdivision. People may hold different conjectures, and there is no direct way for those conjectures to be tested through actions and choices.

This brings us back once again to the absence of the common focal point of residual claimacy. The higher cost of operation may be a source of gain to some people, as a vehicle by which dividends are paid for control over political enterprises. If units of government do not subdivide to secure cost savings, there are three possible paths of explanation. One path is that those claims about cost savings are wrong. A second is that they are there, but existing institutional arrangements render them difficult to see and capture. Both of these paths of explanation treat everyone as alike in sharing a common focal point. A third path would invoke differences in focal points, as illustrated by the possibility that higher costs for some are the instrument by which cash flow is distributed to others.

The empirical challenge for this third path is to illuminate the ways that such cash flow might be distributed in the incomplete agency settings in which governments operate. Let me give a couple of possible illustrations before moving on. Suppose the city labor force can be divided into administrative staff and direct service providers, with the ratio of administrative staff to service providers rising with city size. This would correspond to an increase in the layers of bureaucracy as units of government became larger. It would also translate into increasing pay for administrative personnel who now have larger staffs to supervise, as well as probably into larger and better equipped and furnished office buildings. In a small school, a principal might also teach. In a large school, she might have four assistant principals to buffer her from students and teachers. Alternatively, a larger city might create a downtown park and sponsor weekend festivals to attract people to cultivate patronage for merchants located there. In the absence of residual claimacy in conjunction with the ubiquitous presence of cash flows generated by asset combinations, the capture of those cash flows becomes more complex, akin to the greater complexity of a barter economy over a money economy.

## IV.   CONFLICT AND COORDINATION WITHIN THE COMPOUND REPUBLIC

A simple republic can give rise to problems of opportunism and strategic hold-up when immobile assets present. A simple republic might be constituted under some principle of non-discrimination in taxation, which might initially be thought to require that all property be taxed at the same rate.[7] People locate in that jurisdiction in the presence of those constitutive rules of fiscal conduct. At some later time, the legislature enacts a measure that incorporates tax discrimination among properties. One approach to discrimination would be to create a flat exemption that would apply to all properties. A second approach would be to make the size of exemption vary directly with the number of years for which the present owner had owned that property. These two approaches to exemption would differ in the patterns of gains and losses they created, and so would yet other ways of injecting tax exemption. In one fashion or another, the introduction of tax exemption lowers tax liability for some people while raising it for others.

It is easy enough to see how some such discriminatory measures might be enacted within a simple republic. For instance, suppose the members of the town council are elected by district, with a majority of the council elected from districts where average property values are below the average for the town. It is easy enough to understand how a proposal to create a flat exemption from the tax would gain majority support within the town council, as this would allow a majority of residents to transfer some of what would otherwise have been their tax payments on to taxpayers with properties of above-average value. It is also easy enough to see how a proposal to create an exemption that varied directly with the length of time someone had been a resident of the town might be enacted. Longstanding residents are more likely to secure election to town councils than are relative newcomers. A proposal to give a longevity-based exemption could thus also possibly gain majority support within a town council, and could well be supported by longstanding residents regardless of their particular property values.

Such measures as these which break with the principle of non-discrimination are, of course, manifestations of the general recognition that the best tax is always one that someone else pays. People might have chosen to move into that jurisdiction when non-discrimination is in play, only subsequently to find themselves on the short side of the tax discrimination that tax exemption creates. It could even be the case that non-discrimination was a principle that was given constitutional status, as against being simply a longstanding convention of tax practice that has been suddenly overturned. In the light of this constitutional status for non-discrimination, it might seem as though a taxpayer could claim a fiscal damage from the subsequent tax discrimination. But to whom would such a taxpayer complain, and to whom would he address a request for remedial action? Within the context of a simple republic, the petition for redress must be addressed approximately to the same people who created the program of tax discrimination. The qualifier 'approximately' is added because it is unlikely that the town council would hear complaints *en banc*, though it certainly could within the framework of a simple republic. If it did handle taxpayer complaints this way, the taxpayer's case would surely be hopeless.

That complaint is more likely to be taken to some judicial forum, and there are many ways in which these can be constituted. Within the framework of a simple republic, however, jurists will operate within the same territory as politicians, will often be selected by politicians, will receive appropriations from politicians, and will require the cooperation of politicians in having judicial rulings executed. There may be differences from what would happen if town councils heard complaints, but those differences would surely generally be subtle. Within a simple republic, the separation among legislative, executive and judicial authority is unlikely to have much muscle behind it. A resident might file a complaint against the discriminatory tax. The court will have been appointed by the same legislature that enacted the change in tax regime. If so, that complaint is unlikely to go far. And suppose the court does rule in favor of the taxpayer. Even so, there is no necessity for the executive branch to abide by the court's ruling. The tax collection authority of the executive branch could seize the property for failure to pay tax. The court could do nothing about this because the executive branch wields the policing powers, and orders from the court can be executed only with the concurrence of the executive. Constitutional enforcement within a simple republic depends on a particular type of virtue that would tame the exercise of power, for in a simple republic there is no competing source of power (Wagner 1987, 1993).

It can potentially be different with a compound republic because of the presence of overlapping jurisdictions. In this setting, a relatively new resident could complain to a more encompassing jurisdiction about the violation of what had been constitutionally limited taxing authority. A complaint about a town or county, for instance, could be taken before a state or provincial court. If the principle that people should not be judges in their own causes is extended to corporate bodies, this principle can only be instantiated within a compound republic (Ostrom 1987, 1991). A compound republic opens avenues of contestability about the actions of any particular government that would not be possible within a simple republic.

In a compound republic, at least at sub-federal levels, disputes about the propriety of legislative action within one jurisdiction can be taken to a body constituted within some other jurisdiction. Hence, a complaint against a town can be taken to a county, and a complaint against a county can be taken to a state body. Likewise, a complaint against a state body can be taken to a federal body. To be sure, federalism entails an asymmetry, in that complaints about a federal body cannot be taken outside that body. Symmetry in this respect would require something like an ability to file complaints against federal actions with appropriate bodies at less encompassing levels of governance. Indeed, the original American Constitution recognized this situation, and looked for redress of this asymmetry through the 11th Amendment, which reflected the principle of nullification; this is examined by William Niskanen (1978). In the presence of this constitutional asymmetry, federalist processes can operate to increase the overall size of public squares within a compound republic due to, among other things, the ability of the federal government to organize collusive conduct among public squares.

## V.   TAX COMPETITION AND FISCAL EXTERNALITIES

Charles Tiebout (1956) asserts that there is an analogy between a metropolitan area that contains a large number of local governments and the standard economic model of a competitive industry as likewise containing a large number of producers. That paper has grown to such urban legend status that any reference to competitive jurisdictions invokes the notion of the Tiebout Model, as illustrated by George Zodrow (1983). Tiebout's original exposition was starkly simple, and was put together expressly to emphasize the similarities between a multiplicity of local governments and a competitive industry. Governments were thus assimilated to retail stores. Each government would provide a bundle of services that it thought would attract residents. The central animating idea behind Tiebout's formulation was that the existence of competitive options that is regarded as the central feature of a competitive market carries over to local governments as well.

There subsequently arose an extensive literature that has sought to investigate the similarities and differences between a competitive industry and a fragmented system of local government. Local governments are not expressly organized as profit-seeking firms, and much attention has been given to exploring what differences this might make (Sonstelie and Portney 1978; Boudreaux and Holcombe 1989). This gets into such matters as whether political processes are important to some notion of an efficient Tiebout equilibrium (Epple and Zelnitz 1981), or whether the entrepreneurial creation of localities will entail the creation of constitutive structures that will induce local governments thereafter to act as if they were profit-maximizing firms (Henderson 1985).

One strand of this literature portrays such competition as plagued by a potential 'race to the bottom'. In this regard, it has even been claimed that a nation that has a tax rate that is much below average comprises a tax haven. To be sure, a haven commonly denotes a place of shelter, such as Anne Frank was given in Amsterdam in 1942. But as portrayed by certain conceptual formulations, a tax shelter is debilitating and not protecting. What remains to be explored, though, is precisely for whom and in what respect a tax shelter might be debilitating.[8] A cameralist land that generated its revenues in Disney World fashion through its operation of enterprises would be a tax haven to be closed down and not an experiment to be emulated.[9] Some people and organizations have even wondered whether the time has come to create some form of global tax organization to help combat tax shelters.

The customary claims about tax competition can be illustrated by a simple desert-and-mall model. Two adjacent states are initially equal in all relevant respects. They have the same population and income, and their patterns of taxing and spending are the same. Among other things, each imposes a tax on retail sales and at the same rate. This is a stable equilibrium with no tendency for people to cross the border to shop. Into this serene equilibrium, suppose one of the states lowers its tax on retail sales. This tax reduction creates some incentive for people from the higher tax state to cross the border to shop. Moreover, the greater the tax saving the greater will be the distance they will travel to do so. Speaking metaphorically, the outcome is a thriving retail mall on the low tax side of the border and a retail desert on the other side. Aggregate tax collections have risen in the lower tax state and fallen in the higher tax state. More than this, combined tax collections across both states will have fallen. The tax reduction has done nothing to affect the aggregate budget set, and after the tax reduction people are spending more to travel to the more distant mall. With an increase in the aggregate amount spent on transportation, the aggregate amount of tax collections must fall.

This fall in aggregate tax collections is often characterized as a fiscal externality, typically in the light of a presumption that some measure of social welfare varies directly with total tax revenue. Tax harmonization is often advanced as a remedy for hypothesized fiscal externalities. The common treatment in this respect views governments as individuals, which sets up a framework where tax competition is mutually destructive. It also presents no good reason why taxes are what they are, or why they change.

Suppose we start with a set of what we might characterize as Wicksellian jurisdictions. Each unit of government provides services that its residents desire, and at prices they are willing to pay. Budgetary decisions about taxing and spending are made consensually. One jurisdiction might have a larger budget than the other, but this will not induce any residents to move to the other, lower tax jurisdiction. For taxes to exert independent effects on location, it is necessary to sever the direct connection between taxing and spending. Modern revenue systems are certainly non-Wicksellian, in that the bridge between revenues and expenditures is formal and implicit, and not substantive and explicit. Suppose both states were to finance their activities by taxes on retail sales, with residents of one jurisdiction preferring more collective provision than the other. In this setting, some residents of the higher tax jurisdiction will have some incentive to do their shopping in the jurisdiction with the lower tax rate. As this happens, residents of the higher tax jurisdiction will find their ability to satisfy their demands falling while residents of the lower tax jurisdiction will be able to secure tax rebates made possible by the cross-border shopping.

But what message might we draw from such models as this? If the use of a retail sales tax is held sacrosanct, there is some merit to claims about fiscal externalities. But why is the retail sales tax held sacrosanct? Perhaps it is there out of tradition and inertia. Perhaps it might have encountered fewer competitive problems in times when people walked or rode bicycles than when they drive cars and shop over the internet. Perhaps what we are witnessing is the lack of creativity and a weakness of enterprising spirit among governments that is brought on by the easy recourse to guns instead of handshakes as a way of doing business. Disney World and Hyatt the Hotel, among numerous other examples, have found ways to create contractual arrangements that provide items of collective consumption that its various customers and clients desire. Would Disney World or Hyatt the Hotel have been so creative in their contractual forms and pricing programs had they had the ability to use guns to collect taxes? Perhaps the ability to exercise the martial faculties, one of which involves the collection of taxes, substitutes for the ability to exercise the commercial and contractual faculties, which include the creation of commercially successful enterprises and contractual forms.

A specific form of claim about fiscal externality is the widely prevalent claim that central cities are placed at a competitive disadvantage by the suburbs that surround them. This claim stems from a recognition that the weighted average pattern of movement is one that goes from suburb to city in the morning and from city to suburb in the evening. The most common pattern is one where people live in the suburbs, and commute to work in the city. This pattern is widely claimed to involve a fiscal externality that also entails a systematic exploitation of city residents by suburban residents.

It is easy enough to see the basis for this claim. Suppose governments are financed by a tax on personal income, as based on the location of the taxpayer's residency and not where the income was earned. Commuters generate a demand for government services in their suburbs, but they also generate such demands in the cities where they work. Their tax payments, however, all go to the suburbs where they live. Such considerations as this have inspired a variety of proposals for allowing cities to extend the reach of their taxing ability. One common proposal involves allowing cities to impose a tax on payrolls, though numerous other proposals have been offered as well.

As with tax competition, it must be asked what is so sacred about the income tax in this picture. The issue would not be nearly so clear with a tax on property. While the residential property of commuters is located in the suburbs, they also support the value of commercial and industrial property in the cities to which they commute. This is simple to see by performing the mental experiment of imagining a lock-out of suburban commuters by the central city. With such a lock-out in place, it would be impossible for city officials to claim that they were being exploited by suburban residents who were using city services without paying for them. What would happen in this case would be a depression in the value of commercial and industrial property in the city, along with some movement of commerce and industry to the suburbs.

Some objects of taxation are relatively mobile and some are highly immobile. The degree of mobility, moreover, is a variable that changes with technology. Claims about tax competition and fiscal externality come into play only with respect to tax bases that are relatively mobile. A tax on retail sales is a base that is highly mobile, and increasingly so. An income tax involves less mobility, though perhaps only slightly less in many cases. In contrast, land is the archetypical example of an immobile resource. The Henry George-inspired approach to site value taxation envisions a tax where governments collect increases in site value, based on the belief that improvements that governments produce will lead to increases in the demand for sites within its boundaries (Foldvary 2004). In this manner, governments would operate something like profit-seeking entities, and Hyatt the City would operate similarly to Hyatt the Hotel, as explored by Spencer MacCallum (1970), Fred Foldvary (1994) and Mason Gaffney (2001).

To be sure, there are some organizational considerations surrounding site value taxation that have not been explored in the literature. It is fine to state that government services would be reflected in market demands for sites, thereby putting government on a self-sustaining basis. But what would it take for actual institutional arrangements to operate in this manner? The primary claim on behalf of site value taxation is that it will give city officials strong incentives to provide city services only to the extent that aggregate site values are maximized. A program that increases the value of some sites but reduces even more the value of others will lower the city's total budget. Yet city officials do not have direct interests in the aggregate value of the cities they manage, and site value taxation does nothing by itself to abolish the factionalism that leads to increases in the value of some properties while reducing the value of others. Factionalism cannot be overcome by assumption; indeed, it is doubtful that it could ever be overcome, as against possibly being limited and held in reasonable check.

Along these lines, there are some issues of equity structure that seem worthy of exploration, once it is recognized that units of governments are corporate bodies. One equity structure would be one where each dollar of assessed property value gave one vote to the owner of that property. This would be a voting system that is roughly the same as the one used in publicly traded corporations. Another voting system could still limit the franchise to property holders, but give equal votes regardless of the value of property held within the city. A third voting system would give equal voting rights to owners and residents alike, while at the same time removing voting rights from absentee property owners; this is pretty much the system that is in place now in the United States.

## VI.   THE INSTITUTIONAL FRAMEWORK FOR TERRITORIAL GOVERNANCE

If we look at a federated public square at any moment, we will see a pattern that entails both fragmentation and overlapping. Fragmentation refers to subdivision of some particular geographic territory. Thus a nation is sub-divided into states or provinces. Overlapping refers to the simultaneous connection of any citizen to political enterprises established through multiple parliamentary assemblies. An individual might be a member of federal, provincial, county and town governments, and perhaps even special districts that encompass territory covered by several counties.

The geographical patterns of governments, as well as the patterns of bud-getary activities within governments, are all fashioned through interaction among the competitive efforts of people to replace less-valued options with more-valued options. This universal feature of life plays out by fashioning an immense variety of particular scripts. In all of this, there are processes at work that generate what might be called the industrial organization of the public square. If we compare maps of the public square of some territory through time, we will notice changes in its geographical configuration. In some cases jurisdictions might subdivide, as when Czechoslovakia split into the Czech Republic and Slovakia. Jurisdictions can also combine, as when cities annex unincorporated territory or when governments merge, as illus-trated by the consolidation of Jacksonville and Duval County in the United States. Processes of boundary formation and change are in play in revising the maps of public squares through the years, just as they are in play within the market square.

The institutional arrangements within the public square seem clearly to operate with greater degrees of discontinuity than characterize operation within the market square. Within the market square, enterprises are con-tinually subdividing and consolidating across various activities. Old firms acquire new firms, old firms merge with other old firms, and old firms spin off some of their activities to form new firms. All of these things happen continually in the market square, which leads to continuing change in the boundaries among enterprises.

While boundaries do change in the public square, they do so intermit-tently, sporadically, and generally with great controversy. What would be the equivalent of a simple real estate transaction in the market square becomes highly contentious in its public square equivalent. A city council might decide to try to annex some unincorporated territory. In some American states, cities can do this simply by passing an ordinance to this effect. In other states, approval of some form is required. The form that approval is required to take, moreover, is subject to considerable variation. Where one state might require majority approval within both the city and the targeted area, another state will require only a majority vote within the combined territory. In any case, annexation often proceeds in highly contentious fashion, which surely suggests that it is more about the redistribution of wealth than about creating higher-valued organizational arrangements. If an annexation were thought to increase aggregate value in the public square, it should encounter no opposition. In many cases, of course, annexation involves a transfer of land from county jurisdiction to city jurisdiction where taxes are higher, with the annexed territory having average property values that exceed the average within the city.

Institutional arrangements are surely important in how they shape the geographical organization of public squares. The difficulty of economic calculation in the absence of transferable ownership impinges at many places on any process of boundary adjustment. Transferable ownership makes it easier for people to form similar conjectures about the probable impact of boundary changes. It also provides pay-offs to people from acting in ways that maximize the value of the enterprise. It is easy enough to imagine circumstances under which the value of a city would be larger if it reduced its geographical reach, as in spinning off 30 percent of its territory to some other city. It is also easy enough to imagine an increase in city value through selling off its library operation to some other enterprise. While the equivalent activities happen continually on the market square, they are rare on the public square. The absence of enterprise value, along with the resulting inability to capture capital gains, is surely part of the story of the greater sluggishness in boundary change among enterprises within the public square. Another part of the story surely lies in related differences in executive compensation. Suppose the non-monetary part of compensation varies directly with the size of the activity being managed. Being a police chief of a city of 500 000 would thus confer greater non-monetary status than being chief for a city of 200 000. To the extent that such considerations as these impinge on conduct, we would expect to find greater sluggishness of boundary change among entities within the public square than within the market square.

## NOTES

1. My use of embedded is similar to Granovetter (1985).
2. Actually, it wouldn't truly prevent the appearance of this option within the society, but would only change the organizational channels through which it appeared. For instance, if schools reject martial arts, scouting organizations might embrace it. As noted in an earlier chapter, the American experiment with Prohibition did not prohibit alcohol but merely changed the channels of commerce, along with various other consequences that accompanied this change of channels.
3. For perceptive treatments of some of these issues, see Congleton (1994), Hamlin (1985), Holcombe and Stroup (1993), Kenyon and Kincaid (1991) and Shadbegian (1999).
4. Chucky Cheese is a chain of stores in the United States that offers a combination of food and amusement consumed under roof and aimed at children.
5. For some thoughtful and informative treatments of some of these matters, see Nalbandian (1991), Klingner and Nalbandian (1998) and Frederickson and Nalbandian (2002).

6.  To be sure, the American Constitution initially assigned functions to the federal government through a list of enumerated powers. It has, however, been at least a century since that effort at enumeration had any effect on the actual operation of government.
7.  For an emphasis on non-discrimination over unanimity, see Hutt (1975). In a related vein, see Buchanan and Congleton (1998).
8.  Bruce Benson (2001) provides a thorough examination of these race-to-the-bottom claims which shows them to be without merit.
9.  The cameralist conception of the enterprising state in contrast to the taxing state is explored in Backhaus and Wagner (1987) and Tribe (1984).

# 8.  Fiscal sociology and the challenge of societal agriculture

The systems design or teleological orientation toward public finance construes its object, the state, as intervening in the economy to change the resource allocations that would otherwise have resulted. The seminal articulation of this orientation is Richard Musgrave's (1959) treatise *The Theory of Public Finance*. Musgrave presented a three-fold analytical schema for state intervention that has provided the foundation for fiscal theorizing ever since. Musgrave conceptualized the state as pursuing its tasks within a three-part budgetary framework whose elements were allocation, distribution and stabilization. The dichotomy between allocation and distribution is still in full play in contemporary fiscal theorizing. The interest in stabilization through fiscal policy is also still alive, except that it is now treated as a topic for macro theorizing and not for fiscal theorizing.

The teleological orientation toward public finance bears a mirror image relationship to the theory of welfare economics. This latter is summarized by two theorems. The first asserts that competitive resource allocations are Pareto efficient. The second theorem asserts that one Pareto-efficient allocation can be transformed into an alternative Pareto-efficient allocation through a set of lump-sum taxes and transfers. This two-theorem framework of welfare economics maps directly into a conceptualization of public finance in terms of allocative and distributive branches. The territory to be filled by the allocative branch is the territory where the first theorem of welfare economics fails to hold. In the presence of such alleged failures, various arguments are advanced that states should use their budgetary and regulatory powers to offset market failure by providing public goods and by counteracting externalities. The task of the distributive branch is to adjust market-generated determinations of income and wealth to secure some notion of distributive justice. Welfare economics and public finance differ primarily in the higher degree of abstraction in welfare economics, for fiscal theorizing typically makes more contact with various matters concerning specific tax forms and expenditure programs.[1] It would be accurate to characterize the teleological orientation toward public finance as being applied welfare economics.

From the social-theoretic orientation pursued here, the state is not an agent of intervention but an arena or process of interaction among people who are pursuing ends and whose relationships with one another are governed by the various institutions that constitute those relationships. Fiscal phenomena are thus emergent and not teleological, and the relation between the phenomena that are ascribed to state and those ascribed to market is coeval and not sequential. Orthodox welfare economics is thus not suitable for informing a social-theoretic orientation toward public finance. Yet welfare economics reflects an enduring interest by economists in the goodness of societal patterns of activity. Just because emergence replaces teleology as the organizing analytical orientation does not remove the interest we have in the goodness of a social order. It means only that the analysis of the qualities of that goodness must be approached from within a different conceptual framework.

The different framework that I pursue here is fiscal sociology, a subject that is portrayed in Jürgen Backhaus (2004a). The term fiscal sociology was coined by the Austrian economist Rudolf Goldscheid in the course of a controversy with another Austrian economist, Joseph Schumpeter, regarding the treatment of Austrian public debt after the dissolution of the Austro-Hungarian Empire.[2] Where welfare economics takes as its object the formal structure of relationships among theoretical categories, fiscal sociology takes as its object the substantive character of property-based relationships through which governance proceeds in human societies. It would not be wrong to characterize the object of fiscal sociology as the establishment of a form of societal agriculture (Wagner 2006b). While patterns of fiscal organization and activity are reflectors of human interests and sentiments, they are also shapers of those interests and sentiments, though often in a complex manner that is difficult to discern. Before turning directly to fiscal sociology, this chapter first reviews the standard formulations of welfare economics and their use in organizing theoretical efforts in public finance. The remainder of the chapter examines various facets of how fiscal sociology might serve as an alternative framework for the appraisal of social organization when market and fiscal phenomena are emergent and coeval.

## I.   THE ALLURE OF WELFARE ECONOMICS

Welfare economics provides both an organizational framework and an analytical agenda for a theory of public finance. Fiscal phenomena are enormously complex and exceed the capacity of any scholar to master in any substantive detail. Those details involve hundreds of taxes and thousands of programs. The institutional detail surrounding those taxes and programs, moreover, cannot be comprehended by any single person, as any effort to try would require knowledge of tax codes, legal rulings and processes, and the intricacies of political and budgetary processes across a wide variety of governments. A mastery of all that detail might be found in the combined faculties of economics, law, administration, accounting and politics of a major university, but it will certainly not be found in the head of any one scholar. When confronted with the enormous institutional detail that accompanies fiscal phenomena, analytical coherence can be attained only through massive simplification in some form.

The two theorems of welfare economics offer a convenient approach to achieving such coherence, particularly when the material of public finance is approached from a teleological orientation. This means that fiscal phenomena are construed as the result of some agent's choice that is aimed at the attainment of some objective. It is far simpler to characterize choice than to characterize interaction among choosers, particularly when the number of interacting choosers expands beyond the proverbial handful. One cannot seek to explain patterns of interaction without considering both the effects and the origins of the various institutionalized regularities that frame those interactions. By assimilating fiscal outcomes to the optimizing act of some choosing agent, much institutional detail is consigned to irrelevance.

The ability of teleology to simplify fiscal phenomena is reinforced by the simplification offered by the analytical framework of welfare economics. The two theorems bring a stark simplicity to the organization of a choice-theoretic orientation toward public finance, for any state activity can be expressed in terms of its allocative and its distributive impacts. Welfare economics thus provides a two-layered structure for the theory of public finance. The first layer treats distributive justice, and concerns the preconditions that are thought to be necessary before market outcomes are thought to be warranted even if they are competitively organized. The second layer treats the allocative activities of government, and these activities are conceptualized as arising from a lack of genuine competitiveness in market allocation. That lack of competitiveness is thought to have several dimensions. The one of most immediate relevance to a theory of public finance is the presumed inability of market processes to generate a provision of public goods. Other alleged failures of competitive organization involve claims about uncompensated external effects and market-based monopolization, with these latter claims of failure generally leading more in the direction of regulatory than budgetary activity.

Welfare economics offers a way of reducing complex fiscal phenomena to two simple elements, and once this is done it offers a framework for the application of expertise to the task of achieving societal betterment. It is easy to understand the allure of welfare economics as an instrument for organizing theorizing about fiscal phenomena. It appears to offer a principled and disciplined approach to acting systematically upon the world to promote improvement. That welfare economics offers this advantage for a theory of public finance is clear. Whether that advantage is genuine or illusory is a different matter. There is good reason to think that Paretian welfare economics offers illusory analytical boxes to a theory of public finance.

It is simple enough to postulate sufficient conditions for Pareto efficiency, with violations of those conditions representing Pareto inefficiency. It is not at all simple, however, to construct a correspondence between theoretical category and actual practice. J.H. Clapham (1922) claimed that the theoretical categories of increasing and decreasing returns were empty economic boxes that could not be filled with reference to actual activities. Clapham's claim would seem to apply as well to such fiscal phenomena as public goods and externalities, at least so long as that theory is approached through the Paretian construction. (Clapham's paper elicited a response by A.C. Pigou (1922) and a subsequent commentary by Dennis Robertson (1924).) Similar to Clapham, one can imagine analytical boxes labeled public goods (or market failure) and private goods (or market success). But those boxes cannot be filled appropriately with respect to actual economic activities.

One problem that arises immediately is that all kinds of public goods are provided through market arrangements, with that provision encountering little protestation that would seem even to hint of market failure. Theaters provide public goods, in that a multitude of people are able to see the same performance. Parades are public goods, and yet many of them are organized privately. Shopping centers provide a variety of public goods along with their private stores and shops. And as noted in an earlier chapter, Hyatt the hotel provides pretty much the same menu of public goods as do ordinary cities, but it does so under different organizational and institutional arrangements. The public goods quality that one unit of provision can accommodate multiple units of consumption is clearly no bar to the provision of such services through market arrangements.

It could be objected that market arrangements are able to accommodate only a subset of all instances of public goods, namely those instances where it is feasible to exclude from consumption those who do not pay. While a theater provides a public good for its audience, it can exclude those who do not pay. To be sure, such market-based provision of public goods is still open to a claim of market failure. So long as the theater's capacity has not been reached, the theater's production violates the Paretian conditions so long as there are people who place a positive value on seeing the performance but don't value the performance sufficiently to pay the price. So, merely to observe the market provision of public goods does not allow that provision to be placed in the box labeled market success. Irreducible ambiguity plagues the Paretian construction.

The examination of the boxes could be approached from the other direction by asking how well governmental activities correspond to activities not provided through market arrangements. To the extent that this can be done, it might be concluded that governments are providing services that were not provided through market arrangements. It could not be concluded from such an observation that government was acting to fulfill the Paretian conditions, yet there would be some movement in this direction, in that government was undertaking activities that were not organized through markets. Approaching the task from this direction still leaves empty boxes. There is almost nothing that governments do that is not also organized through market arrangements. Security is generally thought to be the natural province of government, and yet a large volume of security is organized through market arrangements. It is the same with adjudication, in that mediation and other forms for resolving disputes are widely organized through market arrangements. Governments provide parks and other recreational services, but market-based firms likewise organize a huge volume of such services. In short, a dichotomy between public and private goods would seem to be of little use in distinguishing between activities that are organized in the public square and activities that are organized in the market square. One cannot take the world of goods, separate them into public and private categories, and find that the former category is organized in the public square while the latter category is organized in the market square. The analytical boxes cannot be filled.

The Paretian construction provides a grammar that has been used in developing an agenda for public finance that is thought to be suitable for a market-correcting state. According to this agenda, the state engages in two types of corrective activity. One is to correct resource misallocations; the other is to correct mal-distributions of initial endowments. The first type of activity follows the analytical path framed by the first theorem; the second type follows the path framed by the second theorem. The Paretian grammar is necessarily ambiguous to apply because the formal statements it offers in terms of equalities or inequalities among various marginal rates of substitution and transformation are not subject directly to observation. Interpretative substitutes for direct observation, moreover, are likewise invariably ambiguous. Whether one sees a market failure that government corrects or a market success that government disturbs will almost invariably be a matter of what the beholder's eye chooses to see. There is simply no way to tell through observation if the Paretian standard has been met.

A competitive equilibrium is defined by an equality between marginal rates of substitution and transformation, but there is no way to tell by observation whether a particular situation qualifies as competitive by this standard. Consider the claim that a theater that puts on a show while it has unused capacity violates the Paretian condition. This alleged violation reflects a belief that aggregate marginal rates of substitution exceed the marginal rate of transformation. Suppose the theater seats 100 people, charges $5 per seat, and finds that 80 people buy tickets. The orthodox analysis assumes that the marginal cost of allowing 20 more people to watch the show is zero. If so, any arrangement whereby an additional 20 people gained admission would be a Pareto improvement because these people would derive value without imposing cost on anyone. This hypothetical case is the basis of the claim that the market provision of public goods does not overcome alleged market failures associated with public goods. Market pricing in this case allows for exclusion of people who don't pay, but it does not overcome the welfare failures associated with equal consumption. If one production unit can provide 100 consumption units, a market outcome that leads to the theater being filled to anything less than capacity will be a failure on Paretian grounds, provided only that anyone who is excluded placed some non-zero value on watching the performance. The beholder of this scene sees market failure.

Another beholder, however, can look at the same scene and describe it as a market success. The observation that the theater has 20 vacant seats does not imply that it is costless to fill those seats. For one thing, the people who might fill those seats would have to get to the theater. Even if they were offered admission at $1 they might decline because they think this would be a bad deal in the light of the disruption of other plans they had made for that evening. Furthermore, how would the theater manager find these additional 20 people? The standard theoretical formulation simply assumes that they are there, and waiting to enter if allowed. But life never proceeds in this manner. Those potential patrons will have to be attracted, and this will be costly, both to the theater and to the patrons.

If a theater manager were to find people waiting outside as a show was about to start, he might well be inclined to auction available seats and accept less than $5 per seat. But if this practice were repeated with any regularity, fewer patrons would be willing to buy early admission in the first place. This reduction in the initial willingness to buy seats would also be a cost of trying to fill the additional 20 seats. As Kevin Brancato and Richard Wagner (2004) explain, the status of residual claimacy is sufficient in a market setting to promote the *ex ante* exploitation of all gains from trade; a theater that failed to exploit such gains is one that is not maximizing its net worth. From the perspective of this beholder, and in sharp contrast to the previous beholder, the market provision of public goods necessarily fulfills the Paretian conditions once all relevant costs are taken into account, because the contrary is to assume that people are knowingly refusing to try to be effective in their actions.

Roy Cordato (1992) seeks to avoid the ambiguities that necessarily accompany statements in terms of such non-observable magnitudes as marginal rates of substitution. He does this by addressing claims about externality in terms of arguments about economic calculation and common law doctrines. He starts from the impossibility of third parties truly knowing what would have been generated through hypothesized markets that are assumed empirically not to exist. An airport spreads noise over a surrounding area. It is possible to claim, not necessarily correctly to be sure, that the damage done to the surrounding area is sufficient to warrant the employment of some noise abatement equipment and procedures. The prevailing understanding of property might allow the airport to operate as it chooses, and the affected property owners might be sufficiently numerous as to preclude those owners from acting together effectively because of free riding. The conventional claim of market failure proceeds with the analyst postulating demands for noise abatement by the owners that can be summed to determine some aggregate willingness to pay. This exercise is a fictional one that involves a presumption of knowing what a non-existent market would have produced had it existed. Cordato recognizes this problem and turns to common law doctrines to resolve the impasse.

The principal doctrine is that of 'coming to the nuisance'. If people move into an area where an airport is located, it is reasonable to presume that they prefer location there at the price they pay for land to location elsewhere, where the noise would be less and the price of land higher. Without doubt, those landowners would gain by the imposition of noise abatement requirements on the airport, for this would lead to an increase in land prices around the airport. This, however, would be a taking of property. The residents moreover, have already been compensated for their agreement to come to the nuisance in the form of a lower price of land. It doesn't matter if there are many residents that create free rider problems because the residents voluntarily came to the nuisance in the first place. Cordato is able to argue in defense of the status quo and against the claim for state regulation, and does so in a way that appears to give play to latent valuations.

But what kind of a nuisance might the residents have come to? It is easy to imagine a few snapshots of the area taken a few years apart. The first snapshot shows 40 flights per day on planes that carry 30 passengers, with noise levels that never exceed 70 decibels. The next snapshot shows 100 flights daily, with planes carrying 80 passengers and noise levels reaching

110 decibels. The third snapshot shows 500 flights per day, planes carrying 180 passengers, and noise levels reaching 150 decibels. A doctrine of coming to the nuisance begs the question of just what that nuisance might have been. Once again, the analytical boxes must remain empty.

## II.   FORM, SUBSTANCE AND THE OBJECT OF WELFARE ECONOMICS

Someone uninitiated in the culture wherein economists theorize about welfare would surely be excused for expecting to find those theorists engaged in substantive dialogue about the relationship between economic organization and human welfare. Any field of inquiry must have an object at which inquiry is directed. For welfare economics that object would seem surely to be human welfare, particularly as it relates to different forms of economic and social organization. For Paretian welfare economics, however, welfare has no substantive referent and is rendered in a wholly formal manner in terms of equalities between marginal rates of substitution and marginal rates of transformation. This purely formal treatment of welfare is conveyed nicely by the formal equivalence of socialism and capitalism within the Paretian framework.

If welfare economics were nudged in a substantive direction, it would be necessary to organize its categories of thought in some such manner as to make it possible to inquire substantively into the comparative merits of socialist and capitalist forms of social-economic organization on human welfare. Among other things, it would be necessary to craft schema for thought that would make it possible to probe such matters as whether unfettered hedonism is a good thing, or the connection between different forms of economic organization and classical concerns about the well-ordered soul, or any of the myriad possible concerns and issues that have been raised for millennia about goodness and badness as they pertain to life in society.

If there is to be an intellectual construction called welfare economics that allows entry into an examination of substantive issues regarding human welfare, it surely cannot be predicated on some presumption that life is lived within the confines of steady-state equilibrium. Such a model can describe consistency among postulated relationships but it cannot generate those relationships, let alone account for their change. Yet societies are continually changing and regenerating. Asik Radomysler (1946) sketches, in the latter part of his essay, an insightful alternative treatment of the material of welfare economics in an environment of development and conflict that merits consideration today. Joseph Cropsey (1955) and Bertrand de

Jouvenel (1952) explore some of the issues of substance that would surely have to be treated should welfare economics be oriented in a substantive direction.

One topic that would have to be addressed within such a substantively oriented welfare economics is the relationship between mind and society. Within the Paretian orientation, mind is fixed prior to society, as illustrated nicely by George Stigler and Gary Becker (1977). People are endowed with preferences, and society is simply a force for multiplying the extent to which preferences are satisfied through securing the advantages of specialization and the division of labor. This is a model of an autonomous mind, with society serving as a landscape on which individual minds act. Some of those landscapes will provide richer opportunities than other landscapes, but there will be no interaction between landscape and mind. Within such an analytical schema, it could be possible to explore the effect of different societal landscapes on the degrees to which they allow satisfaction of mind. This analytical tack would move beyond the pure formality of Paretian welfare economics through the incorporation of growth into welfare economics. Systems of social-economic organization could then be appraised in terms of such objects as their implications for per capita income.

It is reasonable to wonder whether mind is independent of society. It is conventional for economists to assume such independence, but to be conventional is not necessarily to be correct. The alternative to an autonomous mind is one wherein there is interaction between mind and society, something that is probed with especial clarity in Norbert Elias (1982, 1991). Within this alternative analytical framework, the relation between mind and society is bidirectional. One direction of influence runs from mind to society, as it is the interaction among minds that generates such societal formations as property rights, firms and states. But there is also influence running from society to mind, as the social formations that emerge focus and channel human energy, affecting the content of mind in the process. For instance, a set of people who are interested in some common area of intellectual inquiry will typically generate such societal formations as journals and professional associations. This is the path of influence from mind to society. But those societal formations can also influence subsequent substantive conduct undertaken by minds, as would be illustrated by practitioners modifying their activities to gain professional standing. This path of influence runs from society to mind.

If the relation between mind and society is bidirectional, autonomous individual preferences and their satisfaction can no longer serve as an Archimedean point on which a substantive approach to welfare economics can be grounded. To be sure, to claim that societal structures can influence mind and patterns of human activity is not to assimilate mind to some putty-like substance that can be shaped at will. It is possible to recognize that human nature lends some firmness and texture to the material of mind without denying some scope for societal formations also to work on mind.

Robert Frank (1987) asks *If Homo Economicus Could Choose His Own Utility Function, Would He Want One with a Conscience?* Frank answered his question in the affirmative, arguing that the acquisition of a conscience could be a prudential device for pre-commitment. In this formulation, morality is an object of choice; choosing among moralities is no different from choosing among wines. The mind is thus equated to a tabula rasa on to which morality can be written or erased as a person chooses. This line of analysis treats morality as an argument in a utility function, which means in turn that a person's moral imagination exists on the same plane as a person's taste for wine.

Lexicographical orderings provide a different and surely more illuminating approach to this material. Morality is not an object of choice on the same plane as wine or cheese. An adult can choose or reject an offer of wine or cheese, but does not have the option to choose or reject a morality, for some morality was implanted during childhood, for better or worse.[3] Such morality was implanted through stories, discipline and practice until it became second nature and beyond conscious thought. The content of the moral imagination can transmute after childhood, including transmutation through institutionally organized practice. One person might have been raised to be reliable and to respond to people with some reasonable courtesy, and then finds in subsequent commercial life that such reliability and courtesy are reinforced through commercial success.

Another person might have been similarly raised, but matriculated into bureaucratic life where customers are replaced by supplicants. Market relationships based on contractual equality give way to political relationships based to a significant extent on status and domination. For instance, a person might desire to buy the right to some width of radio spectrum. Within a market setting, she can approach anyone who currently owns rights to spectrum and try to work out a mutually agreeable exchange. The relationship between the parties is grounded on equality and mutuality. Within a bureaucratic setting, however, there is no equality, for the person seeking spectrum is transformed into a supplicant who in various ways must grovel before those who hold the power to grant or reject. To be sure, there are numerous ways that groveling can occur, ranging from forthright begging and pleading to feigned politeness and revolting solicitousness. Furthermore, people in bureaucratic positions who mistakenly treat supplicants as customers will generally not fare as well in those settings relative to others who recognize how to mix obsequiousness and indifference, depending on whether the bureaucrat was facing a political master or a supplicating citizen.

It thus seems plausible that to some extent the forms of social-economic organization can influence the content of the moral imaginations of the citizenry.[4] This is possible to the extent to which the crucible in which the moral imagination is shaped and reshaped is the world of practice and not the world of conscious reflection and intellectual inquiry. To the extent that this is so, the practice of statecraft will be necessarily to engage in soulcraft (Wagner 2006b). A person might not consciously choose to replace a general posture of pleasant courtesy with one that alternates between obsequiousness and indifference depending on the status of the other person, and yet it may happen as an operating characteristic of a particular approach to social-economic organization. More generally, the appraisal of societal formations and societal processes cannot adopt preferences as a fixed point of appraisal but must work instead in terms of the resonance between societal processes and our knowledge of human nature.

## III.   FISCAL SOCIOLOGY AND FISCAL CULTURE

Fiscal sociology is a term developed by the Austrian economist Rudolf Goldscheid in the course of his debate with Joseph Schumpeter over the treatment of Austria's public debt after the end of World War I and the dissolution of the Austro-Hungarian Empire (the contributions are collected in Hickel 1976). While the immediate point of the debate was how to service Austria's large public debt, the intellectual core of the debate was the place of property in the conduct of state activity. Schumpeter supported the imposition of an extraordinary tax that would allow the debt to be extinguished. Once this was accomplished, the state would finance its activities with normal levels of taxation. In contrast, Goldscheid supported a recapitalization of the state, by which he meant a return to the cameralist-type arrangements wherein the state derived significant revenue from property and commercial activity. Goldscheid operated with a notion of an entrepreneurial state, while Schumpeter thought in terms of a tax state (Backhaus 1994, 2004b). Goldscheid thought that a tax state would operate to depress vigorous commercial activity through its taxes, so he advanced the notion of a state as an entrepreneurial actor. Schumpeter thought that the state would act as a poor entrepreneur, and that a tax state would be less damaging on the whole.

There is surely merit in both lines of argument, as well as a great number of imponderable points of ambiguity involved in trying to sort out the issues. Regardless of how such a sorting out might proceed, the central point of contention in this controversy involved the place of property and property-ordered relationships within a theory of public finance. Both

Goldscheid and Schumpeter thought in terms of a participatory as distinct from an interventionist orientation toward public finance, but they had different conceptions of the economic capabilities of states.

In their treatise on fiscal history, Carolyn Webber and Aaron Wildavsky (1986) argue that budgeting is invariably implicated in controversies about how people are to live together. Their formulation brings to mind the conceptualization of structured living together that was central to the Germanic tradition of *Staatswissenschaften*. It is necessary to arrange structures for living together in compact geographical spaces, but there are various ways this might be accomplished. An important consideration with respect to such arrangements concerns the relation between mind and society. The traditional orientation, as noted above, is one where mind is independent of society. Budgetary measures thus reflect some notion of citizen preferences, as befits the standard economic formulation of people as having given preferences which markets just reflect. The central issues thus revolve around notions of aggregation, or of just whose preferences are being reflected in budgetary outcomes. If people differ in their preferred budgetary outcomes, different political and fiscal institutions will affect people differently by generating different outcomes. Whatever the outcome generated, there will be no interaction with mind. Differences in outcome will affect the extent to which different people get their preferences satisfied, but nothing else of interest will occur.

The alternative possibility is one of a reciprocal relationship between mind and society, wherein societal formations exert some feedback on the content of mind. The interaction of minds generates the societal formation we can call fiscal culture, but fiscal culture in turn affects substantive conduct through the ability of institutionalized practice to influence the moral imagination. Such a treatment of the mind–society relationship in terms of budgetary outcomes and fiscal culture is a possibility that can be explored within the rubric of fiscal sociology, where the emphasis is on the generative properties of alternative approaches to fiscal and societal organization.

To work with fiscal culture as a societal formation that can affect the substance of mind, two types of analytical construction are necessary. One type is a mapping of cultural styles or motifs, and this will be considered momentarily. The second type of construction is some analytical framework that can trace a movement from budgetary programs to the substantive content of mind in the form of its moral imagination. To illustrate how this movement might arise while keeping within the framework adopted by Webber and Wildavsky concerning how budgeting involves conflicts among people over how they are to live, consider the simmering controversy over those aspects of the welfare state that concern support in relatively old age, mainly regarding retirement and medical care.

While the controversy has many dimensions and while many particular options and programs have been advanced, for purposes of conceptual clarity it is helpful to collapse the various possible approaches into two polarities: common pooling and individual attribution. Common pooling is currently the predominant approach within democratically-constituted polities. People who are working pay taxes that are placed in a pool from which payments are distributed to people who have reached the age of eligibility. This is social security as a tax-and-transfer program, where there is no contractual relationship between the taxes paid during one interval of life and the payments received during the subsequent interval. Individual attribution is the antipode to common pooling, for here payments made while working become a person's property, and that person alone has the right to claim that property upon reaching an eligible age. Individual attribution is, of course, the way that all market-based investment accounts work, and it has been receiving increasing support as an alternative to the collective pooling approach to social security.

Much of the controversy over different approaches to social security arises out of the large gaps between the present value of projected revenues and the present value of projected payments, when these projections are based on current tax legislation and current demographic projections. These projections show a gap of several trillion dollars in the United States, and similar gaps elsewhere as examined in careful detail by Heinz Grossekettler (2004). Much of the current controversy revolves around just how the gap will be closed, which involves in turn issues of how liability for that gap will be apportioned. Some claim that some of that gap can be closed through the higher return that individual attribution can offer when compared with collective pooling. While there is room for differences in judgment in this respect, as there is in any projection of future magnitudes, no one claims that the gap will disappear through such higher returns. For it to disappear, it will also be necessary for liability for that gap to be made explicit, which in turn will require some combination of higher taxes and reduced payments, with the latter often taking the form of increasing the age of eligibility.

It is not my interest to make a contribution here to the contemporary controversy about social security, though I have done so once (Wagner 1983). My interest rather is in using this controversy as a vehicle for probing issues relating to fiscal sociology and fiscal culture within this particular context. The current debate makes it appear that the only thing at stake is the apportionment of financial liability for the gap. To treat this controversy in terms of its financial implications for different people is to treat mind as independent of society. To explore the alternative possibility, it is necessary to develop some framework that can describe cultural alternatives in a way that can be related to budgetary alternatives.

There are two meanings of culture that probably have some currency in the vocabulary of social theorists, one comparatively shallow and one substantially deeper. By shallow, I mean the various kinds of activities that are often expressed by the notion of cultural goods, and which concern such things as the economic organization of art museums or the relationship between live performances and sales of recordings within an overall strategy of seeking to maximize net worth. Rather than drawing illustrative material from agriculture or manufacture, the analytical material is drawn from the intersecting realms of art, theater and fashion that are normally thought to represent the domain of culture.

By deep, I mean the moral imaginations of the people who populate a society. This use of culture has little to do with the more common use, but it is the use I have in mind here, for it addresses the characters of the inhabitants of a society, and of the possible bi-directional relationship between character and social formation. A bi-directional relationship implies that two distinct currents can be detected flowing between mind and society. One current runs from mind to the generation of societal forms. The other current runs from societal formations to the habits of mind and heart.

While the debate between common pooling and individual attribution is generally pitched as one of comparative financial implications for different people, the debate also reflects some deep cultural differences that point in different directions. By analogy, the two parabolas $X^2$ and $-X^2$ occupy the same territory in the vicinity of their common origin, and yet they point in opposing directions. Something similar would seem to be involved in the clash between common pooling and individual attribution. The question at issue here concerns the ability of a choice between these approaches to contribute to some change in mental orientation that in turn promotes cultural transformation.

It is notable in this regard that Christopher Lasch's (1978) treatment of *The Culture of Narcissism* carried the subtitle: *American Life in an Age of Diminishing Expectations*. Lasch's reference to 'diminishing' refers to a process that is underway and not a condition that has been reached. The object to which the expectations refer is not to some material condition of life but to people's expectations of themselves and of one another. Those are the expectations that Lasch, building upon Philip Rieff's (1966) treatment of a therapeutically ensnarled society, treats as diminishing. The rise of the therapeutic annihilates self-discipline, dignified personal bearing and the interior life, leading many people to bask in public displays of their incompetence. The quest to cultivate the well-ordered soul and the challenge to live virtuously, under which commodious living may follow in its train, gives way to a desire jointly to be liberated from discipline that is accompanied by a self-obsessive materialism. People come to expect less from themselves and yet want more from life while giving less to it.

Alexis de Tocqueville asserted something similar in *Democracy in America* (2002 [1835]) in his chapter on 'What Sort of Despotism do Democracies Have to Fear?' There, he described a despotism that came wearing velvet gloves, mostly. It was a despotism of reduced capacity (the diminished expectations of Lasch's subtitle) where much of the responsibility for prudent living was farmed out to collective authority. It can be a bother to deal with such things as how much to save and where to put it. Governmental agencies can take on these bothers, freeing people to spend more time looking in their mirrors like Narcissus. The opportunity set appears to shift outward while the soul shrinks. In this respect, it should be noted that Lasch associated narcissism not with vanity but with fear.

One of the major lines of argument advanced against full individual attribution, with even advocates of individual accounts often favoring forced saving, is an argument grounded in fear. In particular, the claim is made that if people were free to make their own choices, many would fail to provide for their futures, and this in turn would create problems for others, namely the writers of such claims. What results is an argument grounded in externality that one person's failure to exercise provident judgment will impose costs on other people because those other people subsequently experience anguish, which leads them in turn to offer support. Both of these can be forestalled by forced saving. This, however, does not countenance redistribution, and so does not assuage the fear that the failures of providential conduct are more likely to appear in the presence of lower income. Thus, individual attribution of the forced saving variety often loses support to some type of common pooling. To be sure, these arguments are usually articulated by upper-income professional elites who also happen to think that bowling alleys are museums of primitive culture, and so the incapacitation is a problem that someone else possesses. In any case, the replacement of self-initiative and self-responsibility by collective paternalism can on the one hand be recognized as a manifestation of normal human concerns while on the other hand it can redirect the very exercise of the human faculties in a way that replaces competence with fear, as Vincent Ostrom (1997) examines with particular cogency.

In a treatment that was controversial at the time, Hillary Clinton (1996) advanced the claim that it takes a village to raise a child. There are several things that are notable about this assertion. One is that she is correct, even though she faced strong opposition from many people who claimed instead that the task required only parents. But parents can't raise children on their own. They require help and support beyond what they can provide on their own. It does take a village. While Clinton was right in this respect, she was dead wrong in subsequently assimilating that village to the image of a Health and Human Services bureaucracy and its various allies. Certainly, the needs of children can be complex and require much attention from parents and support that parents will have to obtain from elsewhere in the village. The raising of children requires that parents apply their talents in competent fashion to the task before them, with an important part of this competence involving an awareness of how to make good use of the village that lies around them. By contrast, Clinton's concept of a village promotes fear of the difficulty of the challenges, and tells parents to transfer their concerns to the village bureaucrats, a choice that in turn would allow them to substitute leisure for the exertion that achievement in parenting requires.

## IV.   AGONISTIC THOUGHTS ABOUT EQUALITY

The utilitarian formalization of economic thought leads almost inexorably to an analytical construction that posits some trade-off between total output and the degree of equality with which that output is distributed. While this trade-off appears most explicitly in the various formulations of optimal tax theory, its presence appears throughout economic theory so long as that theory is based upon a utilitarian foundation. The cardinal presumption of that foundation is that people can be characterized as being possessed by a utility function whose arguments are consumption and leisure, with utility increasing at a decreasing rate with consumption. It is also generally assumed that utility is measurable and comparable across people. While a number of critics of equalization seize upon measurability and comparability as the unsupportable presuppositions that invalidate utilitarian conclusions about redistribution, I see no reason to object to these presuppositions, particularly if they are taken simply as expressions of our ability to empathize with others.

My objection to the utilitarian line of argument has two parts.[5] One part, which was noted in an earlier chapter, objects to the presumption that the domain over which people are ruled by utility functions is unlimited. The alternative to such an unlimited domain is a lexicographic ordering, wherein utility functions rule over only some limited domain of action. The second part of my objection is to the standard presumption that utility is separable into consumption and leisure. At first glance, the assumption of separability might seem innocuous, for it simply means that total utility can be expressed by addition across the components of utility. Between two people who can consume the same bundle, the one who can do it with less effort is better off according to this condition. For any individual, the optimum to beat all optimums is to gorge on consumption while doing absolutely nothing, other than to consume.

What this construction says, then, is that effort is a negative aspect of human life and social order. The most desirable of all possible states of affairs is to have all of one's wishes and fantasies fulfilled, and to do so without having to do anything to bring this about. We can all recognize that this situation is impossible, and that some exertion is going to be necessary to satisfy our various wants and desires. Still, this formulation holds up effort and activity as a negative in human life, as a necessary evil that accompanies life this side of Eden. The utility that people derive from life is found by adding the positive utility from consumption and the negative utility from effort.

The alternative to treating utility as separable into consumption and leisure is to treat effort and consumption as joint components of the package by which people participate in life and derive meaning from it. Meaning, moreover, is surely bound up in activity and cannot be reduced to free-standing consumption. Why do people climb mountains (Lowenstein 1999)? After two days hanging on the side of a mountain face, you sit at home beside a fireplace savoring a snifter of cognac. Drinking the cognac and climbing the mountain are not two distinct units of activity, the former involving consumption and the latter effort, with the value of the overall activity set determined through addition across the utilities, positive and negative, associated with the two activities. Rather, both components form a coherent unit of meaningful activity, at least within the context of an ethic of achievement, where pleasure derives from achievement, as distinct from an ethic of pleasure, where achievement is irrelevant, and actually a costly subtraction from pleasure due to the effort it requires.

To approach life through the organization of meaningful activity, as against approaching it hedonistically through consumption, is to seek to reconceptualize welfare in terms of the interesting and challenging adventures that different systems of economic order allow people to have during the course of their lives. Such an alternative formulation would, of course, deny that consumption is the end of economic activity, and would convert consumption into a by-product concomitant of that activity. A society in which people are having interesting and creative adventures will flourish, and what we call high consumption will emerge as a by-product of the activities that flourishing represents.

This reconceptualization of welfare would locate the object of welfare economics proximately in challenging adventures and only derivatively in high consumption, for the latter will follow the former. Consider again the claim from orthodox welfare economics that the formal conditions for optimum welfare are identical under socialism and capitalism. It is often noted that capitalism fares better with respect to production but socialism fares better with respect to various notions of equity and equality. The second theorem of welfare economics, moreover, asserts that a capitalist economy can obtain a socialist distribution through an appropriate set of lump-sum taxes and transfers. From this, we can conclude that welfare economics finds the distinction between capitalism and socialism to be inessential. The alternative approach would treat regimes not directly in terms of measured consumption and its distribution, but in terms of their ability to allow people to generate challenges and pursue meaningful dreams, out of which commodious living emerges as a by-product.

## V.   ORDNUNGSTHEORIE AND TECTONIC SOCIETAL LANDSCAPES

An alternative approach to welfare economics was articulated by the German developers of *Ordnungstheorie* associated with the University of Freiburg, starting in the early 1930s. Among the principal figures were Walter Eucken, Franz Böhm and Wilhelm Röpke, with only Röpke being widely translated into English. *Ordnungstheorie* operated with a two-stage frame of reference that was later adopted within constitutional political economy. The first stage involved a choice among ordering principles for the governance of human relationships; the second stage pertained to the conduct of state activity within the confines of the chosen or preferred framework. As for ordering principle, the basic choice was regarded as between relationships grounded in equality or mutuality and relationships grounded in hierarchy, status and domination.

This distinction between types of ordering relationship brings to mind Henry Maine's assertion in his treatise *Ancient Law* (1864), to the effect that the direction of movement in progressive societies had been one from status to contract. Maine wrote at the close of the 19th century, and the subsequent course of development has surely been mixed. Relationships based on contract are relationships among equals, whereas relationships based on status inject positions of domination and subordination into a society. The continuing debates over such elements of the welfare state as social security and medical care have been largely treated as debates over financial projections and implicit rates of return. This debate, however, also involves matters of how people relate to one another, and of the competencies they are to develop.

A system of designated accounts over which people have ownership creates a relationship among equals. In contrast, existing social security programs involve relationships of domination and subordination, within which supplication becomes a standard mode of conduct. People don't have property in personal accounts, but rather have politically-generated promises to pay benefits under terms to be determined at some future time.

Most people have personal accounts organized in the market square as well as expectations of future payment organized in the public square. The relationships organized in the market square reveal the standard features of relationships of mutual benefit among equals: an account holder typically receives timely and courteous responses to questions and finds vendors generally to be helpful. Likewise, relationships organized in the public square show the standard patterns of hierarchy and supplication: account holders are not treated as account holders, as indeed they are not, for they are supplicants instead. Questions are often addressed neither promptly nor with courtesy, nor are vendors typically particularly helpful, for the people who are asking the questions are not customers but are subordinate supplicants.

The articulators of *Ordnungstheorie* sought to probe the degree of consistency among principles, policies and the arrangements of governance, and to explore processes of institutionalized conflict and societal drift through time. A principle of mutuality or equality did not bar state activity, but rather imposed constitutive requirements that policy measures be 'market conformable'. Market conformability is perhaps one of those ideas whose meaning is better conveyed through illustration. An example that Eucken and Röpke each used a number of times was the comparison between tariffs and quotas. It is easy to give a textbook representation that shows the two to be identical: whatever reduction in imports the tariff achieves can be achieved by a quota. The writers of *Ordnungspolitik* were not fans of tariffs, but they pointed out that tariffs did not violate the principle of market conformability, provided only that they were general and were not so high as to promote smuggling and associated countermeasures. Under those circumstances, the tariff does not violate the central principles of market organization, but only modifies some of the terms of trade within what is still a system of open competition.

In contrast, quotas replace open competition with state allocation. With a tariff on bicycles, which bicycles are imported is still governed by market relationships. With the quota, however, this is no longer the case because vendors are now selected by political officials. Among other things, this increases the scope for venality within politics, thereby injecting elements of hierarchy, domination and supplication into the society, pushing aside mutuality and equality in the process. A vendor who imports bicycles and pays the tariff cannot choose to continue to import bicycles under a quota. It is now necessary to obtain a license. Even if obtained, the license will be for a particular number of bicycles and not for the open-ended number that can be imported in the presence of a tariff.

For a quota to have bite, it will be necessary that people want to import a greater number of bicycles than the quota allows. A political officer will thus select among supplicants. There will thus be competition among supplicants, and this competition can follow any of a large number of channels, all of which represent the effort of people to increase their standing in the competition for licenses. One extreme form of venality is simple bribery of the official who grants the licenses. But there are many channels that don't rely on bribery that can nonetheless represent the effort to gain competitive advantage. Most of these channels involve related lines of activity. For instance, a retired legislator may be hired to lobby for favorable treatment. A public relations firm whose principal owner is cousin to the license-granting official might be hired. A donation might be made to a symphony orchestra for which the public official is a patron and of which his wife is a member. Practically limitless are the channels that a competitive effort might take in the presence of restrictions on bribery.

The formulations from *Ordnungstheorie* are forms of natural law theorizing, keeping in mind that natural law refers to something distinct from references to natural rights. Natural law holds only that there are principles that govern human conduct and social interaction that canot be repealed through legislation. Whether a legislature chooses a quota or a tariff will not repeal any laws of conduct or interaction, but will only change the context within which those laws do their work. Legislation can't repeal natural law any more than a surfer on a board can repeal physics.

## VI.   BEYOND INDIVIDUALISM AND COLLECTIVISM: A PERORATION ON FIRST FEDERALIST

Alexander Hamilton opened *Federalist* #1 (1787) by asking 'whether societies of men are really capable or not of establishing good government from reflection and choice, or whether they are forever destined to depend for their political constitutions on accident and force'. One possibility is that good governance belongs to the realm of the natural, as with such activities as breathing, sleeping and bodily elimination. The alternative is that good governance is a talent or capacity. As such, it can be learned or forgotten and it can be performed in better or worse fashion. Governance would thus be like such activities as skating, singing or writing, in that it can be performed with varying degrees of skill, and with those skills capable of being either strengthened or weakened, depending on the intensity and quality of practice.

If good governance is a talent or capacity, moreover, it is one that must be exercised in coordinated fashion among a collection of interacting people. The task of securing good governance, moreover, requires the exercise of two faculties: one involves cognition and the other involves the moral imagination. In this respect, the challenge of achieving good governance is a form of societal agriculture. Good societal agriculture depends upon both valuation and cognition. At the level of valuation, someone values growing squash more highly than growing peas. How to achieve this valued end depends on the exercise of a variety of cognitive faculties that include such subjects as soil chemistry and plant genetics. Furthermore, the growth of knowledge can influence judgments of valuation. Initially, someone might have fought squash bugs with pesticides. At some later time, someone discovers that squash bugs secrete an enzyme that can be processed to offer protection against AIDS or malaria, which transforms squash bugs into something desired and increases the amount of land people devote to growing squash.

The challenge of societal agriculture, moreover, is far knottier and more tangled than the challenge of regular agriculture, for two reasons. One is that regular agriculture is a relatively simple matter of individual choice, whereas societal agriculture is interactive. The other reason involves a significant point of difference between the natural and the human sciences. People might differ over whether squash bugs should be fought with pesticides or by some sort of green-friendly approach, and those differences might become sufficiently intense as to spill into the public square. Nonetheless, the natural world operates independently of what we think about its operation. Squash bugs will act like squash bugs, regardless of whether someone fights them with chemical sprays or drops of vinegar. This is not so with the social world, for here the institutions we generate and the patterns of conduct we form can influence our activities and practices, which in turn can influence conventional norms about the governance of human relationships.

Good government is not a destination or final resting point. It is a continual, never-ending process. There are two basic though complementary tasks involved in securing good government. One involves the moral imagination, and concerns the principles by which we are to live together. History and our imaginations can present us with many options in this respect. This book rests on an affirmation of the values of a liberal and open society, where human relationships are governed by mutual respect among equals. Ideals are at best realized only imperfectly in practice, of course, and the Faustian character of the bargain that government represents assures us that this will be the case (Ostrom 1984, 1996).

The second task requires us to undertake the cognitive work of relating our institutional arrangements to the types of practice that those arrangements promote or block. This task leads in several directions, and can generate a number of general associations. For instance, it is inconsistent to support an open society and simple democracy, because democratic practice will undermine the values of the open society. It is, however, possible to maintain democratic polities in a federal form of governance, provided that that form of governance operates according to polyarchical and not hierarchical principles. Most fundamentally, governance in a liberal order must be construed in a bottom-up manner. With respect to valuation, democracy is a derivative value, with governance grounded in relationships of mutual respect among equals being primary, and fragmented and overlapping civic association emerging out of the extension of those relationships. With respect to cognition, the actual institutional arrangements of governance must be conformable with those principles of value, otherwise contrary practice can set in motion a process of regime drift, a beautiful example of which was portrayed brilliantly in Charles Warren's (1932) masterful little book *Congress as Santa Claus*.

In the early 14th century, Ambrogio Lorenzetti frescoed the walls of Siena's City Hall with his Allegory of Good and Bad Government (an image of this fresco appears on the cover of Backhaus and Wagner's (2004) *Handbook of Public Finance*). The images contrast starkly. With a government grounded in justice and virtue, commerce is vibrant and people flourish. With tyrannical government, suffering and misery haunt the land. As de Tocqueville (2002 [1835]) reminds us, tyranny need not arrive wearing jack boots and wielding clubs. It can arrive wearing velvet gloves as well, taking the form of a power appearing to be kindly that provides amusements and tutelage, which dampens the spirit by offering the illusion of security in place of genuine adventure. Democratic despotism is not an oxymoronic construction. Moreover, democratic government is a process that contains many independent participants, although the office of a president does inject some of the trappings of monarchy into an otherwise democratic arrangement of offices in the public square. The public square is rooted in human nature, emerging out of that side of our natures that seeks solidarity with others.

There is, however, a significant difference between the public square and the market square in the challenges they pose to orderly living together. To be sure, the market square poses challenges of its own, particularly in its ability to feed vanity by allowing people to exaggerate the extent of their own accomplishments when those accomplishments are deeply encased in the networks of supporting relationships that people are able to craft when they allow their relationships to be governed by the principles of private property. But it is in the public square where the most significant challenges and dangers lie, due primarily to its inherently oligarchic character, that is caused in turn by the inability of people effectively to engage in multipartite discussion.

The grammar of private property limits severely the scope for faction in the market square, for faction violates the grammar of private property through which enterprises are formed and operate. The formation of enterprises in the market square requires unanimity among the participants, even if subsequently quarrels can arise over the distribution of profits. In the public square, however, faction is a necessary condition for it to operate, as an implication of the Chairman's Problem articulated so cogently by Bertrand de Jouvenal (1961). The public square originates in human nature. That nature includes a particular preference for our own projects. On the market square this causes little difficulty because joint projects can go forward only with concurrence among the various participants and their specific preferences and desires. Faction may find expression across corporate bodies organized within the market square but it rarely finds expression within such a corporate body.[6]

In the public square, the operation of faction resides at the core of its operation, with this core surely expanding as the size of the public square expands. A homeowner's association or a town is likely to operate with a good deal of informally organized consensus that is simply validated through formal action. In large representative assemblies, however, most members will not even know one another except as acquaintances. It is easy to understand the growing commingling of market and political enterprises within the overall enterprise map. There are clearly symbiotic opportunities present through the cultivation of relationships between particular market enterprises and particular political enterprises.

Political enterprises, moreover, have two ways of cultivating relationships with market enterprises. One is through rent seeking, the other through rent extraction.[7] Within the market square, both kinds of activity are generally thought wrongful. Within the public square, however, they are integral parts of the square's operation, simply as particular mechanisms through which faction is expressed.

Rent seeking describes what people have in mind by lobbying. It refers to the payments people make to secure political favors. A sports magnate would like special tax treatment for a stadium he is building. He lobbies to get this enacted. Or, more likely, hires someone to do this for him, most likely a defeated or retired legislator. But rent seeking is only part of the story of money and politics, and perhaps only the minor part. Rent extraction may be even more significant. It refers to the payments people make to avoid being victimized by politically harmful measures. If rent seeking were called bribery were it to occur between private persons, rent extraction would be called extortion.

There is one significant difference between rent seeking and rent extraction that should not be ignored, which may explain why the former has received more attention than the latter. With rent seeking, politicians are portrayed as relatively passive victims. They are deluged by lobbyists, and on occasion capitulate to those interests. The politician is caught in a squeeze between the intensity of special interests and the quietude of the public interest.

With rent extraction, politicians are in the forefront of the action. They are the active initiators who continually look for targets. Those targets have a choice. They can ignore the politicians and lose a lot of their wealth. Or they can participate politically, thereby softening their losses. Democratic politicians are a peculiar breed of investment banker where the legislature is organized as a form of professional partnership that has relatively senior and relatively junior partners, with legislators being more interested in promoting their preferred lines of business than in opposing the preferences of other partners. A legislator who opposes the business activity of another partner bears the full cost of that opposition in terms of the sacrificed business that could otherwise have been conducted. The benefits from that opposition, however, are spread among the legislative partners, who each thereby gain some modest potential for doing more business.

Public squares and private squares each derive from human nature. That nature is complex, and contains both good and bad, beautiful and ugly. There is no doubt that the market square can accommodate plenty of badness and ugliness. Yet the conventions of private property surely limit the reach of that badness and ugliness. While the activities of the public square emerge out of our natures, the grammar by which the public square must operate gives special play to the bad and ugly side of the Faustian bargain that necessarily accompanies the use of force in human relationships.

Revolutions do occur in human societies, wherein the environment within which life is experienced changes in the proverbial flash. More commonly, though such changes are gradual and are not even recognized until they are well underway and have established a good deal of momentum that is propelling us into that new world that awaits us. Figure 4.1 compared two enterprise maps. One of them showed market and political enterprises occupying separate locations. The other showed them commingled. The direction of historical movement has been from the former to the latter type of arrangement. Most executives of large American companies now travel regularly to Washington. Not so long ago they stayed home. In that earlier time, New York was the prime location for national trade associations. Now it is Washington. These days, fascism is a slur word that no one embraces and everyone avoids. The fascist theory of social-economic organization was a form of syndicalism where large enterprises were operated with concurrence among representatives of government, labor and capital. Presently, governments don't appoint members of corporate boards, though it is getting increasingly hard to deny the de facto presence of political officials in corporate governance. How such arrangements unfold remains for the future to reveal. We may, however, be confident that what emerges will truly be one more reflection on human nature in its full glory and beastliness.

## NOTES

1. For two careful treatments of the relation between welfare economics and public finance, see Head (1965) and Sobel (2004). The forty years that separate these treatments is the period during which public choice theorizing grew to maturity and the differences between them largely reflects this maturation.
2. For a compilation of papers, see Rudolf Hickel (1976). While Schumpeter's contribution was translated into English, Goldscheid's has not been, though the flavor of Goldscheid's argument can be acquired from the translation in Goldscheid (1958 [1925]). For further discussion, see Musgrave (1980).
3. The same disability infects the numerous Hobbes-like efforts to explain the emergence of order through agreements among adults, for constitutive requisites for such order were already instilled in the minds of the participants by the time they reached adulthood.
4. In place of an influence running from society to mind, it could be claimed that what results instead is a self-selection between activities that varies systematically with differing but invariant minds. This analytical move would represent an *ex post* collapse of a lexico-graphical ordering on to a utility surface. This is a fine, indeed a necessary procedure for natural science, where we have no knowledge of the mental states of the objects we study, but as humans we can recognize the hierarchical order of our moral sentiments.
5. In this regard I recommend particularly highly John Kekes (2003).
6. An exception is the incentive to freeze out minority shareholders, though there are also legal remedies against the exercise of such factional power, remedies that don't exist on the public square.
7. Rent seeking was originated by Gordon Tullock (1967) and is surveyed in Robert Tollison (1982). Rent extraction is explored in Fred McChesney (1997).

# Bibliography

Ackerman, B.A. (1977), *Private Property and the Constitution*, New Haven: Yale University Press.

Adams, C. (1993), *For Good and Evil: The Impact of Taxes on the Course of Civilization*, London: Madison Books.

Alchian, A.A. (1950), 'Uncertainty, Evolution, and Economic Theory', *Journal of Political Economy*, 58, 211–21.

Alchian, A.A. (1965), 'Some Economics of Property Rights', *Il Politico*, 30, 816–29.

Alchian, A.A. and H. Demsetz (1972), 'Production, Information Costs, and Economic Organization', *American Economic Review*, 62, 777–95.

Ammons, D.N. and J.J. Glass (1988), 'Headhunters in Local Government: Use of Executive Search Firms in Managerial Selection', *Public Administration Review*, 48, 687–93.

Anderson, L.R. and C.A. Holt (2004), 'Experimental Economics and Public Choice', in C.K. Rowley and F. Schneider (eds), *The Encyclopedia of Public Choice*, vol. II, Dordrecht: Kluwer Academic Publishers, pp. 240–43.

Ardrey, R. (1968), *The Territorial Imperative*, New York: Atheneum.

Atkinson, A.B. and J.E. Stiglitz (1980), *Lectures on Public Economics*, New York: McGraw-Hill.

Auteri, M. and R.E. Wagner (2007), 'The Organizational Architecture of Nonprofit Governance: Economic Calculation within an Ecology of Enterprises', *Public Organization Review*, 7, 57–68.

Backhaus, J.G. (1992), 'The State as a Club: A Perspective for Public Finance in a Prosperous Democracy', *Journal of Public Finance and Public Choice*, 10, 3–16.

Backhaus, J.G. (1994), 'The Concept of the Tax State in Modern Public Finance Analysis', in Y. Shionoya and M. Perlman (eds), *Schumpeter in the History of Ideas*, Ann Arbor: University of Michigan Press, pp. 65–94.

Backhaus, J.G. (2004a), 'Fiscal Sociology: What For?' in J.G. Backhaus and R.E. Wagner (eds), *Handbook of Public Finance*, Boston, MA: Kluwer Academic Publishers, pp. 521–41.

Backhaus, J.G. (2004b), 'Joseph A. Schumpeter's Contributions in the Area of Fiscal Sociology', *Journal of Evolutionary Economics*, 14, 143–51.

Backhaus, J.G. and R.E. Wagner (1987), 'The Cameralists: A Public Choice Perspective', *Public Choice*, 53, 3–20.

Backhaus, J.G. and R.E. Wagner (eds) (2004), *Handbook of Public Finance*, Boston, MA: Kluwer Academic Publishers.

Backhaus. J.G. and R.E. Wagner (2005a), 'From Continental Public Finance to Public Choice: Mapping Continuity', *History of Political Economy*, Annual Supplement, 37, 314–32.

Backhaus. J.G. and R.E. Wagner (2005b), 'Continental Public Finance: Mapping and Recovering a Tradition', *Journal of Public Finance and Public Choice*, 23, 43–67.

Barnett, A.H. and B. Yandle (2004), 'Regulation by Taxation', in J.G. Backhaus and R.E. Wagner (eds), *Handbook of Public Finance*, Boston, MA: Kluwer Academic Publishers, pp. 217–36.

Barro, R. (1974), 'Are Government Bonds Net Worth?' *Journal of Political Economy*, 82, 1095–118.

Barzel, Y. (1989), *Economic Analysis of Property Rights*, Cambridge: Cambridge University Press.

Barzel, Y. (2002), *A Theory of the State*, Cambridge: Cambridge University Press.

Bast, J.L. (2002), *Municipally Owned Broadband Networks: A Critical Evaluation*, Chicago: Heartland Institute.

Baumol, W.J. (1965), *Welfare Economics and the Theory of the State*, 2nd ed., London: G. Bell and Sons.

Becker, G.S. (1983), 'A Theory of Competition among Pressure Groups for Political Influence', *Quarterly Journal of Economics*, 98, 371–400.

Beito, D.T. (2000), *From Mutual Aid to the Welfare State*, Chapel Hill: University of North Carolina Press.

Bendor, J., S. Taylor and R. van Gaalen (1985), 'Bureaucratic Expertise vs. Legislative Authority: A Model of Deception and Monitoring in Budgeting', *American Political Science Review*, 79, 1041–60.

Benham, F. (1934), [Review of Principii di Economia Finanziaria], *Economica*, 1, 364–67.

Benson, B.L. (1995), 'Understanding Bureaucratic Behavior', *Journal of Public Finance and Public Choice*, 8, 89–117.

Benson, B.L. (2001), 'Fiscal Competition in a Federal System', in D.P. Racheter and R.E. Wagner (eds), *Federalist Government in Principle and Practice*, Boston, MA: Kluwer Academic Publishers, pp. 55–95.

Benson, B.L. and D.W. Rasmussen (1991), 'The Relationship between Illicit Drug Enforcement Policy and Property Crimes', *Contemporary Policy Issues*, 9, 106–15.

Berman, H. (1983), *Law and Revolution: The Formation of the Western Legal Tradition*, Cambridge, MA: Harvard University Press.

Bessley, T. and S. Coate (1997), 'An Economic Model of Representative Democracy', *Quarterly Journal of Economics*, 88, 139–56.

Bish, R.L. (1971), *The Public Economy of Metropolitan Areas*, Chicago: Markham.

Bish, R.L. (1999), 'Federalist Theory and Polycentricity: Learning from Local Governments', in D.P. Racheter and R.E. Wagner (eds), *Limiting Leviathan*, Cheltenham, UK: Edward Elgar, pp. 203–20.

Bish, R.L. and V. Ostrom (1973), *Understanding Urban Government: Metropolitan Reform Reconsidered*, Washington: American Enterprise Institute.

Blankart, C.B. (1991), *Öffentliche Finanzen in der Demokratie*, Munich: Franz Vahlen.

Bode, K. (1943), 'Plan Analysis and Process Analysis', *American Economic Review*, 33, 348–54.

Boettke, P. (2001), *Calculation and Coordination*, London: Routledge.

Boudreaux, D.J. and R.G. Holcombe (1989), 'Government by Contract', *Public Finance Quarterly*, 17, 264–80.

Bowles, S. and H. Gintis (1993), 'The Revenge of Homo Economicus: Contested Exchange and the Revival of Political Economy', *Journal of Economic Perspectives*, 7, 83–102.

Bradford, D.F. and W.E. Oates (1974), 'Suburban Exploitation of Central Cities and Governmental Structure', in H.M. Hochman and G.E. Peterson (eds), *Redistribution through Public Choice*, New York: Columbia University Press, pp. 43–90.

Brancato, K. and R.E. Wagner (2004), 'Inefficient Market Pricing: An Illusory Economic Box', *Journal of Public Finance and Public Choice*, 22, 3–13.

Brennan, G. and J.M. Buchanan (1980), *The Power to Tax: Analytical Foundations of a Fiscal Constitution*, Cambridge: Cambridge University Press.

Brennan, G. and A.P. Hamlin (1985), 'Expressive Voting and Political Equilibrium', *Public Choice*, 95, 149–75.

Brennan, G. and A.P. Hamlin (2000), *Democratic Devices and Desires*, Cambridge: Cambridge University Press.

Brennan, G. and L. Lomasky (1993), *Democracy and Decision: The Pure Theory of Electoral Preference*, Cambridge: Cambridge University Press.

Brennan, G. and P. Pettit (2004), *The Economy of Esteem*, Oxford: Oxford University Press.

Breton, A. (1996), *Competitive Governments: An Economic Theory of Politics and Public Finance*, Cambridge: Cambridge University Press.

Breton, A. and A. Scott (1978), *The Economic Constitution of Federal States*, Toronto: University of Toronto Press.

Breton, A. and R. Wintrobe (1975), 'The Equilibrium Size of a Budget Maximizing Bureau', *Journal of Political Economy*, 83, 195–207.

Breton, A. and R. Wintrobe (1982), *The Logic of Bureaucratic Conduct*, Cambridge: Cambridge University Press.

Brosio. G. (1986), *Economia e Finanza Pubblica*, Rome: La Nuova Italia Scientifica.

Browning, E.K. and W.R. Johnson (1979), *The Distribution of the Tax Burden*, Washington: American Enterprise Institute.

Brownlee, W.E. (1996), *Federal Taxation in America*, Cambridge: Cambridge University Press.

Brownlee, W.E. (2006), 'Social Philosophy and Tax Regimes in the United States, 1763 to the Present', *Social Philosophy and Policy*, 23, 1–27.

Buchanan, J.M. (1959), 'Positive Economics, Welfare Economics, and Political Economy', *Journal of Law and Economics*, 2, 124–38.

Buchanan, J.M. (1960), 'The Italian Tradition in Fiscal Theory', in J.M. Buchanan, *Fiscal Theory and Political Economy*, Chapel Hill: University of North Carolina Press, pp. 24–74.

Buchanan, J.M. (1967), *Public Finance in Democratic Process*, Chapel Hill: University of North Carolina Press.

Buchanan, J.M. (1968), *The Demand and Supply of Public Goods*, Chicago: Rand McNally.

Buchanan, J.M. (1969), *Cost and Choice*, Chicago: Markham.

Buchanan, J.M. (1975), *The Limits of Liberty*, Chicago: University of Chicago Press.

Buchanan, J.M. (1976), 'Taxation in Fiscal Exchange', *Journal of Public Economics*, 6, 17–29.

Buchanan, J.M. and R.D. Congleton (1998), *Politics by Principle, Not Interest: Toward Nondiscriminatory Democracy*, Cambridge: Cambridge University Press.

Buchanan, J.M. and R.A. Musgrave (1999), *Public Finance and Public Choice: Two Contrasting Visions of the State*, Cambridge, MA: MIT Press.

Buchanan, J.M. and W.C. Stubblebine (1962), 'Externality', *Economica*, 29, 371–84.

Buchanan, J.M. and G.F. Thirlby (eds) (1973), *L.S.E. Essays on Cost*, London: Weidenfeld and Nicolson.

Buchanan, J.M. and G. Tullock (1962), *The Calculus of Consent*, Ann Arbor: University of Michigan Press.

Buckle, S. (1991), *Natural Law and the Theory of Property: Grotius to Hume*, Oxford: Oxford University Press.

Buckley, F.H. (ed.) (1999), *The Fall and Rise of Freedom of Contract*, Durham, NC: Duke University Press.

Bulow, J. and K. Rogoff (1989), 'Sovereign Debt: Is To Forgive To Forget?' *American Economic Review*, 79, 43–50.

Calvo, G. (1988), 'Servicing Public Debt: the Role of Expectations', *American Economic Review*, 78, 647–61.

Casson, M. (1982), *The Entrepreneur: An Economic Theory*, Totowa, NJ: Barnes and Noble.

Caves, D.W. and L.R. Christensen (1980), 'The Relative Efficiency of Public and Private Firms in a Competitive Environment: the Case of Canadian Railroads', *Journal of Political Economy*, 88, 958–76.

Cheung, S.N.S. (1973), 'The Fable of the Bees: An Economic Investigation', *Journal of Law and Economics*, 16, 11–33.

Clapham, J.H. (1922), 'Of Empty Economic Boxes', *Economic Journal*, 32, 305–14.

Clark, E.H. (1971), 'Multipart Pricing of Public Goods', *Public Choice*, 11, 17–33.

Clinton, H.R. (1996), *It Takes a Village, and Other Lessons Children Teach Us*, New York: Simon & Schuster.

Coase, R.A. (1974), 'The Lighthouse in Economics', *Journal of Law and Economics*, 17, 357–76.

Coleman, J.S. (1990), *Foundations of Social Theory*, Cambridge, MA: Harvard University Press.

Congleton, R.D. (1994), 'Constitutional Federalism and Decentralization', *Journal of Public Finance and Public Choice*, 12, 15–30.

Congleton, R.D. (2001), 'On the Durability of King and Council: The Continuum between Dictatorship and Democracy', *Constitutional Political Economy*, 12, 193–215.

Cook, P.J. and M.J. Moore (1994), 'This Tax's for You: The Case for Higher Beer Taxes', *National Tax Journal*, 47, 559–73.

Cordato, R. (1992), *Welfare Economics and Externalities in an Open Ended Universe*, Boston, MA: Kluwer Academic Publishers.

Cornes, R. and T. Sandler (1986), *The Theory of Externalities, Public Goods, and Club Goods*, New York: Cambridge University Press.

Coser, L. (1964), *The Functions of Social Conflict*, New York: Free Press.

Cowen, T. (ed.) (1988), *The Theory of Market Failure*, Washington: Cato Institute.

Cowen, T. (2005), 'Self-Deception as the Root of Political Failure', *Public Choice*, 124, 437–51.

Cowen, T. and E. Crampton (2002), *Market Failure or Success: The New Debate*, Cheltenham, UK: Edward Elgar.

Crain, W.M. and N.V. Crain (1998), 'Fiscal Consequences of Budget Baselines', *Journal of Public Economics*, 67, 421–36.

Crain, W.M. and T.J. Muris (1995), 'Legislative Organization of Fiscal Policy', *Journal of Law and Economics*, 38, 311–33.

Crain, W.M. and R.D. Tollison (eds) (1990), *Predicting Politics: Essays in Empirical Public Choice*, Ann Arbor: University of Michigan Press.

Cropsey, J. (1955), 'What is Welfare Economics?' In J. Cropsey, *Political Philosophy and the Issues of Politics*, Chicago: University of Chicago Press, pp. 19–31.

Cullis, J. and P. Jones (1998), *Public Finance and Public Choice*, 2nd ed., Oxford: Oxford University Press.

Da Empoli, A. (1941), *Lineamenti Teorici dell'Economia Corporativa Finanziaria*, Milan: Giuffrè.

Davies, D.D. (1971), 'The Efficiency of Public Versus Private Firms: The Case of Australia's Two Airlines', *Journal of Law and Economics*, 14, 149–65.

De Alessi, L. (1980), 'The Economics of Property Rights: A Review of the Evidence', *Research in Law and Economics*, 2, 1–47.

De Angelo, H. (1981), 'Competition and Unanimity', *American Economic Review*, 71, 18–27.

de Jasay, A. (1985), *The State*, Oxford: Basil Blackwell.

de Jouvenel, B. (1952), 'The Idea of Welfare', in B. de Jouvenel, *Economics and the Good Life*, New Brunswick, NJ: Transaction Publishers, pp. 21–36.

de Jouvenal, B. (1961), 'The Chairman's Problem', *American Political Science Review*, 55, 368–72.

Demsetz, H. (1967), 'Toward a Theory of Property Rights', *American Economic Review, Proceedings*, 57, 347–59.

Denzau, A.T. and M.C. Munger (1986), 'Legislators and Interest Groups: How Unorganized Interests Get Represented', *American Political Science Review*, 80, 89–106.

de Tocqueville, A. (2002 [1835]) *Democracy in America*. Chicago: University of Chicago Press.

De Viti de Marco, A. (1888), *Il Carattere Teorico dell'Economia*, Rome: Pasqualucci.

De Viti de Marco, A. (1934), *Principii di Economia Finanziaria*, Turin: Giulio Einaudi.

De Viti de Marco, A. (1936), *First Principles of Public Finance*, London: Jonathan Cape.

Doig, J. and E. Hargrove (1987), *Leadership and Innovation: A Biographic Perspective on Entrepreneurs in Government*, Baltimore: Johns Hopkins University Press.

Downs, A. (1967), *Inside Bureaucracy*, Boston, MA: Little, Brown.

Dreschler, W. (2001), 'On the Viability of the Concept of Staatswissenschaften', *European Journal of Law and Economics*, 12, 105–11.

Durkheim, E. (1933 [1893]), *The Division of Labor in Society*, London: Macmillan.

Dye, T.R. (2001), 'Liberty, Markets, and Federalism', in D.P. Racheter and R.E. Wagner (eds), *Federalist Government in Principle and Practice*, Boston, MA: Kluwer Academic Publishers, pp. 1–17.

Eckert, R.D. and G.W. Hilton (1972), 'The Jitneys', *Journal of Law and Economics*, 15, 293–325.

Edgeworth, F.Y. (1958 [1897]), 'The Pure Theory of Taxation', in R.A. Musgrave and A.T. Peacock (eds), *Classics in the Theory of Public Finance*, London: Macmillan, pp. 119–36.

Eisinger, P. (1988), *The Rise of the Entrepreneurial State*, Madison: University of Wisconsin Press.

Elias, N. (1982), *The Civilizing Process*, New York: Pantheon Books.

Elias, N. (1991), *The Society of Individuals*, Oxford: Basil Blackwell.

Enelow, J.M. and M.J. Hinich (1984), *The Spatial Theory of Voting*, Cambridge: Cambridge University Press.

Enelow, J.M. and M.J. Hinich (1990), *Advances in the Spatial Theory of Voting*, Cambridge: Cambridge University Press.

Epple, D. and A. Zelnitz (1981), 'The Implications of Competition among Jurisdictions: Does Tiebout Need Politics?' *Journal of Political Economy*, 89, 1197–217.

Epstein, R.A. (1985), *Takings: Private Property and the Power of Eminent Domain*, Cambridge, MA: Harvard University Press.

Epstein, R.A. (1993), *Bargaining with the State*, Princeton: Princeton University Press.

Epstein, R.A. (1995), *Simple Rules for a Complex World*, Cambridge, MA: Harvard University Press.

Eucken, W. (1990 [1952], *Grundsätze der Wirtschaftpolitik*, 6th ed., Tübingen: J.C.B. Mohr.

Fama, E.F. (1980), 'Agency Problems and the Theory of the Firm', *Journal of Political Economy*, 88, 288–307.

Fama, E.F. and M.C. Jensen (1983), 'Agency Problems and the Theory of the Firm', *Journal of Law and Economics*, 26, 327–49.

Fiorina, M. (1976), 'The Voting Decision: Instrumental and Expressive Aspects', *Journal of Politics*, 38, 390–415.

Foldvary, F. (1994), *Public Goods and Private Communities*, Cheltenham, UK: Edward Elgar.

Foldvary, F. (2004), 'Public Revenue from Land Rent', in J.G. Backhaus and R.E. Wagner (eds), *Handbook of Public Finance*, Boston, MA: Kluwer Academic Publishers, pp. 165–94.

Foss, N. (1993), 'Theories of the Firm: Contractual and Competence Perspectives', *Journal of Evolutionary Economics*, 3, 127–44.

Frank, R.F. (1987), 'If Home Economicus Could Choose His Own Utility Function, Would He Want One with a Conscience?' *American Economic Review*, 77, 593–604.

Frederickson, H.G. and J. Nalbandian (eds) (2002), *The Future of Local Government Administration*, Washington: International City/County Management Association.

Friedman, D. (1978), *The Machinery of Freedom: Guide to a Radical Capitalism*, New Rochelle, NY: Arlington House.

Frohlich, N., J. Oppenheimer and O. Young (1971), *Political Leadership and Collective Goods*, Princeton: Princeton University Press.

Fukuyama, F. (1995), *Trust: The Social Virtues and the Creation of Prosperity*, New York: Simon & Schuster.

Gaffney, M. (2001), 'Liberty, Markets, and Federalism', in D.P. Racheter and R.E. Wagner (eds), *Federalist Government in Principle and Practice*, Boston, MA: Kluwer Academic Publishers, pp. 97–109.

Goldscheid, R. (1958 [1925]), 'A Sociological Approach to Problems of Public Finance', in R.A. Musgrave and A.T. Peacock (eds), *Classics in the Theory of Public Finance*, London: Macmillan, pp. 202–13.

Gordon, S. (1999), *Controlling the State: Constitutionalism from Ancient Athens to Today*, Cambridge, MA: Harvard University Press.

Gouyette, C. and P. Pestieau (1999), 'Efficiency of the Welfare State', *Kyklos*, 52, 537–53.

Granovetter, M. (1985), 'Economic Action, Social Structure, and Embeddedness', *American Journal of Sociology*, 91, 481–510.

Grossekettler, H. (2004), 'Social Insurance', in J.G. Backhaus and R.E. Wagner (eds), *Handbook of Public Finance*, Boston, MA: Kluwer Academic Publishers, pp. 323–83.

Grossman, H.I. and J.B. Van Huyck (1988), 'Sovereign Debt as a Contingent Claim: Excusable Default, Repudiation, and Reputation', *American Economic Review*, 78, 1088–97.

Groves, T. and M. Loeb (1975), 'Incentives and Public Inputs', *Journal of Public Economics*, 4, 211–26.

Hall, R.E. and A. Rabushka (1983), *Low Tax, Simple Tax, Flat Tax*, New York: McGraw-Hill.

Hamilton, A. (1787), 'Federalist No. 1: General Introduction', in *The Federalist Papers*, http://thomas.loc.gov/home/histdox/fed_01.html, accessed 7 November 2006.

Hamlin, A.P. (1985), 'The Political Economy of Constitutional Federalism', *Public Choice*, 46, 187–95.

Hammond, T.H. (1986), 'Agenda Control, Organizational Structure, and Bureaucratic Politics', *American Journal of Political Science*, 30, 379–420.

Hansen, S.B. (1983), *The Politics of Taxation: Revenue without Representation*, New York: Praeger.

Harper, D.A. (1996), *Entrepreneurship and the Market Process: An Inquiry into the Growth of Knowledge*, London: Routledge.

Hayek, F.A. (1945), 'The Use of Knowledge in Society', *American Economic Review*, 35, 519–30.

Hayek, F.A. (1960), *The Constitution of Liberty*, Chicago: University of Chicago Press.

Hayek, F.A. (1973), *Rules and Order*, Chicago: University of Chicago Press.

Head, J.G. (1965), 'The Welfare Foundations of Public Finance Theory', *Rivista di Diritto Finanziario e Scienza delle Finanze*, 24, 379–428.

Henderson, J.V. (1985), 'The Tiebout Model: Bring Back the Entrepreneurs', *Journal of Political Economy*, 93, 248–64.

Hettich, W. and S.L. Winer (1988), 'Economic and Political Foundations of Tax Structure', *American Economic Review*, 78, 701–12.

Hettich, W. and S.L. Winer (1999), *Democratic Choice and Taxation*, Cambridge: Cambridge University Press.

Hickel, R. (ed.) (1976), *Die Finanzkrise der Steuerstaats*, Frankfurt: Suhrkamp.

Himmelfarb, G. (1984), *The Idea of Poverty*, New York: Alfred A. Knopf.

Himmelfarb, G. (1992), *Poverty and Compassion: The Moral Imagination of the Late Victorians*, New York: Vintage.

Hirshleifer, J. (2001), *The Dark Side of the Force: Economic Foundations of Conflict Theory*, Cambridge: Cambridge University Press.

Holcombe, R.G. and M.D. Stroup (1993), 'Federal Funding and the Cartelization of State Governments', *Journal of Public Finance and Public Choice*, 11, 101–9.

Homans, G.C. (1958), 'Social Behavior as Exchange', *American Sociological Review*, 29, 597–606.

Homans, G.C. (1974), *Social Behavior: Its Elementary Forms*, New York: Harcourt Brace.

Hughes, J.R.T. (1965), *The Vital Few: American Economic Progress and its Protagonists*, New York: Oxford University Press.

Hughes, J.R.T. (1977), *The Governmental Habit: Economic Controls from Colonial Times to the Present*, New York: Basic Books.

Hutt, W.H. (1975), 'Unanimity versus Non-discrimination (as Criteria for Constitutional Validity)', in S. Pejovich and D. Klingaman (eds), *Individual Freedom: Selected Essays of William H. Hutt*, Westport, CT: Greenwood Press, pp. 14–33.

Ikeda, S. (1997), *Dynamics of the Mixed Economy*, London: Routledge.

Jha, R. (1998), *Modern Public Economics*, London: Routledge.

Johnson, D.B. (1973), 'Meade, Bees, and Externalities', *Journal of Law and Economics*, 16, 35–66.

Justi, J.H.G. von (1969 [1771]), *Natur und Wesen der Staaten*, Darmstadt: Scientia Verlag Aalen.

Kato, J. (1994), *The Problem of Bureaucratic Rationality*, Princeton: Princeton University Press.

Kayaalp, O. (2004), *The National Element in the Development of Fiscal Theory*, Houndmills, UK: Palgrave Macmillan.

Kekes, J. (2003), *The Illusions of Egalitarianism*, Ithaca, NY: Cornell University Press.

Kenyon, D.A. and J. Kincaid (eds) (1991), *Competition among States and Local Governments*, Washington: Urban Institute.

Keynes, J.M. (1936), *The General Theory of Employment, Interest, and Money*, New York: Harcourt, Brace.

Kirzner, I.M. (1973), *Capitalism and Entrepreneurship*, Chicago: University of Chicago Press.

Kirzner, I.M. (1979), *Perception, Opportunity, and Profit*, Chicago: University of Chicago Press.

Kirzner, I.M. (1985), *Discovery and the Capitalist Process*, Chicago: University of Chicago Press.

Klein, D.B. (1997), *Curb Rights: A Foundation for Free Enterprise in Urban Transit*, Washington: American Enterprise Institute.

Klingner, D.E. and J. Nalbandian (1998), *Public Personnel Management*, 4th ed., Upper Saddle River, NJ: Prentice-Hall.

Knight, F.H. (1921), *Risk, Uncertainty, and Profit*, New York: Harper.

Koppl, R. (2002), *Big Players and the Economic Theory of Expectations*, New York: Palgrave Macmillan.

Kraan, D. (1996), *Budgetary Decisions: A Public Choice Approach*, Cambridge: Cambridge University Press.

Kuran, T. (1995), *Private Truths, Public Lies: The Social Consequences of Preference Falsification*, Cambridge, MA: Harvard University Press.

Lachmann, L. (1971), *The Legacy of Max Weber*, Berkely, CA: Glendessary Press.

Lachmann, L. (1977), *Capital, Expectations, and the Market Process*, Kansas City: Sheed Andrews and McMeel.

La Manna, M. and G. Slomp (1994), 'Leviathan: Revenue Maximizer or Glory Seeker?' *Constitutional Political Economy*, 5, 159–72.

Landa, J.T. and G. Tullock (2003), 'Why Ants Do but Honeybees Do Not Construct Satellite Nests', *Journal of Bioeconomics*, 5, 151–64.

Lasch, C. (1978), *The Culture of Narcissism: Life in an Age of Diminishing Expectations*, New York: Norton.

Lawson, T. (1997), *Economics and Reality*, London: Routledge.

Lawson, T. (2003), *Reorienting Economics*, London: Routledge.

Le Bon, G. (1960 [1895]), *The Crowd*, New York: Viking.

Leibowitz, A. and R.D. Tollison (1980), 'A Theory of Legislative Organization', *Quarterly Journal of Economics*, 94, 261–77.

Leijonhufvud, A. (1967), *On Keynesian Economics and the Economics of Keynes*, Oxford: Oxford University Press.

Leipold, H. and I. Pies (eds) (2000), *Ordnungstheorie und Ordnungspolitik: Konzeptionen und Entwicklungsperspektiven*, Stuttgart: Lucius & Lucius.

Levi, M. (1988), *Of Rule and Revenue*, Berkeley: University of California Press.

Levy, D.M. (1990), 'The Bias in Centrally Planned Prices', *Public Choice*, 67, 213–36.

Lewis, E. (1980), *Public Entrepreneurship: Toward a Theory of Bureaucratic Power*, Bloomington: Indiana University Press.

Littlechild, S.C. (1978), *The Fallacy of the Mixed Economy*, London: Institute of Economic Affairs.

Loasby, B. (1982), 'The Entrepreneur in Economic Theory', *Scottish Journal of Political Economy*, 29, 235–45.

Loasby, B. (1991), *Equilibrium and Evolution*, Manchester: Manchester University Press.

Loasby, B. (1998), 'The Organization of Capabilities', *Journal of Economic Behavior and Organization*, 35, 139–60.

Loewenstein, G. (1999), 'Because It Is There: The Challenge of Mountaineering . . . for Utility Theory', *Kyklos*, 52, 315–43.

Lovejoy, A.O. (1961), *Reflections on Human Nature*, Baltimore: Johns Hopkins University Press.

MacCallum, S.H. (1970), *The Art of Community*, Menlo Park, CA: Institute for Humane Studies.

Macey, J.R. (2006), 'Government as Investor: Tax Policy and the State', *Social Philosophy & Policy*, 23, 255–86.

Mack, E. (2002), 'Self-Ownership, Taxation, and Democracy: A Philosophical-Constitutional Perspective', in D.P. Racheter and R.E. Wagner (eds), *Politics, Taxation, and the Rule of Law*, Boston, MA: Kluwer Academic Publishers, pp. 9–31.

Mack, E. (2006), 'Non-Absolute Rights and Libertarian Taxation', *Social Philosophy and Policy*, 23, 109–41.

Maine, H.S. (1864), Ancient Law, 5th ed., New York: Henry Holt.

Makowski, L. (1983), 'Competition and Unanimity Revisited', *American Economic Review*, 73, 329–39.

Manne, H.G. (1965), 'Mergers and the Market for Corporate Control', *Journal of Political Economy*, 73, 10–20.

Marlow, M.L. and W.P. Orzechowski (1997), 'The Separation of Spending from Taxation: Implications for Collective Choices', *Constitutional Political Economy*, 8, 151–63.

McChesney, F. (1997), *Money for Nothing: Politicians, Rent Extraction, and Political Extortion*, Cambridge, MA: Harvard University Press.

McCormick, R.E. and R.D. Tollison (1981), *Politicians, Legislation, and the Economy*, Boston, MA: Kluwer Academic Publishers.

McGee, R.W. (2004), *The Philosophy of Taxation and Public Finance*, Boston, MA: Kluwer Academic Publishers.

Meade, J.E. (1952), 'External Economies and Diseconomies in a Competitive Situation', *Economic Journal*, 62, 54–67.

Meckling, W.H. and M.C. Jensen (1976), 'Theory of the Firm: Managerial Behavior, Agency Costs, and Ownership Structure', *Journal of Financial Economics*, 3, 305–60.

Menger, C. (1981 [1871]), *Principles of Economics*, New York: New York University Press.

Menger, C. (1985 [1883]), *Investigations into the Method of the Social Sciences*, New York: New York University Press.

Migué, J. and G. Bélanger (1974), 'Toward a General Theory of Managerial Discretion', *Public Choice*, 17, 27–43.

Miller, F.D., Jr (1995), *Nature, Justice, and Rights in Aristotle's Politics*, Oxford: Oxford University Press.

Miron, J.A. and J. Zwiebel (1991), 'Alcohol Consumption during Prohibition', *American Economic Review, Proceedings*, 81, 242–47.

Mirrlees, J.A. (1994), 'Optimal Taxation and Government Finance', in J.M. Quigley and E. Smolensky (eds), *Modern Public Finance*, Cambridge, MA: Harvard University Press, pp. 213–31.

Mises, L. von (1944), *Bureaucracy*, New Haven, CT: Yale University Press.

Mises, L. von (1957), *Theory and History: An Interpretation of Social and Economic Evolution*, New Haven, CT: Yale University Press.

Mises, L. von (1966), *Human Action*, 3rd ed., Chicago: Regnery.

Mitchell, W.C. and R.T. Simmons (1994), *Beyond Politics: Markets, Welfare, and the Failure of Bureaucracy*, Boulder, CO: Westview Press.

Moe, T.M. (1984), 'The New Economics of Organization', *American Journal of Political Science*, 35, 512–46.

Moe, T.M. (1991), 'Politics and the Theory of Organization', *Journal of Law, Economics, and Organization*, 6, 213–53.

Moe, T.M. and M. Caldwell (1994), 'The Institutional Foundations of Democratic Government: A Comparison of Presidential and Parliamentary Systems', *Journal of Institutional and Theoretical Economics*, 150, 171–95.

Morris, C.W. (1998), *An Essay on the Modern State*, New York: Cambridge University Press.

Murphy, L. and T. Nagel (2002), *The Myth of Ownership*, Oxford: Oxford University Press.

Musgrave, R.A. (1959), *The Theory of Public Finance*, New York: McGraw-Hill.

Musgrave, R.A. (1980), 'An Essay on Fiscal Sociology', in H. Aaron and M. Boskin (eds), *The Economics of Taxation*, Washington: Brookings Institution, pp. 361–90.

Musgrave, R.A. and A.T. Peacock (eds) (1958), *Classics in the Theory of Public Finance*, London: Macmillan.

Nalbandian, J. (1991), *Professionalism in Local Government*, San Francisco: Jossey-Bass.

Nelson, R.R. and S.G. Winter (1982), *An Evolutionary Theory of Economic Change*, Cambridge, MA: Harvard University Press.

Neyman, J. (1950), *First Course in Probability and Statistics*, New York: Henry Holt.

Niskanen, W.A. (1971), *Bureaucracy and Representative Government*, Chicago: Aldine.

Niskanen, W.A. (1975), 'Bureaucrats and Politicians', *Journal of Law and Economics*, 18, 617–43.

Niskanen, W.A. (1978), 'The Prospect for Liberal Democracy', in J.M. Buchanan and R.E. Wagner (eds), *Fiscal Responsibility in Constitutional Democracy*, Leiden: Martinus Nijhoff, pp. 157–74.

Niskanen, W.A. (2003), *Autocratic, Democratic, and Optimal Government*, Cheltenham, UK: Edward Elgar.

Oates, W.E. (1972), *Fiscal Federalism*, New York: Harcourt Brace.

Oates, W.E. (1997), 'On the Welfare Gains from Fiscal Decentralization', *Journal of Public Finance and Public Choice*, 15, 83–92.

Oates, W.E. (1999), 'An Essay on Fiscal Federalism', *Journal of Economic Literature*, 37, 1120–49.

Olson, M. (1965), *The Logic of Collective Action*, Cambridge, MA: Harvard University Press.

Olson, M. (2000), *Power and Prosperity*, New York: Basic Books.

Osborne, D. and T. Gaebler (1992), *Reinventing Government: How the Entrepreneurial Spirit is Transforming the Public Sector*, Reading, MA: Addison-Wesley.

Ostrom, E. (1990), *Governing the Commons*, Cambridge: Cambridge University Press.

Ostrom, E. (2005), *Understanding Institutional Diversity*, Princeton, NJ: Princeton University Press.

Ostrom, V. (1962), 'The Water Economy and Its Organization', *Natural Resources Journal*, 2, 55–73.

Ostrom, V. (1973), *The Intellectual Crisis in American Public Administration*, Tuscaloosa, AL: University of Alabama Press.

Ostrom, V. (1984), 'Why Governments Fail: An Inquiry into the Use of Instruments of Evil to do Good', in J.M. Buchanan and R.D. Tollison (eds), *Theory of Public Choice II*, Ann Arbor: University of Michigan Press, pp. 422–35.

Ostrom, V. (1987), *The Political Theory of a Compound Republic*, 2nd ed., Lincoln: University of Nebraska Press.

Ostrom, V. (1991), *The Meaning of American Federalism*, San Francisco: ICS Press.

Ostrom, V. (1996), 'Faustian Bargains', *Constitutional Political Economy*, 7, 303–8.

Ostrom, V. (1997), *The Meaning of Democracy and the Vulnerability of Societies: A Response to Tocqueville's Challenge*, Ann Arbor: University of Michigan Press.

Ostrom, V. (1999), 'Polycentricity', in M.D. McGinnis (ed.), *Polycentricity and Local Public Economics*, Ann Arbor: University of Michigan Press, pp. 52–74, 119–38.

Ostrom, V., C.M. Tiebout and R. Warren (1961), 'The Organization of Government in Metropolitan Areas: A Theoretical Inquiry', *American Political Science Review*, 55, 831–42.

Pantaleoni, M. (1911), 'Considerazioni sulle Proprieta di un Sistema di Prezzi Politici', *Giornale degli Economisti*, 42, 9–29, 114–33.

Pareto, V. (1935), *The Mind and Society: A Treatise on General Sociology*, New York: Harcourt Brace.

Pauly M.V. and M.R. Redisch (1973), 'The Not-For-Profit Hospital as a Physicians' Cooperative', *American Economic Review*, 63, 87–99.

Pechman, J.A. and B.A. Okner (1974), *Who Bears the Tax Burden?* Washington: Brookings Institution.

Peirce, W.S. (1999), 'Government: An Expensive Provider', in D.P. Racheter and R E. Wagner (eds), *Limiting Leviathan*, Cheltenham, UK: Edward Elgar pp. 56–73.

Penrose, E.T. (1959), *The Theory of the Growth of the Firm*, Oxford: Oxford University Press.

Pescatrice, D.R. and J.M. Trapani (1980), 'The Performance and Objectives of Public and Private Utilities', *Journal of Public Economics*, 13, 259–76.

Peukert, H. (2001), 'The Multifaceted Balance of the Concept of Staatswissenschaften in the Tradition of the Historical School', *European Journal of Law and Economics*, 12, 113–22.

Pfiffner, J.P. (1987), 'Political Appointees and Career Executives: The Democracy–Bureaucracy Nexus in the Third Century', *Public Administration Review*, 47, 57–65.

Pigou, A.C. (1922), 'Empty Economic Boxes: A Reply', *Economic Journal*, 32, 458–65.

Plott, C.R. and M.E. Levine (1978), 'A Model of Agenda Influence on Committee Decisions', *American Economic Review*, 68, 146–60.

Popper, K.R. (1962), *Conjectures and Refutations*, New York: Basic Books.

Poterba, J.M. (1996), 'Budget Institutions and Fiscal Policy in the U.S. States', *American Economic Review, Proceedings*, 86, 395–400.

Potts, J. (2000), *The New Evolutionary Microeconomics: Complexity, Competence, and Adaptive Behaviour*, Cheltenham, UK: Edward Elgar.

Puviani, A. (1903), *Teoria della Illusione Fianziaria*, Palermo: Sandron.

Radomysler, A. (1946), 'Welfare Economics and Economic Policy', *Economica*, 13, 190–204.

Ramsey, F.P. (1927), 'A Contribution to the Theory of Taxation', *Economic Journal*, 37, 47–61.

Rath, C. (1998), *Staat, Gesellschaft, und Wirtschaft bei Max Weber und bei Walter Eucken*, Egelsbach: Hänsel-Hohenhausen.

Ratner, S. (1942), *Taxation and Democracy in America*, New York: John Wiley.

Read, L.E. (1958), 'I, Pencil: My Family Tree', as told to Leonard E. Read. www.econlib.org/LIBRARY/Essays/rdPncl1.html, accessed 7 November 2006.

Rescher, N. (2000), *Process Philosophy*, Pittsburgh: University of Pittsburgh Press.

Resnick, M. (1994), *Turtles, Termites, and Traffic Jams: Explorations in Massively Parallel Microworlds*, Cambridge, MA: MIT Press.

Reynolds, M. and E. Smolensky (1977), *Public Expenditure, Taxes, and the Distribution of Income*, New York: Academic Press.

Rieff, P. (1966), *The Triumph of the Therapeutic*, Chicago: University of Chicago Press.

Robert, H.M. (2000), *Robert's Rules of Order*, 10th ed., New York: Parseus Books.

Roberts, P.C. (1971), *Alienation and the Soviet Economy*, Albuquerque: University of New Mexico Press.

Robertson, D.H. (1924), 'Those Empty Boxes', *Economic Journal*, 34, 16–30.

Robertson, D.H. (1940), *Essays in Monetary Theory*, London: P.S. King.

Romer, T. and H. Rosenthal (1978), 'Political Resource Allocation, Controlled Agenda, and the Status Quo', *Public Choice*, 33, 27–43.

Rosen, H.S. (2005), *Public Finance*, 7th ed., New York: McGraw-Hill.

Rothbard, M.N. (1973), *For a New Liberty*, New York: Macmillan.

Salanié, B. (2003), *The Economics of Taxation*, Cambridge, MA: MIT Press.

Samuelson, P.A. (1954), 'A Pure Theory of Public Expenditure', *Review of Economics and Statistics*, 36, 387–89.

Samuelson, P.A. (1955), 'Diagrammatic Exposition of a Theory of Public Expenditure', *Review of Economics and Statistics*, 37, 350–56.

Sandel, M. (1996), *Democracy's Discontent: America in Search of a Public Philosophy*, Cambridge, MA: Harvard University Press.

Sautet, F.E. (2000), *An Entrepreneurial Theory of the Firm*, London: Routledge.

Savas, E.S. (1987), *Privatization: The Key to Better Government*, Chatham, NJ: Chatham House.

Schlesinger, M., S. Mitchell and B. Gray (2004), 'Public Expectations of Nonprofit and For-Profit Ownership in American Medicine', *Health Affairs*, 23, 181–91.

Schneider, M. and P. Teske (1995), *Public Entrepreneurs: Agents for Change in American Government*, Princeton: Princeton University Press.

Schoeck, H. (1969), *Envy: A Theory of Social Behaviour*, New York: Harcourt Brace.

Schoenblum, J. (2006), 'Taxation, the State, and the Community', *Social Philosophy and Policy*, 23, 210–34.

Schumpeter, J.A. (1934), *The Theory of Economic Development*, Cambridge, MA: Harvard University Press.

Schumpeter, J.A. (1954 [1918]), 'The Crisis of the Tax State', *International Economic Papers*, 4, 5–38.

Shackle, G.L.S. (1961), *Decision, Order, and Time in Human Affairs*, Cambridge: Cambridge University Press.

Shackle, G.L.S. (1972), *Epistemics and Economics*, Cambridge: Cambridge University Press.

Shadbegian, R.J. (1999), 'Fiscal Federalism, Collusion, and Government Size', *Public Finance Review*, 27, 262–81.

Shepsle, K.A. and B.R. Weingast (1981), 'Structure Induced Equilibrium and Legislative Choice', *Public Choice*, 37, 503–19.

Sherman, R. (1967), 'A Private Ownership Bias in Transit Choice', *American Economic Review*, 57, 1211–17.

Sherwood, F.P. and Lee J. Breyer (1987), 'Executive Personnel Systems in the States', *Public Administration Review*, 47, 410–16.

Shoup, D.C. (2005), *The High Cost of Free Parking*, Chicago: American Planning Association.

Simmel, G. (1978 [1900]), *The Philosophy of Money*, London: Routledge.

Simons, H.C. (1937), [Review of First Principles of Public Finance], *Journal of Political Economy*, 45, 712–17.

Smith, A. (1991 [1776]), *The Wealth of Nations*, London: Everyman's Library.
Sobel, R.S. (2004), 'Welfare Economics and Public Finance', in J.G. Backhaus and R.E. Wagner (eds), *Handbook of Public Finance*, Boston, MA: Kluwer Academic Publishers, pp. 19–51.
Sonstelie, J.C. and P.R. Portney (1978), 'Profit Maximizing Communities and the Theory of Local Public Expenditure', *Journal of Urban Economics*, 5, 263–77.
Spruynt, H. (1994), *The Sovereign State and Its Competitors*, Princeton, NJ: Princeton University Press.
Stigler, G.J. and G.S. Becker (1977), 'De Gustibus non est Disputandum', *American Economic Review*, 67, 76–90.
Stonier, A. and K. Bode (1937), 'A New Approach to the Methodology of the Social Sciences', *Economica*, 4, 406–24.
Streit, M. (1992), 'Economic Order, Private Law, and Public Policy: The Freiberg School of Law and Economics in Perspective', *Journal of Institutional and Theoretical Economics*, 148, 675–704.
Surowiecki, J. (2004), *The Wisdom of Crowds*, New York: Doubleday.
Taylor, M. (1982), *Community, Anarchy, and Liberty*, Cambridge: Cambridge University Press.
Thomas, J.H. (1933), *Town Government in the Sixteenth Century*, London: George Allen & Unwin.
Thornton, M. (1991), *The Economics of Prohibition*, Salt Lake City: University of Utah Press.
Tideman, T.N. and G. Tullock (1976), 'A New and Superior Process for Making Social Choices', *Journal of Political Economy*, 84, 1145–60.
Tiebout, C.M. (1956), 'A Pure Theory of Local Expenditures', *Journal of Political Economy*, 64, 416–24.
Tollison, R.D. (1982), 'Rent Seeking: A Survey', *Kyklos*, 35, 575–602.
Tononi, G., O. Sporns and G.M. Edelman (1999), 'Measures of Degeneracy and Redundancy in Biological Networks', *Proceedings of the National Academy of Sciences*, 96, 3257–62.
Tribe, K. (1984), 'Cameralism and the Science of Government', *Journal of Modern History*, 56, 263–84.
Tuerck, D.G. (ed.) (1978), *The Political Economy of Advertising*, Washington: American Enterprise Institute.
Tullock, G. (1965), *The Politics of Bureaucracy*, Washington: Public Affairs Press.
Tullock, G. (1967), 'The Welfare Costs of Tariffs, Monopolies, and Theft', *Economic Inquiry*, 5, 224–32.
Tullock, G. (1970), *Public Wants, Private Means*, New York: Basic Books.
Tullock, G. (1987), *Autocracy*, Boston, MA: Kluwer Academic Publishers.

Tullock, G. (1994), *The Economics of Non-Human Societies*, Tucson, AZ: Pallas Press.

Usher, D. (1992), *Welfare Economics of Markets, Voting, and Predation*, Ann Arbor: University of Michigan Press.

Vanberg, V. (1975), *Die zwei Soziologien: Individualismus und Kollektivismus in der Sozialtheorie*, Tübingen: J.C.B. Mohr.

Vihanto, M. (1992), 'Competition between Local Governments as a Discovery Procedure', *Journal of Institutional and Theoretical Economics*, 148, 411–36.

Viner, J. (1961), 'Hayek on Freedom and Coercion', *Southern Economic Journal*, 27, 230–36.

Voigt, S. (1999), *Explaining Constitutional Change*, Cheltenham, UK: Edward Elgar.

Wagner, R.E. (1983), 'Funded Social Security: Collective and Private Options', *Cato Journal*, 3, 581–602.

Wagner, R.E. (1987), 'Parchment, Guns, and the Maintenance of Constitutional Contract', in C.K. Rowley (ed.), *Democracy and Public Choice: Essays in Honor of Gordon Tullock*, Oxford: Basil Blackwell, pp. 105–21.

Wagner, R.E. (1988), 'The Calculus of Consent: A Wicksellian Retrospective', *Public Choice*, 56, 153–66.

Wagner, R.E. (1993), *Parchment, Guns, and Constitutional Order*, Cheltenham, UK: Edward Elgar.

Wagner, R.E. (1994), 'Economic Efficiency, Rent Seeking, and Democracy: Zenoistic Variations on Coasian Themes', in P.J. Boettke and M.J. Rizzo (eds), *Advances in Austrian Economics I*, Greenwich, CT: JAI Press, pp. 129–44.

Wagner, R.E. (1997a), 'Choice, Exchange, and Public Finance', *American Economic Review, Proceedings*, 87, 160–63.

Wagner, R.E. (1997b), 'Parasitical Political Pricing, Economic Calculation, and the Size of Government', *Journal of Public Finance and Public Choice*, 15, 135–46.

Wagner, R.E. (2002a), 'Some Institutional Problematics of Excess Burden Analytics', *Public Finance Review*, 30, 531–45.

Wagner, R.E. (2002b), 'Complexity, Governance, and Constitutional Craftsmanship', *American Journal of Economics and Sociology*, 61, 105–22.

Wagner, R.E. (2003), 'Public Choice and the Diffusion of Classic Italian Public Finance', *Il Pensiero Economico*, 11, 271–82.

Wagner, R.E. (2005), [Review of Orhan Kayaalp's The National Element in the Development of Fiscal Theory], *Journal of the History of Economic Thought*, 27, 223–26.

Wagner, R.E. (2006a), 'Choice, Catallaxy, and Just Taxation: Contrasting Architectonics for Fiscal Theorizing', *Social Philosophy and Policy*, 23, 235–54.

Wagner, R.E. (2006b), 'States and the Crafting of Souls: Mind, Society, and Fiscal Sociology', *Journal of Economic Behavior and Organization*, 59, 516–24.

Warren, C. (1932), *Congress as Santa Claus: National Donations and the General Welfare Clause of the Constitution*, Charlottesville, VA: Michie.

Watts, R. and J. Zimmerman (1983), 'Agency Problems, Auditing, and the Theory of the Firm', *Journal of Law and Economics*, 26, 613–33.

Webber, C. and A. Wildavsky (1986), *A History of Taxation and Public Expenditure in the Western World*, New York: Simon and Schuster.

Weingast, B.R. (1984), 'The Congressional–Bureaucratic System: A Principal–Agent Perspective', *Public Choice*, 44, 147–91.

Weingast, B.R. and M.J. Moran (1983), 'Bureaucratic Discretion or Congressional Control? Regulatory Policy Making by the Federal Trade Commission', *Journal of Political Economy*, 91, 765–800.

Weinrib, L.L. (1987), *Natural Law and Justice*, Cambridge, MA: Harvard University Press.

Weisbrod, B.A. (1964), *External Benefits of Public Education*, Princeton, NJ: Industrial Relations Section, Princeton University.

Wicksell, K. (1896), *Finanztheoretische Untersuchungen*, Jena: Gustav Fischer.

Wicksell, K. (1958 [1896]), 'A New Principle of Just Taxation', in R.A. Musgrave and A.T. Peacock (eds), *Classics in the Theory of Public Finance*, London, Macmillan, pp. 72–118.

Williamson, O.E. (1985), *The Economic Institutions of Capitalism*, New York: Free Press.

Williamson, O.E. (1996), *The Mechanisms of Governance*, New York: Oxford University Press.

Wilson, E.O. (1971), *The Insect Societies*, Cambridge, MA: Harvard University Press.

Wilson, E.O. (1975), *Sociobiology: The New Synthesis*, Cambridge, MA: Harvard University Press.

Wilson, J.Q. (1989), *Bureaucracy: What Government Agencies Do and Why They Do It*, New York: Basic Books.

Wittman, D. (1989), 'Why Democracies Produce Efficient Results', *Journal of Political Economy*, 97, 1395–424.

Wittman, D. (1995), *The Myth of Democratic Failure*, Chicago: University of Chicago Press.

Zodrow, G. (ed.) (1983), *Local Provision of Public Services: The Tiebout Model after Twenty Five Years*, New York: Academic Press.

# Index